THE INSURANCE REIMBURSEMENT MANUAL

For America's Bodyworkers, Bodytherapists and Massage Professionals

The only <u>officially</u> <u>approved</u> insurance reimbursement home study course for Bodytherapists!

Revised 1999 Edition

Contains new documentaion, forms, and sample letters, etc.

Exp... ...ractice Incr... ...r Income!

D1541141

- **Learn how you can join the Nation's top ten managed care networks!**
- **Increase your referral business by 300%**
- **Establish a hospital-based massage therapy program!**

■ **Bodytherapy is finally gaining acceptance as a legitimate healing art**. However, insurance companies still dictate which procedures will be reimbursed and who can perform them. Many clients could not afford your services without some type of insurance coverage. You can get your share of this major source of income, but <u>only</u> if you know how the system works. This manual will show you how to work with doctors and insurance companies, serve many more people, and make more money.

■ *Newly updated, revised 5th Edition for 1999 contains*: — The latest on charting and documentation! —1999 CPT and ICD 9-CM Codes — Easy to use forms and Letters! — Key reference Materials listing Insurance companies that cover your services! — How to establish a hospital-based massage therapy program!

What You'll Learn . . .

- A simple step-by-step billing approach that minimizes red tape, paperwork, and stress - and gets you paid a lot faster!

- How to work professionally & effectively with Personal Injury insurance claims, Worker's Compensation claims and Major Medical insurance claims.

- How to determine current fees for all types of bodytherapy services in your local market area

- How to establish effective, profitable business relationships with Medical Doctors (MDs), Chiropractors (DCs) & other health professionals

- How to write a business relationship agreement with an MD or DC in any State in the country

- Seven tried & proven ways to market your services to health care providers & individuals!

- How to design your own professional-looking referral forms to get business from licensed health care providers (many sample forms & letters are provided in the extensive manual)

- How to define and promote your services

- How to understand and use the appropriate Standard Procedure Codes for insurance reimbursement.

- How to make Electronic Billing and Computerized Billing work for you

- The 5 best ways to get ongoing referrals from other health care professionals in your area

- Current legal guidelines and professional roles

- Troubleshooting and how to solve insurance problems fast!

- Answers to your most frequently asked questions on billing and marketing

- Plus a whole lot more!

- **Order today at NO RISK! Your satisfaction is guaranteed!**

About The Author

Christine Rosche, M.A., M.P.H., author, educator, and consultant, is America's leading authority in the field of marketing and insurance reimbursement for massage professionals and body-therapists. Chris has carefully researched and developed insurance reimbursement and marketing procedures based on 15 years in the health care field, including 5 years at Stanford University Medical Center. She received her B.A. in Psychology from Stanford University and a Master's Degree in Public Health from San Jose State University. As a Certified Trager® Practitioner and Certified Massage Practitioner, Chris maintains a successful private practice with medical doctors and chiropractors in Northern California.

THE INSURANCE REIMBURSEMENT MANUAL

For America's Bodyworkers, Bodytherapists
and Massage Professionals

FIFTH EDITION

Christine Rosche, MA, MPH

Bodytherapy Business Institute

Continuing Education for America's Bodyworkers™
Books • Seminars • Consulting

Palo Alto, California

This book is intended as a guide for insurance reimbursement for bodytherapy practitioners. While it presents helpful legal and financial information, it is not a substitute for professional legal or tax opinions. Consult with the appropriate professional in your state.

Revised and Updated for 1999

Copy Editor: Monica Meffort
Cover Design: R. Kharibian & Associates
Text Design & Compositor: R. Kharibian & Associates
Production Consultant: Chris Smith
Production Coordinator: Jack Halliday, Topping House

ISBN 0-9646428-1-6

Bodytherapy Business Institute
Continuing Education for America's Bodyworkers SM
4157 El Camino Way, Suite C
Palo Alto, California 94306

Contents

Bodytherapy Business Institute

Continuing Education for America's Bodyworkers™
Books • Seminars • Consulting

Christine Rosche, MPH
Founder and Director

READ ME FIRST!

Dear Reader,

Thank you for purchasing *The Insurance Reimbursement Manual*. I know this book will guide and empower you towards increasing your professional success. Congratulations for taking this important career step!

Thousands of America's bodyworkers, bodytherapists, and massage professionals have benefited from the proven, practical approach offered here.

Because I am committed to maintaining the highest possible quality and effectiveness of this material, I want to invite you to help me make the manual even better.

In the back of the book are two important forms I want you to know about. Please turn to pages 261 through 263. Let me explain.

- **Page 261 — Book Evaluation Form**
  After you have read the book, please take just 5 minutes to give me your evaluation and comments. Then, cut or tear out the form and mail it to the address indicated at the bottom of the page.

- **Page 263 — Reader's Feedback Form**
  Please use this form to send us your feedback, updates, and improvements so we can make the manual even better with each new edition. Feel free to suggest revisions, new ideas, or information that could be added—or even removed. If you find any typos or errors, please point them out to us and they will be corrected in the next printing. We re-print almost monthly.

I have recently added a page for **Notes** and a page for **Things to Do** at the end of the book. Please use these pages to jot down your thoughts as you read and learn.

I look forward to receiving your evaluations, endorsements, and feedback.

Sincerely,

Chris Rosche

Acknowledgements

Milton Trager, M.D., the founder of Trager Psychophysical Integration, encouraged me to pursue my career as an adjunctive therapist to the health professions.

Ruth Winkler and Five Associates, Inc., were my first associates in offering the Business Symposium for Bodytherapy Professionals, where I taught this material to my fellow professionals. They also encouraged me to write this book.

David Palmer guided me in seeking out the people and materials I needed. He also printed my articles in his newsletter, *The Bodywork Entrepreneur*, which formed the early foundation of this book.

Jocelyn Olivier of Alive and Well Institute of Bodytherapy, San Anselmo, California, offered my classes and encouraged me. Her students also insisted I publish this information.

Robert Calvert, editor and publisher of *Massage Magazine*, has assisted with providing information on massage laws nationwide.

Hal Bennett and **Susan Sparrow** were invaluable assistants and supporters during the writing of the manuscript.

Norman Early gave me support, encouragement and important information.

Dennis Briskin, of Catalyst Creative Services, worked closely with me on writing, editing and producing this book.

Cherie Sohnen-Moe gave me important feedback and editorial advice.

I am also grateful to the doctors who were interested in adding my services to their practices. The satisfying business relationships we formed showed me the mutual benefit that can come from this type of collaboration.

Preface to the Fifth Edition

In May 1989, when this book first appeared, massage/bodytherapy was a cottage industry of low-ranking practitioners viewed at best as "alternative" healthcare providers. Only a small percentage of us thought about reimbursement issues and the possibility of actually working with doctors, clinics and hospitals.

Now, in late 1996, we have grown to become a recognized, insurance-eligible member of mainstream healthcare. This important change came through the efforts of a few hard-working, determined bodytherapy professionals. Working alone and with other healthcare providers, their efforts focused on ways to raise our credibility and status among insurance companies and healthcare providers while becoming better known and appreciated by the public. This shift in public and professional perceptions and insurance industry practices promises to bring long-term benefits to all of us.

Consider these recent developments:

- Insurers are becoming more open to including our profession in their preferred provider pools (PPOs) and health maintenance organizations (HMOs). Several managed care networks are recruiting therapists to join their provider pool.

- In 1996, Washington became the first state to legally require all insurance companies to pay for alternative therapies, including massage therapy. Other states have similar legislation pending and a growing number of insurance carriers are including massage therapy in their benefit plans.

- Worker's Compensation and personal injury insurance companies have urged me to help educate massage/bodytherapists in proper billing procedures because they increasingly look for more therapists to serve their subscribers.

- Many physicians, chiropractors, osteopaths and other providers want to see changes in laws and professional standards which support bodytherapy. They also support our using case studies and articles which communicate the benefits of our work to insurance companies.

- Studies continue to show that consumers use massage and bodytherapy services regularly and want insurance coverage for them.

For example, 34% of respondents in a recent survey reported using at least one unconventional therapy in the past year (*New England Journal of Medicine,* January 28, 1993). In 1990, Americans made an estimated 425 million visits to providers of unconventional therapy and spent $13.7 billion. (About 75% of these payments were "out-of-pocket" or not covered by insurance.) This number exceeds the number of visits to all

U.S. primary care physicians (388 million) and suggests a long-term shift in how patients choose their medical services and providers.

Television, radio, magazine and newspaper coverage, especially in the past year, calls attention to this "healthcare revolution." Traditional (allopathic) medicine and alternative/complementary therapies are blending and cooperating to offer more integrated treatment. For example, *Life Magazine* (September 1996) ran a healthcare article with the headline, "Surgery or Acupuncture? Antibiotics or Herbs? Both are Better." The subhead underneath read, "More and more M.D.s are mixing ancient science and new science to treat everything from the common cold to heart disease."

- The Touch Research Institute of Miami, Florida, has published several significant research findings on the clinical benefits of massage.
- The new Office of Alternative Medicine at the National Institutes of Health continues to fund ongoing research in massage and bodytherapy.

As these changes occur, the licensing and credentialing of practitioners promises to become the universal standard for our profession. However, I see a wide range of training and ability within the different bodytherapy disciplines. Lower standards make it more difficult for legislators to consider establishing a license for our profession in their state. As of Fall 1996, only 20 states plus the District of Columbia offer some type of credential to practicing massage therapists—usually a license, certificate or registration. When we succeed in raising the educational requirements and appropriate standards, the remaining states will be more likely to establish licensure.

With national certification fast becoming the standard of competence in our profession, especially in unlicensed states, practitioners must give higher priority to lobbying and other efforts to bring full professional accreditation and stature.

In many states, bodytherapy professionals are developing campaigns to educate legislators and insurance companies on the nature and application of our work. With the establishment of national certification and the spread of licensing laws, the profession can now move towards full accreditation, recognition and credibility. All these are necessary to fully establish yourself within the healthcare profession and insurance reimbursement system.

I encourage you to do as many of the following as your time and resources permit:

- Become nationally certified in your profession.
- Join state and national educational campaigns in your specialty.
- Join professional associations working towards setting appropriate educational and accreditation standards.
- Ask the doctors and healthcare providers you work with to support your efforts by documenting your work and case examples.

I look forward to an exciting future as this field moves toward full integration and becomes a part of mainstream health and preventive care.

I welcome your letters and telephone calls with information about developments in your state and your professional practice.

Introduction

Why You Should Read This Book

Clients usually ask bodytherapy practitioners, "Can my insurance cover your fees?" Many clients cannot afford your services without insurance coverage.

You can receive payments from the insurance reimbursement system, but only if you know how the system works and how you fit into it. If you study this book and learn how to work with insurance companies and licensed healthcare providers, you will be able to serve many more people and add this large source of income to your business.

This book is primarily a guide to insurance reimbursement for massage therapists and other bodytherapy professionals. It covers insurance claims procedures, legal guidelines and appropriate professional roles within the current healthcare system. It also provides background information on career options for those new to the field or considering entering the profession.

This information fills an important gap in understanding how the U.S. healthcare system operates. While it does not cover every possible situation, (and is not a substitute for competent legal advice), it does show you step-by-step how to minimize delays and paperwork and get paid as fast as possible. It also helps educate, reassure and guide the serious bodytherapy professional on how to adopt regular, proven strategies to process claims efficiently so you can focus on the rest of your profession.

As a professional colleague, I offer you both caution and reassurance. What you need to know is complex, sometimes confusing and often technical. It also requires learning something about the law, the current state of our healthcare system and professional licensing regulations in various states. Read this book carefully, studying the legal guidelines, insurance claims procedures, sample forms and billing case studies. Also, you may need to refer back to it often as you begin to use the information.

Here's the reassurance: You CAN master this information and use it to build and sustain a more successful practice. Both in my own experience and in teaching hundreds of others, I have found that a few months of carefully studying and applying these guidelines enable even someone with no billing background to feel comfortable and confident to handle insurance matters.

Whether we like it or not, insurance company rules and guidelines on reimbursement play an ever-increasing role in paying for U.S. healthcare and often determine what procedures are done and by whom. Licensed healthcare providers (physicians, chiropractors and acupuncturists) now receive about two-thirds of their income from insurance companies. As bodytherapy professionals gain increasing public and professional acceptance for their work, they have greater access to a previously unavailable source of revenue.

How This Book is Organized

This book is reorganized from earlier editions into 17 chapters and 4 appendices. Also new in this fifth edition: The key chapters now begin with brief summaries which emphasize the most important points to help you quickly skim and find just the information you need. I hope this new feature will make the book even easier to use. As with earlier editions, the book includes samples of all the forms you need to establish insurance billing, whether you work in your own office or as an adjunctive therapist in a licensed provider's office. Following standard practice guidelines, we have used the term patient when referring the physician and client when referring to the massage therapist.

Chapters 1 & 2 show the legal and medical context in which bodytherapists work. They also help you define and promote your professional services and select the best career option for you.

Chapters 3 through 5 cover how to determine which type of working relationship with a licensed provider is best for you and how to create the contract to define your rights and responsibilities. It also teaches you how to use the proper forms for intake and case histories (with samples), and the best wording for doctor's prescription and referral letters.

Chapters 6 through 10 show you how to establish yourself as a member of the insurance reimbursement system and how to submit claims for major medical, personal injury and Worker's Compensation insurance.

Chapter 11 shows you how to identify and solve difficult billing problems and trace delinquent claims. It also gives specific recommendations and immediate actions you can take to collect promptly. In addition, included is information on how to document your work with accurate charts and records, follow patient progress and substantiate your claims for reimbursement.

Chapter 12 introduces electronic billing, which will help you lower your expenses, submit more accurate claims and get paid faster. The chapter also shows you what to look for in buying billing software.

Chapter 13 discusses documentation for massage therapy, using SOAP charting.

Chapter 14 contains important research information and outcome studies you can use to show insurance companies and medical providers that your work is supported by scientific methods.

Chapter 15 explains managed care and contains crucial information on how to join a managed care network with the various options available to bodytherapists.

Chapter 16 presents a current overview of hospital-based massage therapy.

Chapter 17 provides answers to the most frequently asked questions drawn from 10 years of talking with therapists, providers and insurance companies nation-wide.

The list of references includes insurance companies that reimburse for adjunctive therapies, where to look for liability insurance and important professional resources and organizations. The list of suggested readings includes important books and journals for the bodytherapy professional.

The four appendices give specific information on laws affecting your profession, promotional materials and important terminology. This fifth edition also contains updated versions of all the sample forms you need for insurance billing, recordkeeping and working in a medical office. The author grants permission to duplicate forms copyrighted by Chris Rosche.

How To Use This Book

Are you not yet working as a bodytherapy practitioner, either because you are doing something else and considering a career change or because you are still a student in training? Read the whole book but begin with career options, pay scales, and the pros and cons of the insurance field.

Are you an entry level massage practitioner who has just finished a 100- to 500-hour training program? Read Chapters 1 through 3, which will show you how to market yourself to medical doctors and healthcare providers, and what to do once you are hired.

Are you an established, advanced bodytherapy practitioner who is already working in a doctor's office, has some experience and wants to be sure the billing is done properly? Or are you considering making a change to work for another doctor? Go directly to Chapter 6, How to Get Reimbursed by an Insurance Company. Follow it with Chapters 7 through 10. These chapters explain procedure codes, insurance claim procedures, how to communicate your services and insurance expertise appropriately, both in your present position and in the new job.

Also be sure to read Chapter 14 on research information and Chapter 15 on managed care to determine how you can best present your services to doctors and insurance companies and determine your eligibility to join a managed care organization.

Are you an advanced bodytherapist not in a doctor's office? Do you periodically encounter insurance cases? Are you uncertain of all the options available to you? Are you considering joining a managed care network? The most frequently asked questions are:

Can I get a larger percentage of claims covered if I work through a doctor's office?

What are the options for a doctor billing for me?

Can I get reimbursed by a managed care company?

For these answers, refer to Chapter 6, How to Get Reimbursed by an Insurance Company, and Chapters 7 through 10 for detailed information, forms and documentation for billing Worker's Compensation, major medical and personal injury. Most importantly, look at Chapter 15 on how to join a managed care network. Also see the sections in Chapter 17 (questions and answers) that discuss practice management and insurance coverage.

How to Find Quickly What You Need to Know about Insurance Billing and Collection

Do you have…

No experience filing claims and billing insurance?
See Chapters 1–6, pages 1–74.

Some experience and basic knowledge of insurance billing?
Be sure to read Chapters 7–11, pages 75–146.

Extensive experience but some uncertainties?
Go to Chapters 8–17, pages 85–202.

Frequent problems collecting from insurers?
Go to Chapter 11, Troubleshooting and Tracing Delinquent Claims
Go to Chapter 17, Answers to Frequently Asked Questions

How I Came to Write This Book

Within a year of opening my private practice in Trager and massage therapy, I began working in a chiropractic healthcare center. I was the adjunctive therapist working with clients to release tension and stress from their muscles before their chiropractic adjustments. When I began at the clinic, the doctor asked me how to bill for my services, since he knew little about it. He also wanted me to set up his insurance billing system and teach the front office staff how to use it.

As I searched for answers, I found little information available to guide bodytherapy practitioners in working with insurance. Understanding insurance guidelines, billing systems and procedure codes became a critical function of my job in order to get paid for my services.

After I had worked at the chiropractic clinic for several months, the doctor's practice had increased significantly, as many clients sent their friends and relatives to experience the benefits of massage and Trager bodytherapy. My practice doubled in three months and became a valuable adjunct to the doctor's treatment program as well as adding to his income. Because we were using correct insurance billing procedures, clients were getting reimbursed for 80% of my services. At this healthcare center, the doctors began to recognize bodytherapy as an important part of a patient's overall treatment program.

With no guidelines, publications or references available to help others, I decided to develop this book using what I learned from my research and 12 years of work in healthcare.

I also began teaching seminars at bodytherapy schools for healthcare practitioners around the country on how to work effectively with a variety of primary healthcare providers. These seminars also included how to use insurance billing procedures to get paid promptly and be a recognized partner in the healthcare system.

I have worked with hundreds of practitioners over the past several years, coaching and consulting with them on marketing, insurance reimbursement and practice management issues. Due to many requests from practitioners and bodytherapy schools nationwide, I have fully updated and expanded the book and added seven chapters which contain the latest, up-to-date research and information for bodytherapists of all levels of expertise nationwide. Among the new chapters are two (13 and 16) written by therapists, Diana Thompson of Washington State, author of "Hands Heal: The Proof is in the SOAP Chart " and Laura Koch, LMT, who put together an excellent summary of hospital-based massage therapy programs.

I look forward to working together to continue to incorporate massage and bodytherapy into mainstream medical care and become fully recognized as effective healthcare providers. Given the more favorable climate for our profession, together we can build a new future in healthcare.

Background, the Law and the Bodytherapy Practitioner

Chapter 1

Quick Summary of Key Points

- Overview of Western medical practice versus Eastern medical practice
- Understanding the insurance industry
- Licensing regulations

    Licensed states

    Unlicensed states

- Bodytherapy as an adjunctive therapy to a medical treatment program
- Legal definitions and guidelines
- Determine the scope of your bodytherapy practice

The Medical Model and the Health Insurance System

To solve the insurance reimbursement puzzle you need to understand a few basic facts about medicine as it is practiced in the Western world and the insurance system that has grown up around it. In the West (meaning all those societies that trace their cultural and scientific origins from Greece and Rome) doctors have traditionally practiced what is called allopathic medicine based on the Western medical model. Common symptoms are classified into *disease entities* and *scientific conclusions* which are based on verifiable observations. The Western doctor cures disease by treating the patient, who tends to passively receive it. Also, in the West health has been defined as the absence of disease or physical symptoms.

By contrast, Eastern medicine is based on what might be called the growth or balance model. The Oriental health practitioner studies *life force* or *vital energy*. He or she considers subjective sources of data, takes a broader view of the individual that includes his energetic and spiritual dimensions, and defines health as a range of states along a continuum of internal and environmental balance. This approach seeks to understand and consider all possible factors affecting a person's health and wellbeing. The Eastern practitioner (and his increasing number of Western students) sees the client as an active, contributing partner in the health treatment plan.

The Insurance Industry

Insurance as it operates can be quite complicated, but the idea behind it is simple. Insurance pools together the money of a large number of people in order to have a fund to reimburse the few individuals who experience a loss. Regardless of the kind of risk it protects against, (fire, theft, accident, disease, etc.) an insurance company makes money by taking in more money in premiums than it pays out in claims. (A "claim" is a formal request by the insured to receive money to pay for his or her "loss.") The insurance company also makes money by investing its surplus funds in various profit-making ventures.

Given the above, it's understandable that insurance companies are concerned about the cost of health care. More people making more claims for more money will reduce insurance company profits unless premiums are raised or people make fewer claims for less money. Faced with healthcare costs rising even faster than the rate of general inflation, insurance companies have worked to both raise premiums and reduce the number and size of medical insurance claims.

In deciding what is a valid claim under a medical insurance policy, the insurance industry has structured itself to fit the Western medical model of disease. As a practical consequence, **insurance companies pay only for the treatment of disorders or diseases diagnosed by a healthcare professional who is licensed to practice in his or her state**. The amount of reimbursement for such services varies with each insurance company, but the client must have a diagnosed disorder or recognized medical condition in order to be eligible for reimbursement.

Although insurance companies increasingly recognize the role of prevention and early detection of disease in holding down healthcare costs, the health insurance system is still based on reimbursement only for treatment of a diagnosed disorder or disease. Only some consumer-oriented insurance companies will reimburse for preventive services and check-ups. (See Suggested Readings and Reference Materials for insurance companies that pay for adjunctive services.) Usually, services which aim only to enhance wellbeing or prolong life without correcting or relieving a diagnosed disease or disorder are not eligible for coverage. In short, **insurance pays to relieve sickness but not to enhance wellness.**

Fortunately, more doctors and healthcare providers are willing to consider the Eastern view of health and disease, and to take a whole person approach to health care. They understand the need to see health as a process of internal and external balance. For example, lifestyle factors such as stress and tension are becoming recognized as important contributors to one's overall health profile. What this means for bodytherapy professionals whose discipline is based on the Eastern model is that healthcare centers are being formed which recognize the importance of adding the services of bodytherapy professionals to traditional Western medical treatment. For example, a clinic may include several medical doctors working with acupuncturists, psychologists, chiropractors and bodytherapy practitioners. Also, traditional doctors and clinics frequently refer their patients for various adjunctive services which have proven helpful.

Therefore, until insurance companies reimburse routinely for the services of bodytherapy professionals, **the only way you can get paid by insurance companies is to establish a legally-acceptable, medically effective relationship with a licensed healthcare provider who will refer clients to you as part of a supervised treatment program.** Once a licensed provider establishes you as an effective adjunct to regular prescribed treatments, then many insurance companies will pay for your services.

Licensing Regulations

The word "license" may be used in at least two different ways that often lead to confusion for bodytherapy practitioners, especially those just getting started. You must understand the difference between 1) a license to provide health care; and 2) a business license from your city to practice massage/bodytherapy.

1) A licensed provider of health care is a professional who has passed licensing examinations by his or her state professional board (such as the Board of Medical Quality Assurance in California, the State Medical Board in Ohio, and the Florida Board of Massage) after completing degree and educational requirements. For example, licensed healthcare providers are medical doctors, chiropractors, osteopaths, registered physical therapists, psychologists and clinical social workers. As of the printing of this book in 1997, massage therapists are licensed providers in the 21 states that have passed laws to regulate massage through state professional boards.

2) A business license is simply legal permission from a city or county to sell a product or perform a service for money at a certain location. As of May 1998, there are 22 states (including Washington, Oregon, Hawaii, Utah, New Mexico, Texas, Arkansas, Iowa, Louisiana, Florida and South Carolina, Ohio, New York and Maine) that offer statewide licensure for professionals in the massage and bodywork field. There are approximately 8 states with legislative activity in process or with regulation passed but not yet finalized. There are 16 states (including California, Nevada, Montana, Wyoming, Colorado, Arizona, Idaho, South Dakota, Kansas, Oklahoma, Illinois, Michigan, Kentucky, North Carolina) without licensure or statewide registration for practicing massage or bodytherapy.

In California, cities and counties have authority to enact an ordinance to regulate the business of massage. The counties and cities vary widely in their massage regulation.

> **NOTE:** In this book I am calling states that do not offer or require a bodytherapy license an "unlicensed state." States that do license bodytherapy professionals are "licensed states." State licenses are not based on approving or disapproving bodytherapy professionals work, but rather on the state's decision to regulate bodytherapy professionals. For information on licensing regulations in your state, see the Resource List of State Boards and Agencies in Appendix A.

Unlicensed State Laws

Bodytherapy practitioners in unlicensed states need to work directly under the supervision of a licensed provider of medical care (medical doctor, chiropractor, or osteopath.) "Supervision" means the doctor is on the premises at least 50% of the work week. For a more complete discussion of supervision in California, see the Chiropractic Practice Act of the State of California. Check with your state massage board/department of licensing (if licensed) or the chiropractic and medical boards to determine supervision requirements.

If a doctor's referral letter is required by the insurance company (as is often the case with insurance claims), the letter must designate bodytherapy services as ancillary and adjunctive to the medical treatment program.

Licensed State Regulations

In licensed states, bodytherapy practitioners are recognized by many insurance companies as adjunctive practitioners and, in most cases, may bill for their services from their own offices by submitting a statement of services as well as a letter of referral from the doctor. For more recent information, check with your state agencies listed in Appendix A.

The client's insurance company specifies how much reimbursement is allowed for the adjunctive service. In most cases, the service needs to be part of a medical treatment program and requires a diagnosis and written referral from a doctor. This referral letter or prescription must follow the guidelines in Chapter 5 on Doctor's Referral Letter. The treatment program includes regular meetings between the bodytherapy practitioner and the doctor to discuss the case and obtain necessary supervision.

To summarize, in a licensed state you may work independently with a client who has been referred to you by a doctor who supervises your work. (Be sure to confirm your eligibility for reimbursement when you verify coverage with the insurance company.) Many insurance companies may recognize you as a practitioner, since you have met the state requirements for your professional license, and you are considered to be an adjunctive therapist.

In an unlicensed state, the insurance company requires the practitioner to work directly under the license and supervision of the primary healthcare provider who is referring the patient. For major medical and Worker's Compensation insurance claims the doctor must be on the premises at last 50% of your work week. For personal injury claims such as car accidents you may bill from your own office with a doctor's referral letter.

> **NOTE:** Despite these legal requirements, my research indicates that in unlicensed states practitioners frequently work in their own offices, with the doctor's office billing for them. This good faith practice has become established because doctors want these services available to their patients but often do not have physical space for a practitioner in their offices.

About the Bodytherapy Industry

The field of massage therapy and bodytherapy is going through an important transition period.

In May 1989, when this book first appeared, massage/bodytherapy was a cottage industry of low-ranking practitioners viewed at best as "alternative" healthcare providers. Only a small percentage of us thought about reimbursement issues and the possibility of actually working with doctors, clinics and hospitals.

Now in 1998 to the present, when the first edition of this book was published, we have grown to become a recognized, insurance-eligible member of mainstream healthcare. This important change came through the efforts many hard-working, determined bodytherapy professionals. Working alone and with other healthcare providers, their efforts focused on ways to raise our credibility and status among insurance companies and healthcare providers while becoming better known and appreciated by the public. This shift in public and professional perceptions and insurance industry practices promises to bring long-term benefits to all of us.

The bodytherapy professional can practice his or her profession in several different sectors. The service industry is comprised of clients who seek your services to relax, reduce stress and promote their general health. These clients may find you at health spas, fitness centers and beauty salons. Although some of these clients may have a health problem, the service industry focuses on enhancing and maintaining health. Since insurance companies reimburse only for adjunctive therapy for a diagnosed physical disorder or disease, in the service industry eligibility for insurance reimbursement is determined by the presence or absence of a diagnosed medical disorder.

Probably more relevant to readers of this book is the newly developing field of clinical and therapeutic massage and bodytherapy, which emphasizes the use of body therapy as an adjunctive therapy to a medical treatment program for a diagnosed physical disorder. Clients have a presenting problem that can be diagnosed by a licensed doctor. Bodywork is done either in the clinical setting (the doctor's office) or in the bodywork professional's office. The referring and supervising licensed provider of health care (remember that this is required for insurance companies to reimburse for bodytherapy services) may be a medical doctor, chiropractor or other licensed healthcare professional.

Legal Definitions and Guidelines

Working with insurance also requires that you understand current laws governing the practice of medicine and physical therapy in your state. Each state has their own departments of professional regulations for massage therapy (if applicable), physical therapy and medicine. Refer to Appendix A for information on the massage laws in your state and contact your state department of professional licensing (for licensed states) to clarify specific regulatory constraints in your state.

A medical license is completely different from a state bodytherapy license or a local business license to practice your bodytherapy specialty. From the standpoint of the law and insurance regulations, the most important definition you must understand is "the practice of medicine."

For example, according to the California Medical Practice Act, a licensed physician or surgeon is allowed "to use drugs or devices in or upon human beings and to sever or penetrate the tissues of human beings and to use any and all other methods in the treatment of diseases, injuries, deformities, and other physical and mental conditions."

That defines what a licensed medical professional MAY do. Even more important for the bodytherapy practitioner is what all other persons who do not have a medical license MAY NOT do. Section 2052 of the California Medical Practice Act defines "Unlawful Practice of Medicine," as the main prohibited action you must avoid. A person commits a misdemeanor if he or she "…practices…any system or mode of treating the sick or afflicted…or…diagnoses, treats, operates for, or prescribes for any ailment, blemish, deformity, disease, disfigurement, disorder, injury, or other physical or mental condition of any person…"

If you need legal advice about your profession, see an attorney. As a practical matter the key words in the definition are "diagnose" and "treatment". **Without a medical license you may not tell people what's wrong with them ("diagnose") and you may not on your own prescribe therapy ("treatment") to correct any condition.** Be sure to contact the appropriate professional boards in your state for further information.

While a bodytherapy professional may not diagnose or prescribe treatment, in many unlicensed states your services are categorized under the Physical Therapy Practice Act, which most closely describes what you do. In California, for example, Section 2620 of the Physical Therapy Practice Act defines physical therapy as "...the art and science of physical or corrective rehabilitation or of physical or corrective treatment of any bodily or mental condition of any person by the use of physical, chemical, and other properties of heat, light, water, electricity, sound, massage, and active, passive, and resistive exercise..."

According to California law, a physical therapist may evaluate and do treatment planning in consultation with a medical doctor. Your services as a bodytherapy practitioner are an adjunctive modality to the overall physical therapy program designed and supervised by a person with a medical license, such as a physician. Contact your state medical board or physical therapy board to learn how the Physical Therapy Practice Act in your state affects your professional practice.

Among the states that license massage therapy there is considerable variance in the definition of a massage therapist and how the therapist relates to the healthcare system. (See Appendix A for a list of state agencies.) For example, in New York massage is defined as "applying a scientific system of manipulation to the soft tissues of the human body with joint range of motion exercises; including but not limited to heat, cold, hydrotherapy for the purpose of improving and maintaining general health and effecting the rehabilitation of injury and disease."

In Florida massage is defined as "The manipulation of the superficial tissues of the human body with the hand, foot, arm or elbow whether or not such manipulation is aided by hydrotherapy, including colonic irrigation, or thermal therapy; any electrical or mechanical device; or the application to the human body of a chemical or herbal preparation."

In Ohio, massage is regulated through the state medical board and falls into the category of "limited branch of medicine." The definition of massage includes the "treatment of disorders of the human body by systematically applied friction, heat, or by stroking, slapping, kneading, tapping or hand manipulation only. Swedish movement is the treatment of disorders of the human body by applied or advised exercise."

Determine the Scope of Your Practice

If you are already working with licensed healthcare providers or are considering establishing a clinical massage/bodytherapy practice, you should answer the following questions to help you determine the scope of your practice. This list was developed by Jerry Green, an attorney specializing in preventive and adjunctive therapies.

1. How does your work differ from medical practice?

2. How do you distinguish a referral for your work from a prescription for medical treatment?

3. How do you convey these distinctions to your clients?

4. Describe specifically the allocation of responsibility in your relationship with your client. List the decisions which belong to each of you.

5. What form of client feedback do you have in place to determine what your client understands about his/her treatment? For example, do you have a written contract which describes the scope of your work and defines your responsibilities to your client?

6. How do you provide for the periodic redefinition of your client relationship in accord with his changing needs, desires, and expectations?

7. What kind of record, chart, form or journal entry do you use to assist your client in exercising his responsibility in your relationship? (For example, a chart may let your client know whether he is actually doing the exercises he agreed to.)

8. What kind of record, chart, form or journal entry do you use to assist you in your work?

9. What information do you need from your client on a regular basis? How can you get it?

10. What information does your client need from you on a regular basis? How can you provide it?

11. What kind of information would you benefit from receiving from your client's physician? What kind of information could you provide him?

Career Concerns, Defining
Your Professional Services and
Promoting Your Business

Chapter 2

Quick Summary of Key Points

- How to establish yourself as an adjunctive practitioner in the healthcare field
- Networking and interfacing with primary healthcare providers
- Determining the appropriate provider to work with
- Strategies for establishing professional relationships with licensed providers
- Career options and pay scales
- Prerequisites for insurance reimbursement for bodytherapy/massage therapy
- Sample letters
    1) To Doctor's office introducing yourself and your practice
    2) Follow-up letter to the Doctor's office

Career Concerns, Defining Your Professional Services and Promoting Your Business

This chapter helps you decide which of several bodytherapy professional career options may be best for you given your preferences, education and previous experience. It then outlines strategies for finding and interviewing the appropriate licensed professional with whom you may want to establish a working relationship. The chapter ends with sample written materials to help introduce you to the doctor's office and reach a mutually beneficial agreement.

In order to work effectively within the current health insurance system you must work as an adjunctive bodytherapy practitioner. An adjunctive practitioner's service complements and supports a doctor's treatment plan. For example, a bodytherapy practitioner may do massage therapy to prepare a patient for a chiropractic adjustment. The practitioner helps to release restricted neuromuscular holding patterns, which facilitates the patient's response to and maintenance of chiropractic adjustments.

To establish yourself as an effective adjunct, carefully study the prerequisites for insurance reimbursement in this chapter. Before you begin working as an adjunctive practitioner, determine and clearly define how your skills can work best with the doctor's practice. For example:

- Determine the type of healthcare provider you want to work with. The values clarification process in this section will also help you find the right person or group.

- Design a brochure and promotional literature which highlights your skills, education and training, as well as your career goals. This information should be easy to read and emphasize the benefits of your work for the doctor's practice. See Appendix B for sample promotional materials.

- Investigate what career options and pay scales are available to you, depending on the state you work in and the type of relationship you establish with the licensed healthcare professional (see Career Options and Pay Scales on pages 17–20.

When you've completed your research and self-evaluation, you are ready to begin your job search.

Networking and Interfacing with Primary Healthcare Providers

If you are interested in working with a doctor, how do you locate the appropriate person? The primary answer is first to define your goals and values in doing your specific bodytherapy practice. Begin by answering the questions in the Value Clarification Process section of this chapter.

When you are clear about the type of practice you are looking for, ask your friends, clients and acquaintances for names of doctors they enjoyed working with or being treated by.

Talk with members and staff of your professional organizations. Also visit several doctors and interview them about their scope of practice, style, goals of practice and primary value system. What is their purpose in providing health care? The following pages contain a step-by-step guide on how to find and interview the doctor of your choice.

Before you talk with the doctor, ask yourself the following questions: How can my service benefit the client and the doctor? What is the market value of my service? How do I want to get paid?

Be prepared to answer logistical details such as: Will I supply the massage table, sheets and oil and, if so, how do I figure that into the overall payment plan? How many hours a week do I want to work and how do I want to structure my practice? How many insurance payments can I have outstanding each month? How long can I wait to be reimbursed for my services?

Doctors who have large amounts of outstanding insurance payments often expect you to wait for payment until the insurance company reimburses them. For Worker's Compensation, this can mean waiting 3-8 weeks. Personal injury claims may take 1-2 years. Deciding in advance how much you want to be paid each week and presenting an appropriate proposal to the doctor will improve your chances of being paid. State that you need to be paid for your services at regular intervals, for example, every 2 weeks, except in cases of special arrangements between you, the client and the doctor. For example, you might agree when you are hired to wait 6–8 weeks to be paid so that the doctor's office can begin receiving insurance payments for your services, after which you will be paid every 2 weeks.

When you go to the doctor's office to interview him/her, talk with other staff members to find out what it is like working there. If you will be the first bodytherapy practitioner to work there, realize that you may have to educate the doctor and his patients on the value and benefits of your services. If other bodytherapy practitioners have worked at the office, ask them about their experiences there.

Your professional presence and competence communicates your self-worth. Remember that **as an adjunctive practitioner you are a valuable asset to the doctor's practice.** You are working in an area that is vitally important to the patient's health and wellbeing. Besides providing a quality service, you add revenue to the doctor's practice in the form of new referrals from satisfied patients.

For example, a Hellerwork practitioner began working in a doctor's office 3 days per week, 4 hours per day. Besides providing care for the doctor's patients, she generated 10 new referrals each month from satisfied patients. She produced $1,500 per month additional income for the doctor (the portion of her fee that went to the doctor as part of their financial arrangement.) After six months, the doctor's practice had doubled due to the positive benefits received from her services. This significantly increased the practitioner's income.

It is not enough to <u>assert</u> your value to the doctor's practice. You must prove it in order to be taken seriously. It is strongly recommended that you document the number of clients you have seen, the number of clients you have referred and your results.

Appendix B shows examples of promotional materials outlining the benefits of massage therapy and Trager bodytherapy. These materials will help you define and promote your professional services to doctors and healthcare centers.

VALUE CLARIFICATION PROCESS

Do this exercise before making contact with the doctor.

Think back to a time when you had a particularly positive visit with a health-care provider

1. What did you like about that visit?

   - doctor's professionalism

   - types of questions he/she asked you

   - office environment

   - courtesy of staff

2. What was the doctor's value system?

   - primary goal was financial and welfare of patient came second

   - primary goal was patient care, the doctor spent time listening and clarifying the needs of the patient

3. How did the doctor communicate his/her value system and beliefs to you?

   - verbal, non-verbal and visual factors such as office environment

4. What type of practice does this doctor have?

   - number of patients seen per day

   - type of patient

   - percentage of practice composed of patients with major medical insurance, Worker's Compensation or personal injury

   - doctor's attitude towards incorporating bodytherapy services and referring to an adjunctive practitioner

5. In your private practice, what are your primary objectives, goals and values?

   - describe how you interact with a client in your own office, including time spent talking, office environment, your professional standards and ethics.

   - what are the above communicating to your client?

6. Describe the type of practice and doctor you want to work with. Include specific details of the type of office environment you are looking for, location of your work space, number of staff, etc.

Recommended Strategies for Establishing Professional Relationships with Licensed Providers

1. Make a list of people you know in your medical and personal community. Ask friends, clients and medical professionals for the names of doctors who are oriented towards the type of care you want to give clients.

2. Determine a target market. Through personal references and referrals, determine the names of the healthcare providers who are recognized in the community and who share your values and beliefs. (Answer the questions in the Values Clarification Process to determine the appropriate value fit.)

3. Send a letter to each provider, indicating your interests and background. (See sample letters in this chapter.) Follow up with a telephone call to arrange an appointment at the doctor's convenience, usually early morning, lunch or after hours.

4. Present your portfolio to the doctor, including resume, letters of referral from current and former employers and testimonials from satisfied clients. Do research before your meeting to learn the background/orientation of this provider. What are his/her interests and achievements? What is their philosophy of health care? If appropriate, during your meeting present concise, clear examples of how you and the doctor can assist patients by working together adjunctively. Prepare a brief description of your services and skills and how they can benefit the doctor's patients.

5. If appropriate, arrange a follow up meeting with the doctor. Be prepared to demonstrate your work to the doctor and/or a staff member.

6. If it seems like an appropriate job fit and you may work together, design a contractual agreement such as in Chapter 3.

7. Be clear and concise in your contract. Determine a mutually agreeable trial period and evaluation process (usually six months). At that time, a revised contract may be written.

8. Determine educational and assessment tools to teach clients about your work and evaluate their progress. This is usually done in conjunction with the doctor and may include specifics such as using a goniometer to measure joints, range of motion and flexibility of specific muscle groups.

❖   ❖   ❖

**Take a deep breath and stretch
before you go on to the next section.**

❖   ❖   ❖

CAREER OPTIONS AND PAY SCALES

1. **OFFICE RENTAL** – You may rent space in the same office as the doctor or in another office in the same building. In the San Francisco Bay Area rentals vary from $600 per month and up for a bodytherapy room, depending on the location of the office and the size of the space/facilities. Check with other professionals in your area to determine rental fees.

   Primary advantages of this option are accessibility to supervision by the doctor and professional autonomy. Remember that eligibility for insurance reimbursement depends on the legal requirements in your state.

   This is a viable option for the practitioner who already has a private practice of his own which he could bring to this office, thus also bringing referrals to the doctor. A practitioner beginning his practice in a doctor's office will need to do marketing, outreach and patient education to expand his practice.

2. **EMPLOYEE OR INDEPENDENT CONTRACTOR IN A DOCTOR'S OFFICE** – This option gives the practitioner maximum visibility in a medical setting, access to clients and insurance billing, opportunities to educate clients and ongoing referrals.

   In the San Francisco Bay Area, the current rate for clinical bodytherapy in a doctor's office is $65-75 per hour, $40 per half hour and $25-30 for 15 minutes. Ask other bodytherapy professionals working with doctors in your area to determine the current rates.

   For an independent contractor the current reimbursement rate to doctors is 30-40% of the $65-75 per hour if the practitioner provides the massage table, all supplies and also brings her own clients to the office.

   If the doctor provides the massage table and supplies as well as refers most of the clients to the practitioner, the reimbursement rate to the doctor is 50% of all hourly fees charged.

   As an employee, the practitioner pay rate varies from region to region. The average is between $12-20 per hour, depending on types of services rendered. This means that you have set hours in the doctor's office and, in some cases, may be required to do other work such as administering physical therapy equipment.

3. **PAYMENT** – An important consideration is how long you must wait for payment by the doctor after you have worked with a client. In some cases, at the time of the interview the doctor may ask if you are prepared to wait for payment until the insurance company reimburses the doctor for services rendered. This can be anywhere from 2-4 weeks for major medical services and up to 1-2 years for personal injury cases. If the doctor's office accepts assignment of benefits by an insurance company (this means that the client pays

the doctor 20% and the rest is billed to the insurance company, who then is obligated to pay the doctor) you need to clarify how much money you can afford to have outstanding at any one time.

One option is for you to determine exactly how much you can have outstanding and then divide your practice into cash-paying clients (a certain percentage who need to pay you directly) and clients who have assigned benefits to the doctor.

Many doctors have cash-only practices where the client pays the doctor at the time of his visit and is given a pre-printed billing statement (called a superbill) which contains all the information he needs to bill the insurance company. In this case, office policy is that payment for services is due at the time the service is rendered. Payment is the obligation of the client regardless of insurance involvement. The office staff assists the client with filling out the appropriate insurance forms. However, it is the client's responsibility to collect on the insurance claim and negotiate settlement of a disputed claim. The insurance company will usually reimburse the client within 2-6 weeks. In this type of practice, the doctor will pay you every two weeks for the hours you have worked.

In a doctor's practice where a large percentage of clients have major medical claims assigned to the doctor, personal injury or Worker's Compensation cases the doctor may ask you to wait until the office has received payment. You can suggest to the doctor the following system when you begin working. You can wait 6-8 weeks until some insurance money begins to come in regularly and then ask to be paid every 2 weeks after that, based on the hours you worked. With an effective billing system and an efficient office staff, major medical and Worker's Compensation claims are received regularly every 2-6 weeks. If the claim is a personal injury case with no medical payment coverage by the client's auto insurance, you will need to wait for payment until the case is settled. You can ask to be reimbursed directly by the client.

Clarify all of the above at the time of your initial and follow-up meetings and in your contract with the doctor. A clear written agreement in advance will protect both of you against future misunderstandings.

Professional Career Options

A variety of career options are available to bodytherapy professionals as this growing field integrates with mainstream healthcare and defines its roles and responsibilities. An increasing number of physicians, osteopaths and chiropractors are using bodytherapy professionals as part of their overall healthcare programs with excellent results. The patients are benefitting from the integration of bodytherapy with their medical treatment program, and, as a result, are referring their family and friends.

Physicians and providers of general and preventive medicine say that in many cases bodytherapy facilitates their patients' recovery. In addition, it enables doctors to offer a unique service, thus producing more satisfied patients and referrals for the office. Often an adjunctive professional is able to educate the patient in preventive care and perform services for which the doctor has no time available.

According to the American Massage Therapy Association (AMTA), the benefits of massage include reducing tension and stress, increasing flexibility, mobility and strength of joints, improving circulation as well as influencing chiropractic adjustments to stay in place longer. As many chiropractors use massage therapy before an adjustment, they report that clients are more relaxed during an adjustment and respond more favorably to the doctor's overall treatment program. (See the article by Robert Calvert on "Chiropractic and Massage: A Healing Combination." in Issue 10 of *Massage Magazine*).

In addition to increased patient and doctor satisfaction with this adjunctive service, there is a significant financial benefit of bodytherapy to both the doctor and the practitioner. On the average, if a practitioner works 20 hours per week in a doctor's office, he or she earns $2,000 per month based on an average hourly income of $25, and the doctor earns approximately $2,000 per month. This is based on an arrangement of dividing the total income of $50 per hour between the doctor and the practitioner. Adding bodytherapy to the practice also contributes significantly to patient satisfaction, thus generating new referrals for the doctor and the practitioner. The bodytherapy practitioner is also able to generate a regular, stable income without the time or expense usually needed to market a private practice. In this case, the practitioner and the doctor can work out an insurance billing system with the front office staff and all bodytherapy services can be billed from the doctor's office.

To summarize, the first option of working with a physician or chiropractor on the premises has numerous benefits, among them increased visibility which leads to an ongoing, stable practice for the practitioner and the satisfaction of being part of a growing healthcare team. For the doctor, the increased patient satisfaction, income and new referrals are important benefits.

A second option is to work out of your own office with clients referred by a primary healthcare provider. This option is most common among practitioners who are unable to secure space in the doctor's office. Your office may be located in the same building as the doctor's office or in a separate building. In most unlicensed states, in order to be reimbursed by Major Medical and Worker's Compensation insurance, the doctor must be physically present on the premises, at least 50% of the time, during your sessions. Be sure to check the legal requirements in your state.

A third option is for the bodytherapy professional to rent space on the premises of a referring healthcare provider's office while still maintaining his own private practice. In this case, there may be some referrals from the doctor's office but the practitioner is working independently. In order for the practitioner's clients to receive insurance reimbursement they must be evaluated by the supervising doctor. Once a diagnosis is made, the doctor's office may bill the insurance company, or the practitioner can assist the client in billing his insurance company using the pre-printed billing form from the doctor's office (superbill). This option requires ongoing supervision by the licensed healthcare provider.

Important Prerequisites for Insurance Reimbursement for Bodytherapy/Massage Therapy

To be an effective member of the healthcare team, you must have:

- A good understanding of **medical terminology**. Most community colleges and medical assisting schools have courses in this area.

- A thorough **knowledge of anatomy and physiology.** Take a two-semester course in anatomy and physiology at a junior college or university, since many massage certification programs are inadequate in this area.

- The ability to **define what you do and explain it** to medical professionals in their language. For example, massage is "soft-tissue mobilization." Trager or Hellerwork are called "neuromuscular re-education."

- **Good communication skills.** You must be able to explain to doctors how your skills can help their patients.

- **Work experience in a medical/chiropractic setting.** A few hours a week in a doctor's office will help you understand how the healthcare delivery and health insurance systems work.

- **Accurate, concise progress records** on all clients. Record your findings, subjective and objective, along with procedures and recommendations.

- **Accurate accounting records** on all clients, using a bookkeeping system with receipts, ledger cards and insurance log.

- **Supervision** from your primary healthcare provider. In many licensed states practitioners work in their own office with telephone supervision from the doctor, as needed. In many <u>unlicensed</u> states, supervision means working in the doctor's office at least half the time. Verify supervision requirements with your state agency or professional association.

- Your own **professional liability insurance**, regardless of the doctor's coverage. See Suggested Readings and Reference Materials after Chapter 17 for names of companies offering liability insurance for practitioners.

Sample Letter to Doctor's Office

(Introducing yourself and your practice - Letter A)

Dear Dr. Jones:

I have been referred to you by your patient, Susan Weinstein. I am interested in meeting with you to discuss the possibility of working together.

I am a NATIONALLY CERTIFIED MASSAGE THERAPIST member of the American Massage Therapy Association and specialize in myofascial trigger point therapy and deep tissue massage therapy. The purposes of my form of bodytherapy are to: assist patients to identify and release neuromuscular holding patterns, particularly in the neck and shoulders; release stress and tension throughout the body; modify old postural habits and gait patterns; allow tight, restricted areas of the body to be more open and available for chiropractic adjustments and enhance the patient's response to chiropractic treatment.

Many doctors are utilizing massage therapy as an effective adjunctive and ancillary method in their patient care programs. Benefits include increased patient satisfaction and referrals. An example is Judith Hamilton, a current client who is receiving my service as well as chiropractic adjustments in her doctor's office. She states that, "Your bodytherapy has helped decrease the tension and stress in my body and allowed me to be much more relaxed during and after the chiropractic adjustments. Your method is a perfect combination with chiropractic."

I am enclosing my brochure as well as an article on my form of bodytherapy. I will call you next week to set up an appointment time. I look forward to talking with you.

Sincerely,

John Davis

John Davis, B.A., C.M.T.
Certified Massage Therapist
123 Maple Lane
Palo Alto, CA 94303

Follow-Up Letter to Doctor's Office

(Letter B)

Dear Dr. Jones:

Thank you for meeting with me on Tuesday. I feel your practice and focus on treating the whole person are in agreement with my approach. The thorough health history assessment you do is indicative of your concern for early detection and preventive care for each patient.

I am interested in discussing with you the possibility of incorporating massage therapy/bodytherapy as part of your practice. Current practice indicates that my services can help your patients be better prepared for your adjustments. The addition of massage therapy to your practice will help to maintain your treatments and promote stress reduction and preventive care.

I will contact you next week to set up a follow-up meeting to discuss possible arrangements for working together.

Sincerely,

John Davis

John Davis, B.A., C.M.T.
Certified Massage Therapist
123 Maple Lane
Palo Alto, CA 94303

Forming a Professional Relationship with a Licensed Healthcare Provider: Independent Contractor or Employee?

Chapter 3

Quick Summary of Key Points

Forming a professional relationship with a licensed healthcare provider as

- Independent contractor
- Employee

Sample contracts

- Employment contract
- Independent contractor agreement
- Professional contract

Forming a Professional Relationship with a Licensed Healthcare Provider

In order to establish and maintain an effective working relationship, you and the doctor's office must draft an appropriate contract defining your agreement, including financial arrangements and criteria for terminating the agreement. Many bodytherapy professionals have based their working relationship with a doctor on a verbal agreement, only to terminate later due to misunderstandings and assumptions that were never clarified. To be more fully professional, have a clear, written agreement.

Specifically, in order to avoid violating the tax and labor laws, you and the doctor both must understand and honor the distinction between an independent contractor and an employee. The exact determination of contractor versus employee status can be somewhat complicated and you may wish to consult a tax advisor, attorney or tax office for a definitive answer.

The following guidelines will help you understand whether you are an independent contractor or an employee. For example:

Independent contractor, you set your own hours, fees and method of working and work for a number of different people. You are required to make quarterly payments of your estimated federal taxes, which include the self-employment tax. Self-employed persons pay 2 times as much in Social Security taxes as employees because there is no employer contributing to the retirement fund.

Employee, you work on the doctor's premises only, according to terms he sets (fees, hours and method of working). <u>If you are an employee of the doctor</u>, he is required by law to withhold from your wages payments for state and federal income taxes, as well as Social Security and unemployment deductions. He must also forward that money to the proper tax collecting agencies according to established schedules.

Unfortunately, not every situation is quite so clearcut. The rules are complex and vary from state to state, which is further reason why you should seek competent advice. Abuses by licensed healthcare providers have come to light and the Internal Revenue Service has recently announced a special enforcement program to prosecute doctors who are illegally treating their employees as if they were independent contractors. Understanding the law and your rights and obligations should help you avoid problems. See a professional tax advisor in your state for further information on this important area.

The next section contains samples of three types of contracts: 1) employment contract (working in a doctor's office), 2) independent contractor agreement, and 3) professional contract.

Employment Contract

The following is an agreement between Healthcare Chiropractic, Inc., (referred to as "office") and Karen Davis, Ms. T., (referred to as "therapist.")

HOURS: Massage Therapy will be provided by the therapist on Tuesdays and Thursdays between the hours of 2:00 p.m. and 7:00 p.m., as appointments are scheduled.

EQUIPMENT: Healthcare Chiropractic shall provide massage table, oil, lotions, linens, music and sound system.

COMPENSATION: The office shall provide a guaranteed salary at the rate of $27 per hour paid every two weeks on the first (1st) and fifteenth (15th) day of each month. Healthcare Chiropractic shall be responsible for all payroll deductions such as state and federal tax. "No shows" shall be deemed the responsibility of the office, and the therapist shall be compensated at the same hourly rate.

CLERICAL: The office shall have sole responsibility to do all scheduling of appointments, necessary billing and various paperwork requirements.

OFFICE RATES: Office staff, which includes all doctors, shall schedule appointments through the normal channels and will be charged by the therapist at the rate of $65 per hour, $20 for each additional fifteen (15) minutes or fraction thereof. Payment shall be due and payable upon completion of the massage.

TERMINATION: Each party shall have the right to cancel or amend this contract. Cancellation shall require two (2) weeks notice. Amendments may be made by notifying the other party in writing and must be mutually agreeable.

The intention of all parties is to provide a clear understanding of the method of operations and payments in order that no misunderstandings occur. It is hereby mutually agreed on and witnessed by the parties below.

_____   _____
CHIROPRACTIC OFFICE   MASSAGE THERAPIST

_____
DATE

INDEPENDENT CONTRACTOR AGREEMENT

The following is an agreement between Sally Moore and Dr. Susan Smith, Medical Doctor.

Sally Moore is working on the premises of Dr. Susan Smith 3 days per week. The hours, as determined by Sally, are 9 a.m. to 4 p.m.

Sally provides massage therapy services to the patients of Dr. Susan Smith and her own personal clients, as needed.

Sally provides massage table, oil, sound and music systems. Dr. Susan Smith provides linen service and office space, insurance billing by the office staff and scheduling of all appointments.

The financial arrangement is as follows: Dr. Susan Smith receives 40% ($26) of $65 charged per clinical massage hour. When seeing her own clients at the office, Sally pays Dr. Susan Smith $20 per hour for use of the office space and the linen service. Sally shall be responsible for payment of federal and state taxes, as applicable.

It is agreed that Sally gets paid bi-weekly, every 14 days, by the office of Dr. Smith, regardless of insurance reimbursements received by the office.

Each party shall have the right to cancel or amend this contract. Cancellation or amendment shall require two (2) weeks notice. Amendments must be in writing and mutually agreeable.

_____

MEDICAL OFFICE   MASSAGE THERAPIST

_____

DATE

PROFESSIONAL CONTRACT

This contract specifies the terms and conditions of the professional working relationship of John Smith and Dr. Wayne Jones.

John Smith works as an adjunctive bodytherapy practitioner out of his own office on 420 Emerson Street, the same building which houses Dr. Wayne Jones's practice.

John Smith agrees to provide bodytherapy services, in his own office, to patients of Dr. Wayne Jones as scheduled by appointment and on an emergency basis, as needed.

Dr. Wayne Jones will give his patients a brochure and card and they will call John Smith to arrange their appointments. Dr. Wayne Jones will call John Smith with the patient's medical history, diagnosis and specific recommendations for bodytherapy.

Dr. Wayne Jones's office will bill the patient's insurance company or give the patient the doctor's billing form to submit to the insurance company, as appropriate.

John Smith will pay Dr. Jones a fee of $20 per patient visit, at the end of each month, for the insurance billing and necessary supervision. John Smith will keep progress notes on file in his office for each patient seen and will submit copies to Dr. Jones's office at the end of each month.

For tax purposes John is considered an independent contractor, responsible for declaring his own income and paying his own taxes.

Each party shall have the right to cancel or amend this contract. Cancellation or amendment shall require two (2) weeks notice. Amendments must be in writing and mutually agreeable.

_____   _____
CHIROPRACTIC OFFICE   MASSAGE THERAPIST

_____
DATE

Forms for Intake and Case Histories

■■■■■

Chapter 4

Quick Summary of Key Points

Sample forms for intake and case histories

- Medical Concern Disclosure
- Notification of Referral
- Professional Service Agreement
- Client Intake
- Client Personal Health Information
- Practitioner's Policy Statement on Insurance Reimbursement
- Practitioner/Client Payment Agreement

Forms for Intake and Case Histories

This section focuses on the forms and information you need to evaluate a client's needs, take a case history at the first visit and make appropriate referrals.

The Intake Application in this chapter is for healthcare practitioners working out of their own office. This applies particularly to bodytherapy practitioners who are licensed by their state. It is designed to assist the client and the practitioner in evaluating the need for diagnosis or treatment of a medical condition.

The form, "Medical Concern Disclosure," is an important part of your first interview and deals primarily with clients who are concerned about receiving the appropriate medical diagnosis, prognosis and treatment alternatives. This will be done in conjunction with a referral to a licensed provider of medical care. When a new client first asks about insurance reimbursement, it is your responsibility to inform him that to receive reimbursement he must have a diagnosed medical disorder. Remember that you may not make the diagnosis, but must refer the client to his own doctor or other licensed professional.

This chapter contains several examples of Client Intake and Case History forms to be filled out by the client at the first visit. These forms give you the information you need for appropriate care and referrals. You can adapt the forms for your practice or choose one that best serves your needs. Doctors' offices usually have an intake interview form which is in the chart of every new patient. If you work in a doctor's office, you may want to add questions to his form to help you better serve the patient.

Most importantly, **before you begin work with a new client, either in the doctor's office or your office, you must know his previous medical history and possible contraindications to bodytherapy.** It is suggested that you do an extensive interview to determine his specific needs. You may wish to include a simple body diagram like the example shown in this chapter in order to mark the specific areas of the body that need your work.

The Professional Service Agreement in this chapter is designed to assist you, along with the client, in defining your professional role and responsibilities. Often this agreement will clarify important issues before the course of therapy begins and will enhance compliance and commitment to the healing process.

The Financial Policy Agreement is designed to communicate the policy of your office regarding fees and insurance reimbursements. Whether you work in your own office or the doctor's office, you need to determine your financial policy.

Questions on Your Financial Policy

1. Do you request payment for services as they are rendered?
2. What percentage of your practice will be clients who pay you immediately as opposed to clients who have outstanding balances?

3. Will you request monthly payments from clients who have outstanding balances? Or will you wait for the insurance company to reimburse you?

The financial agreement shown is a suggested example for an independent contractor/bodytherapy practitioner working in his own office and affiliated with a medical doctor who refers clients. The doctor's practice may be in the same office, the same building or elsewhere.

If you work in a doctor's office, discuss your preferred financial policy with the doctor. Be sure to include the specific financial terms you and the doctor agreed to in your contract. (See Chapter 3.)

MEDICAL CONCERN DISCLOSURE

1. HEALTH PRACTITIONER

Name __Gregory Johnson__

Clinic/etc. __Neuromuscular Institute__

Address __1234 Georgia Ln.__ Suite __A__

City/Sate/Zip __Anytown, U.S.A. 12345__

Phone (234) __987-3456__ Fax (234) __986-9800__

2. CLIENT

Name __Robert Allen__

Address __1234 Town Lane__ Suite __N/A__

City/State/Zip __Anytown, U.S.A. 12345__

Phone (201) __123-4567__ Fax (201) __555-4567__

Referred by __Wendy Goldsmith__

It is my policy that before we begin our work together, we must first determine whether you have a medical condition that may require diagnosis and treatment by a licensed physician (Doctor of Medicine, Doctor of Chiropractic, etc.). Such condition may be a disease, disorder, injury, or other mental or physical condition. I am not trained nor licensed to diagnose or treat medical conditions. Therefore, I must request that we discuss your possible need for medical services. If we determine that you have an illness, physical symptoms, or a medical condition that warrants referral to a physician, I will recommend that you seek appropriate medical diagnosis, advice, and/or treatment prior to our work.

3. CLIENT'S DISCLOSURE OF MEDICAL CONCERN: Please answer the following questions:

a. Do you have any current concerns about the diagnosis or treatment of any medical condition you may have? ☑ Yes ☐ No

Please explain __I have had severe headaches and insomnia for 3 weeks.__

b. Please check any of the following areas of concern you may have about your health:

☑ **PHYSICAL** behavior patterns and/or imbalances

☑ **EMOTIONAL** behavior patterns and/or imbalances

☑ **ENERGY/MUSCULAR** behavior patterns and/or imbalances

☐ Other _____

Please explain __Insomnia, Pain radiating down my neck, shoulders and arms; difficulty concentrating__

4. CLIENT'S CHOICE OF ALTERNATIVES ABOUT MEDICAL CONCERN:

☑ Client will seek advice from a physician regarding diagnosis, prognosis, and treatment alternatives.

☐ Client will obtain the services of a physician for the purposes of monitoring an acknowledged pathological condition during a course of neuro-muscular re-education and/or other procedures.

☐ Client will receive diagnosis and treatment from a physician.

☐ Client's current concern is not sufficient to warrant referral to a physician at this time. Practitioner is satisfied that Client understands each alternative and has made an informed and reasonable choice.

5. ACKNOWLEDGMENT AND AGREEMENT:

Client has fully disclosed to practitioner all current medical concerns and has discussed with practitioner the implications of each of the alternatives above. As a result, Client has made, and agrees to abide by, the choice(s) indicated above.

X _Gregory Johnson_ _1/5/1997_   X _Robert Allen_ _1/5/1997_

Practitioner's Signature   Date   Client's Signature   Date

MEDICAL CONCERN DISCLOSURE

1. HEALTH PRACTITIONER

Name _____

Clinic/etc. _____

Address _____ Suite _____

City/Sate/Zip _____

Phone ( ) _____ Fax ( ) _____

2. CLIENT

Name _____

Address _____ Suite _____

City/State/Zip _____

Phone ( ) _____ Fax ( ) _____

Referred by _____

It is my policy that before we begin our work together, we must first determine whether you have a medical condition that may require diagnosis and treatment by a licensed physician (Doctor of Medicine, Doctor of Chiropractic, etc.). Such condition may be a disease, disorder, injury, or other mental or physical condition. I am not trained nor licensed to diagnose or treat medical conditions. Therefore, I must request that we discuss your possible need for medical services. If we determine that you have an illness, physical symptoms, or a medical condition that warrants referral to a physician, I will recommend that you seek appropriate medical diagnosis, advice, and/or treatment prior to our work.

3. CLIENT'S DISCLOSURE OF MEDICAL CONCERN: Please answer the following questions:

a. Do you have any current concerns about the diagnosis or treatment of any medical condition you may have? ☐ Yes ☐ No

Please explain _____

_____

b. Please check any of the following areas of concern you may have about your health:

☐ **PHYSICAL** behavior patterns and/or imbalances

☐ **EMOTIONAL** behavior patterns and/or imbalances

☐ **ENERGY/MUSCULAR** behavior patterns and/or imbalances

☐ Other _____

Please explain _____

4. CLIENT'S CHOICE OF ALTERNATIVES ABOUT MEDICAL CONCERN:

☐ Client will seek advice from a physician regarding diagnosis, prognosis, and treatment alternatives.

☐ Client will obtain the services of a physician for the purposes of monitoring an acknowledged pathological condition during a course of neuro-muscular re-education and/or other procedures.

☐ Client will receive diagnosis and treatment from a physician.

☐ Client's current concern is not sufficient to warrant referral to a physician at this time. Practitioner is satisfied that Client understands each alternative and has made an informed and reasonable choice.

5. ACKNOWLEDGMENT AND AGREEMENT:

Client has fully disclosed to practitioner all current medical concerns and has discussed with practitioner the implications of each of the alternatives above. As a result, Client has made, and agrees to abide by, the choice(s) indicated above.

X _____   X _____

Practitioner's Signature   Date   Client's Signature   Date

1. To: CLIENT

Name **Gregory Johnson**

Address **1234 Town Lane** Suite **N/A**

City/State/Zip **Anytown, U.S.A. 12345**

Phone (**201**) **123-4567** Fax (**201**) **555-4567**

Referred by **Wendy Goldsmith**

2. From: HEALTH PRACTITIONER

Name **Robert Allen**

Clinic/etc. **Neuromuscular Institute**

Address **1234 Georgia Lane** Suite **A**

City/Sate/Zip **Anytown, U.S.A. 12345**

Phone (**234**) **987-3456** Fax (**234**) **986-9800**

3. HEALTH PRACTITIONER'S REFERRAL STATEMENT:

On the Medical Concern Disclosure form that you completed and signed, I stated that it is my policy that before we begin our work together we must first determine whether you have a medical condition that may require diagnosis and treatment by a licensed physician (Doctor of Medicine, Doctor of Chiropractic, etc.). Such condition may be a disease, disorder, injury, or other mental or physical condition.

On that form, and in our subsequent conversation, you disclosed a concern about your health.

I am not trained nor licensed to diagnose or treat medical conditions. Therefore, I must request that you seek appropriate medical diagnosis, advice, and/or treatment prior to beginning our work.

You may select a doctor of your choice, or one that I may refer you to. After you have seen a doctor about this condition, please furnish me with his/her name, address, telephone number, and fax number so that I may consult with him/her about your condition.

After I have received appropriate information from your doctor, we may proceed.

4. CLIENT'S AREA OF HEALTH CONCERN:

Your health concern is in the following area(s):

- ☑ **PHYSICAL** behavior patterns and/or imbalances
- ☑ **EMOTIONAL** behavior patterns and/or imbalances
- ☑ **ENERGY/MUSCULAR** behavior patterns and/or imbalances
- ☐ Other **Insomnia, Pain radiating down my neck, shoulders**

    and arms; difficulty concentrating

5. CLIENT'S REFERRAL ALTERNATIVES:

- ☑ Client will see the doctor of his/her choice.
- ☐ Client will see the doctor recommended by practitioner on Referral Memo to Doctor

6. ACKNOWLEDGMENT AND AGREEMENT:

Client acknowledges this Notification of Referral, and agrees to seek appropriate medical diagnosis, advice, and/or treatment before beginning work with practitioner.

X *Gregory Johnson* 1/6/1997   X *Robert Allen* 1/6/1997

Practitioner's Signature   Date   Client's Signature   Date

Notification of Referral

NOTIFICATION OF REFERRAL

1. To: CLIENT

Name _____

Address _____ Suite _____

City/State/Zip _____

Phone ( ) _____ Fax ( ) _____

Referred by _____

2. From: HEALTH PRACTITIONER

Name _____

Clinic/etc. _____

Address _____ Suite _____

City/Sate/Zip _____

Phone ( ) _____ Fax ( ) _____

3. HEALTH PRACTITIONER'S REFERRAL STATEMENT:

On the Medical Concern Disclosure form that you completed and signed, I stated that it is my policy that before we begin our work together we must first determine whether you have a medical condition that may require diagnosis and treatment by a licensed physician (Doctor of Medicine, Doctor of Chiropractic, etc.). Such condition may be a disease, disorder, injury, or other mental or physical condition.

On that form, and in our subsequent conversation, you disclosed a concern about your health.

I am not trained nor licensed to diagnose or treat medical conditions. Therefore, I must request that you seek appropriate medical diagnosis, advice, and/or treatment prior to beginning our work.

You may select a doctor of your choice, or one that I may refer you to. After you have seen a doctor about this condition, please furnish me with his/her name, address, telephone number, and fax number so that I may consult with him/her about your condition.

After I have received appropriate information from your doctor, we may proceed.

4. CLIENT'S AREA OF HEALTH CONCERN:

Your health concern is in the following area(s):

- ☐ **PHYSICAL** behavior patterns and/or imbalances
- ☐ **EMOTIONAL** behavior patterns and/or imbalances
- ☐ **ENERGY/MUSCULAR** behavior patterns and/or imbalances
- ☐ Other _____

_____

_____

5. CLIENT'S REFERRAL ALTERNATIVES:

- ☐ Client will see the doctor of his/her choice.
- ☐ Client will see the doctor recommended by practitioner on Referral Memo to Doctor

6. ACKNOWLEDGMENT AND AGREEMENT:

Client acknowledges this Notification of Referral, and agrees to seek appropriate medical diagnosis, advice, and/or treatment before beginning work with practitioner.

X _____   X _____
Practitioner's Signature   Date   Client's Signature   Date

PROFESSIONAL SERVICE AGREEMENT

1. HEALTH PRACTITIONER

Name   Susan Jaccoby

Clinic/etc.   Health Associates

Address   345 Bruce Ln.   Suite   A

City/Sate/Zip   Anytown, U.S.A. 12345

Phone (123)   456-7890   Fax (123)   456-7891

2. CLIENT

Name   Ellen Steele

Address   405 Linden Ln.   Suite   N/A

City/State/Zip   Anytown, U.S.A. 12345

Phone (123)   456-6789   Fax (123)   567-8907

Referred by   Dr. Jack Martin, D.C.

3. PURPOSE OF WORK: _____

_____

4. PRACTITIONER'S RESPONSIBILITIES:

☑ Assess and evaluate Client

☑ Recommend specific exercises

☑ Neuromuscular re-education and other procedures

☑ Evaluate and assess Client's progress

☐ Other (specify): _____

_____

5. CLIENT'S RESPONSIBILITIES:

☑ Arrive on time for all scheduled sessions

☑ Promptly report to practitioner any changes in health

☑ Do the recommended exercises

☐ Other (specify): _____

_____

6. COURSE OF PROCEDURE:

___2___ times per week for ___2___ weeks, and then ___1___ times per week for ___4___ weeks

7. ACKNOWLEDGMENTS:

(A) Practitioner makes no claims, representations, or guarantees about specific results.

(B) Payment for service is due at the time the service is performed unless prior arrangements are made. Payment is Client's personal obligation regardless of insurance or other third-party involvement.

(C) Appointments cancelled with less than 24 hours notice beforehand will be charged for.

(D) Client is currently taking the following medications: Coumadin _____

_____

(E) Client has the following condition(s) which may warrant special concern or precautions: _____

Hypertension

X _Susan Jaccoby_ 2/1/1997   X _Ellen Steele_ 2/1/1997

Practitioner's Signature   Date   Client's Signature   Date

PROFESSIONAL SERVICE AGREEMENT

1. HEALTH PRACTITIONER

Name _____

Clinic/etc. _____

Address _____ Suite _____

City/Sate/Zip _____

Phone ( ) _____ Fax ( ) _____

2. CLIENT

Name _____

Address _____ Suite _____

City/State/Zip _____

Phone ( ) _____ Fax ( ) _____

Referred by _____

3. PURPOSE OF WORK: _____

_____

4. PRACTITIONER'S RESPONSIBILITIES:

☐ Assess and evaluate Client

☐ Recommend specific exercises

☐ Neuromuscular re-education and other procedures

☐ Evaluate and assess Client's progress

☐ Other (specify): _____

_____

5. CLIENT'S RESPONSIBILITIES:

☐ Arrive on time for all scheduled sessions

☐ Promptly report to practitioner any changes in health

☐ Do the recommended exercises

☐ Other (specify): _____

_____

6. COURSE OF PROCEDURE:

_____ times per week for _____ weeks, and then _____ times per week for _____ weeks

7. ACKNOWLEDGMENTS:

(A) Practitioner makes no claims, representations, or guarantees about specific results.

(B) Payment for service is due at the time the service is performed unless prior arrangements are made. Payment is Client's personal obligation regardless of insurance or other third-party involvement.

(C) Appointments cancelled with less than 24 hours notice beforehand will be charged for.

(D) Client is currently taking the following medications: _____

_____

(E) Client has the following condition(s) which may warrant special concern or precautions: _____

_____

X _____   X _____

Practitioner's Signature   Date   Client's Signature   Date

(PRACTITIONER'S LETTERHEAD)

CLIENT INTAKE FORM

WELCOME TO THE OFFICE OF _____

Client Information
(please print)

Name : _____   Sex: M __ F __

Address:_____

City:_____   State _____ Zip_____

Telephone Number: (____)_____

Soc. Sec. No. _____   Driver's Lic. No. _____

Age: _____   Date of Birth:_____   Number of Children:____

Marital Status: Single ( )   Married ( )   Widow(er) ( )   Divorced ( )   Separated ( )

Occupation _____   Employer _____

Address:_____

City:_____   State_____ Zip_____

Telephone Number: (____)_____

Spouse's Name: _____

Occupation _____

Employer _____   Address: _____

City:_____   State _____ Zip_____

Telephone Number: (____)_____

Family Physician _____

Address:_____

City:_____   State _____ Zip _____

Telephone Number: (____)_____

CLIENT INTAKE FORM (Continued)

Insurance Information:
*Primary Carrier*_____

Address:_____

City:_____ State _____ Zip_____

Telephone Number: (___)_____

Subscriber's Name_____ ID# _____ Policy# _____

*Secondary Carrier*_____

Address:_____

City:_____ State_____ Zip_____

Telephone Number: (___)_____

Subscriber's Name_____ ID#_____ Policy#_____

Who referred you to this office? _____

Have you ever been treated by a counselor? No ( ) Yes ( ) Last Visit_____

In case of emergency, please notify:_____

Telephone Number: (___)_____

Financial Policy: We ask our clients to pay at the end of each visit, unless other specific arrangements are made.

Cancellation Policy: The time of your appointment is reserved for you.
Please give us 24 hours notice if you are unable to keep your appointment. Appointments cancelled less than 24 hours beforehand will be charged for payment in full.

Signature:_____ Date_____

Witness:_____ Relationship (if minor client) _____

CLIENT PERSONAL HEALTH INFORMATION

Date _____

Name _____

How did you hear of my services? _____

Describe reason for this visit: _____

Date of last medical examination:_____

Are you currently under a doctor's care?____ If yes, give name of physician and reason for consulting

him/her: _____

Are you presently taking any medications?_____

If yes, please describe: _____

Are you now or have you ever been under the care of a psychotherapist? ____ If yes, give name and

reason for care: _____

Have you ever received bodytherapy? ___ If yes, please describe: _____

_____

List any other therapies you are receiving: _____

_____

Have you ever had any type of accident?_____

If yes, please describe: _____

_____

_____

Do you have trouble with varicose veins or blood clots?_____

Have you had any type of surgery?_____

Do you have any limitations of mobility?_____

_____

CLIENT PERSONAL HEALTH INFORMATION (continued)

Are you on an exercise program? _____

Describe type of excercise & frequency: _____

_____

_____

Describe methods you use to manage your stress: _____

_____

_____

Any additional comments regarding your health: _____

_____

_____

CLIENT INTAKE FORM

Check specific areas where you experience pain or discomfort:

_____ Head	_____ Arms	_____ Knees
_____ Neck	_____ Hands	_____ Lower Legs
_____ Shoulders	_____ Abdomen	_____ Ankles
_____ Chest	_____ Pelvis	_____ Feet
_____ Lower Back	_____ Hips	
_____ Middle Back	_____ Thighs	

Shade in areas
of pain

Shade in areas
of pain

PRACTITIONER'S POLICY STATEMENT ON INSURANCE REIMBURSEMENT

To all clients with health insurance:

In order to bill for bodytherapy services, your primary care physician must diagnose your condition. Also, the primary care physician must supervise this work and recommend further bodytherapy.

Charges for bodytherapy are due at the time the service is performed, unless prior arrangements are made with the doctor's office and the bodytherapy practitioner. Payment is your obligation regardless of insurance or other third-party involvement.

This office cannot accept responsibility for collecting your insurance claim, nor negotiating a settlement for a disputed claim.

NOTE: You can use the following format and wording to establish your payment policy with your clients.

You may mail the superbill and/or the claim form directly to your insurance company.

PRACTITIONER/CLIENT AGREEMENT REGARDING INSURANCE REIMBURSEMENT

I understand and agree that health and accident insurance is a contract between an insurance carrier and me. Any amount authorized to be paid directly to my doctor's office will be credited to my account upon receipt. However, I understand and agree that all services rendered to me are charged directly to me, and that I am personally responsible for payment.

Signature: _____ Date: _____

Client's Printed Name: _____

Address: _____

Phone Number: (___)_____

SAMPLE

PRACTITIONER/CLIENT PAYMENT AGREEMENT

The usual policy of this office is for clients to pay as services are rendered regardless of insurance reimbursement.

The following is an extended payment agreement between the practitioner and the client whose name and signature appear below. The agreement consists of those completed paragraphs whose initial letter (A, B, and/or C) are circled.

The unpaid balance to date is $<u>750.00</u>.

PAYMENT ARRANGEMENTS:
(Circle the letter and fill in the paragraphs that apply.)

   A. I agree to pay the balance due of $ _____ on_____.

   B. After your insurance has paid the covered amount, any remaining balance is due when billed. If no insurance payment is received 30 days after service is rendered, monthly payments will begin.

   C. Monthly payments in the amount of $<u>100.00</u> will be due on the <u>1st</u> day of each month, beginning <u>MAY 1, 1997</u>, and continuing on the same day of each month and every month thereafter until paid in full.

Interest will accrue at the rate of <u>15%</u> (Annual Percentage Rate).

THE RESPONSIBILITY OF PAYMENTS RESTS WITH THE CLIENT, NOT THE CLIENT'S INSURANCE COMPANY. PAYMENT MUST BE MADE BY CASH, PERSONAL CHECK, CASHIER'S CHECK OR MONEY ORDER.

To secure the payment of this obligation, I, without process, confer judgment in favor of <u>ALEX JONES, C.M.T.</u>, for the sum due and unpaid and authorize judgment to be entered in that amount against me. I will also be responsible for all costs of collection and reasonable attorney fees.

_____

Client's Signature (Parent, if Minor)

Witness_____ Date <u>APRIL 15, 1997</u>

Practitioner/Client Payment Agreement

The usual policy of this office is for clients to pay as services are rendered regardless of insurance reimbursement.

The following is an extended payment agreement between the practitioner and the client whose name and signature appear below. The agreement consists of those completed paragraphs whose initial letter (A, B, and/or C) are circled.

The unpaid balance to date is $_____.

PAYMENT ARRANGEMENTS:
(Circle the letter and fill in the paragraphs that apply.)

A. I agree to pay the balance due of $ _____ on_____.

B. After your insurance has paid the covered amount, any remaining balance is due when billed. If no insurance payment is received 30 days after service is rendered, monthly payments will begin.

C. Monthly payments in the amount of $_____will be due on the___day of each month, beginning _____, and continuing on the same day of each month and every month thereafter until paid in full.

Interest will accrue at the rate of_____% (Annual Percentage Rate).

THE RESPONSIBILITY OF PAYMENTS RESTS WITH THE CLIENT, NOT THE CLIENT'S INSURANCE COMPANY. PAYMENT MUST BE MADE BY CASH, PERSONAL CHECK, CASHIER'S CHECK OR MONEY ORDER.

To secure the payment of this obligation, I, without process, confer judgment in favor of _____*, for the sum due and unpaid and authorize judgment to be entered in that amount against me. I will also be responsible for all costs of collection and reasonable attorney fees.

*insert practitioner's name

_____

Client's Signature (Parent, if Minor)

Witness_____   Date _____

Chapter 5

Letter Formats for Doctor's Prescription and Referral

Quick Summary of Key Points

Description and examples of

- Prescription form: How a prescription must be worded for maximum reimbursement.
- Referral memo: What is a referral memo and how to use it.

Letter Formats for Doctor's Prescription and Referral

Before you can legally deliver your service, the client's primary healthcare provider must write a referral memo and a prescription ordering your particular service as an adjunct to a supervised treatment plan.

In licensed states, prescriptions for massage and bodytherapy services are customary, since a practitioner is licensed by the state to perform services as an adjunctive therapist to the doctor's treatment plan. The definition of adjunctive therapist varies with the state licensing and examining board for the bodytherapy profession.

In unlicensed states (such as California) in the case of a personal injury or automobile accident claim, the insurance company may require a prescription and/or a referral memo to you from the licensed provider of care.

What is a Prescription Form?

The prescription form in this chapter also includes the names of muscles, which the referring doctor can easily check off. The prescription forms in this chapter are shown both blank and filled in so you can see how they look.

In unlicensed states, if a prescription format is required by the client's personal injury or accident insurance company, I recommend that you also ask the doctor to write a memo of referral, a copy of which you keep in your files to protect you.

What is a Referral Memo?

The referral memo format shown in this chapter is preferred in unlicensed states, as it clearly indicates that bodytherapy is an adjunctive service to the medical treatment program. In my consulting practice I have talked with several practitioners who have not been reimbursed for their services because the referral memo and/or prescription was not correctly worded. In some cases the doctor gave the wrong name for the bodytherapy. For example, when the doctor prescribed Hellerwork or Trager® work the insurance company responded that it needed more information on this type of service. Therefore, **the doctor should use the terms "neuromuscular re-education" and "soft-tissue therapy" when ordering your services, since they are recognized by insurance companies.**

Why do you need both?

According to Jerry Green, legal expert for healthcare practitioners, a prescription for your services which does not state that you are an adjunctive therapist may be interpreted by a court of law as a prescription for a treatment program, which you are not licensed to give. Therefore, the referral memo should specifically say that you are an adjunctive therapist.

The prescription and/or referral memo must contain the client's name, diagnosis, the name of the adjunctive procedure referred for and the number of sessions prescribed. (For example, 3 sessions per week for 2 weeks, then one session per week for 8 weeks.) Insurance companies look for terminology they recognize with specific recommendations for duration of the service performed. At the end of that time, if sessions are to continue the client must be re-evaluated by the doctor and a new prescription/referral memo submitted to the insurance company.

These two documents together may help protect you against a charge of practicing medicine without a license. For further information on this issue contact Jerry Green directly at:

Jerry Green, J.D.
P.O. Box 5094
Mill Valley, CA 94942

Date __1/15/97__   Name of Patient Referred __Howard Green__

1. To: HEALTH PRACTITIONER

Name __Karen Jones__

Organization __Myotherapy Clinic__

Address __12345 Hill Road__   Suite __A__

City/Sate/Zip __Anytown, U.S.A. 12345__

Phone (415) __234-5678__   Fax (415) __345-6789__

2. From: DOCTOR

Name __Jack Friedberg, M.D.__

Clinic/etc. __Neurology Center__

Address __123 Maple Lane__   Suite __C__

City/State/Zip __Anytown, U.S.A. 12345__

Phone (123) __678-9845__   Fax (123)__567-4567__

3. REFERRAL UNDERSTANDING:

I am referring to you the patient named above. I am the primary care provider for this patient. Your health care service(s) will be an ancillary and/or adjunctive part of my primary treatment program, and you will work under my direction. Please advise me of your progress with this patient and call me if you need more information or wish to discuss any aspect of this patient's care.

4. RECOMMENDATION:

I recommend the following procedure(s):

☑ Soft-tissue therapy   ☑ Neuromuscular re-education   ☐ Muscle rehabilitation & exercise

☐ _____

Course of procedure(s):

__2__ times per week for __2__ weeks, and then __1__ times per week for __6__ weeks

5. FOLLOW-UP EVALUATION:

I will evaluate this patient __one__ time(s) per month and make further recommendations regarding the patient's treatment plan.

6. FOR YOUR INFORMATION:

(A) I am currently treating this patient for: __headaches and fibromyalgia__

(B) My current regimen of treatment for this patient is: __Medications, Ultrasound__

(C) This patient is currently taking the following medications: __Coumadin, Tetracycline__

(D) This patient has the following conditions which may warrant special concern or precautions:

__He has a history of hypertension and heart disease.__

X _~~Jack Friedberg, M.D.~~_

Doctor's Signature and Title

REFERRAL MEMO TO HEALTH PRACTITIONER

Date _____   Name of Patient Referred _____

1. To: HEALTH PRACTITIONER

Name _____

Organization _____

Address _____ Suite _____

City/Sate/Zip _____

Phone (___) _____ Fax (___) _____

2. From: DOCTOR

Name _____

Clinic/etc. _____

Address _____ Suite _____

City/State/Zip _____

Phone (___) _____ Fax (___) _____

3. REFERRAL UNDERSTANDING:

I am referring to you the patient named above. I am the primary care provider for this patient. Your health care service(s) will be an ancillary and/or adjunctive part of my primary treatment program, and you will work under my direction. Please advise me of your progress with this patient and call me if you need more information or wish to discuss any aspect of this patient's care.

4. RECOMMENDATION:

I recommend the following procedure(s):

☐ Soft-tissue therapy   ☐ Neuromuscular re-education   ☐ Muscle rehabilitation & exercise

☐ _____

Course of procedure(s):

_____ times per week for _____ weeks, and then _____ times per week for _____ weeks

5. FOLLOW-UP EVALUATION:

I will evaluate this patient _____ time(s) per month and make further recommendations regarding the patient's treatment plan.

6. FOR YOUR INFORMATION:

(A) I am currently treating this patient for: _____

_____

(B) My current regimen of treatment for this patient is: _____

_____

(C) This patient is currently taking the following medications: _____

_____

(D) This patient has the following conditions which may warrant special concern or precautions:

_____

X _____

Doctor's Signature and Title

REFERRAL MEMO TO DOCTOR

3

Date __1/15/97__ Name of Patient Referred __Susan Weinstein__

1. To: DOCTOR

Name __Allen Jones, M.D.__

Clinic/etc. __New Brighton Clinic__

Address __1234 Lane Rd.__ Suite __A__

City/Sate/Zip __Allentown, PA 11121__

Phone (805) __111-3456__ Fax (805) __444-5555__

2. From: HEALTH PRACTITIONER

Name __Karen Friedberg__

Organization __Neuromuscular Associates__

Address __224 Pine Lane__ Suite __B__

City/State/Zip __Georgia, PA 12344__

Phone (341) __111-7890__ Fax (341) __555-6789__

3. REFERRAL UNDERSTANDING:

I am referring to you the client named above who has come to me for health care services. This client has expressed concern about an illness/physical symptoms/health condition which may require your diagnosis, advice, and/or treatment prior to, or concurrent with, my services. Please use your professional judgment regarding this individual and advise me accordingly. Also, please advise me of your ongoing progress with this client and call me if you need more information. In the client's best interest, I will not provide my services until hearing from you.

4. RECOMMENDATION:

I recommend the following:

☑ Your advice regarding diagnosis, prognosis, and possible treatment alternatives

☐ Monitoring a recognized pathological condition

☐ Diagnosis and treatment of client's health condition(s)

☐ _____

5. FOR YOUR INFORMATION:

(A) This client has come to me for:

☑ Soft-tissue therapy ☑ Neuromuscular re-education ☐ Muscle rehabilitation & exercise

☐ _____

(B) This client has the following conditions which may warrant your treatment or special concern:

History of automobile accident one year ago diagnosed as lumbar sprain/strain.

Thank you for your cooperation,

x _Karen Friedberg, LMT_

Practitioner's Signature and Title

Referral Memo to Doctor from Health Practitioner

REFERRAL MEMO TO DOCTOR

Date _____ Name of Patient Referred _____

1. To: DOCTOR

Name _____

Clinic/etc. _____

Address_____ Suite _____

City/Sate/Zip _____

Phone (   )_____ Fax (   ) _____

2. From: HEALTH PRACTITIONER

Name _____

Organization_____

Address_____ Suite _____

City/State/Zip_____

Phone (   )_____ Fax (   ) _____

3. REFERRAL UNDERSTANDING:

I am referring to you the client named above who has come to me for health care services. This client has expressed concern about an illness/physical symptoms/health condition which may require your diagnosis, advice, and/or treatment prior to, or concurrent with, my services. Please use your professional judgment regarding this individual and advise me accordingly. Also, please advise me of your ongoing progress with this client and call me if you need more information. In the client's best interest, I will not provide my services until hearing from you.

4. RECOMMENDATION:

I recommend the following:

☐ Your advice regarding diagnosis, prognosis, and possible treatment alternatives

☐ Monitoring a recognized pathological condition

☐ Diagnosis and treatment of client's health condition(s)

☐ _____

5. FOR YOUR INFORMATION:

(A) This client has come to me for:

☐ Soft-tissue therapy   ☐ Neuromuscular re-education   ☐ Muscle rehabilitation & exercise

☐ _____

(B) This client has the following conditions which may warrant your treatment or special concern:

_____

_____

_____

_____

_____

Thank you for your cooperation,

X _____

Practitioner's Signature and Title

Referral Memo to Doctor from Health Practitioner

SAMPLE

DOCTOR'S PRESCRIPTION FORM

DECEMBER 5, 1996
Date

I have been treating ___Trudy Dennis___ since ___12/1/97___ for the following condition:

DIAGNOSIS: ___Cervical Subluxation, Thoracic Subluxation___

I prescribe soft-tissue therapy (and exercise, if indicated) on the muscles indicated below:

Rx ___3___ TIMES PER WEEK FOR ___6___ weeks.

CONTRAINDICATIONS/PRECAUTIONS: _____

Jim Friedman, M.D.
Doctor's Signature

CERVICAL

RT	LT	B/L	MUSCLE
	✓		__ Suboccipital
✓	✓		__ Trapezius
✓	✓		__ Splenius capitis
✓			__ Levator scapulae

THORACIC

RT	LT	B/L	MUSCLE
		✓	__ Trapezius
			__ Longissimus thoracis
	✓		__ Latissimus dorsi
	✓		__ Rhomboid Maj/Min
		✓	__ Serratus Post/Sup

SHOULDER

RT	LT	B/L	MUSCLE
	✓		__ Deltoid
	✓		__ Pectoralis major
		✓	__ Teres major
		✓	__ Trapezius

LUMBOSACRAL

RT	LT	B/L	MUSCLE
	✓		__ Gluteus maximus
		✓	__ Piriformis
	✓		__ Iliocostalis lumborum
	✓		__ Erector spinae
		✓	__ Quadratus lumborum

DOCTOR'S PRESCRIPTION FORM

_____

Date

I have been treating _____ since _____ for the following condition:

DIAGNOSIS: _____

I prescribe soft-tissue therapy (and exercise, if indicated) on the muscles indicated below:

Rx _____ TIMES PER WEEK FOR _____ weeks.

CONTRAINDICATIONS/PRECAUTIONS: _____

_____

Doctor's Signature

CERVICAL

RT	LT	B/L	MUSCLE
—	—	—	__ Suboccipital
—	—	—	__ Trapezius
—	—	—	__ Splenius capitis
—	—	—	__ Levator scapulae

THORACIC

RT	LT	B/L	MUSCLE
—	—	—	__ Trapezius
—	—	—	__ Longissimus thoracis
—	—	—	__ Latissimus dorsi
—	—	—	__ Rhomboid Maj/Min
—	—	—	__ Serratus Post/Sup

SHOULDER

—	—	—	__ Deltoid
—	—	—	__ Pectoralis major
—	—	—	__ Teres major
—	—	—	__ Trapezius

LUMBOSACRAL

—	—	—	__ Gluteus maximus
—	—	—	__ Piriformis
—	—	—	__ Iliocostalis lumborum
—	—	—	__ Erector spinae
—	—	—	__ Quadratus lumborum

S A M P L E

DOCTOR'S PRESCRIPTION FORM

It is my recommendation that _____<u>Susan Smith</u>_____
undergo the following adjunctive procedure:

      ☑ Soft-Tissue Therapy

      ☐ Neuromuscular Re-education

Sessions to be scheduled:

      ☑ 3 times per week for ____<u>1</u>____ weeks

      ☑ 2 times per week for ____<u>4</u>____weeks

      ☐ Once per week for _____ weeks

Diagnosis:

_____<u>Cervical Subluxation, Thoracic Subluxation</u>_____

<u>December 9, 1996</u>____
Date

_<u>Susan Jones, D. C.</u>_____
Physician's Signature

DOCTOR'S PRESCRIPTION FORM

It is my recommendation that _____
undergo the following adjunctive procedure:

        ☐ Soft-Tissue Therapy

        ☐ Neuromuscular Re-education

Sessions to be scheduled:

        ☐ 3 times per week for _____ weeks

        ☐ 2 times per week for _____weeks

        ☐ Once per week for _____ weeks

Diagnosis:

_____

_____
Date

_____
Physician's Signature

DOCTOR'S REFERRAL FORM

SAMPLE

In your overall health care program, your doctor is sensitive to providing quality care and long-term cost reduction.

If your doctor has determined that you have:
☑ *muscle spasms*   ☑ *stiffness*   ☐ *backache*
☑ *headache*   ☑ *a physical injury*   ☐ *neuro-muscular disorder*   ☐ *other_____*

_____

*your doctor may suggest that you make an appointment with Chris Rosche, Certified Trager*_{SM} *Practitioner and Massage Therapist for:*   ☑ *clinical massage therapy*   ☑ *neuromuscular re-education*   ☐ *soft-tissue mobilization*   ☐ *release of accumulated stress*   ☐ *increased circulation*   ☑ *enhanced flexibility and range of motion*   ☐ *increased body awareness*   ☐ *other*

_____

_____

Chris Rosche M.A., M.P.H., specializes in neuro-muscular and movement re-education and offers personalized attention to guide you toward greater health.

She is available to meet with you as needed to provide the necessary guidance and support during your physical recovery.

Trager® and Massage therapy can be a considered adjunctive to primary medical care, chiropractic and physical therapy.

To make an appointment in Palo Alto, please call (408) 732 3376

This personalized service is designed to provide quality preventive and adjunctive health care with your doctor's referral.

Referring physician ___Wayne Jones, MD___

Diagnosis ___Neck Muscle Spasm Whiplash Injury___

Date ___5/1/96___

DOCTOR'S REFERRAL FORM

In your overall health care program, your doctor is sensitive to providing quality care and long-term cost reduction.

If your doctor has determined that you have: ☐ *muscle spasms* ☐ *stiffness* ☐ *backache* ☐ *headache* ☐ *a physical injury* ☐ *neuro-muscular disorder* ☐ *other_____*

_____

*your doctor may suggest that you make an appointment with Chris Rosche, Certified Trager*_{SM} *Practitioner and Massage Therapist for:* ☐ *clinical massage therapy* ☐ *neuromuscular re-education* ☐ *soft-tissue mobilization* ☐ *release of accumulated stress* ☐ *increased circulation* ☐ *enhanced flexibility and range of motion* ☐ *increased body awareness* ☐ *other*

_____

_____

Chris Rosche M.A., M.P.H., specializes in neuro-muscular and movement re-education and offers personalized attention to guide you toward greater health.

She is available to meet with you as needed to provide the necessary guidance and support during your physical recovery.

Trager® and Massage therapy can be a considered adjunctive to primary medical care, chiropractic and physical therapy.

To make an appointment in Palo Alto, please call (408) 732 3376

This personalized service is designed to provide quality preventive and adjunctive health care with your doctor's referral.

Referring physician _____

Diagnosis _____

Date _____

How to Get Reimbursed by an Insurance Company

Chapter 6

Quick Summary of Key Points

- Basic professional requirements
- Importance of verifying client coverage and billing options
- Distinguishing between types of insurance & source of injury complaints
- Basic billing procedures for all claim types
- Establishing rapport with Insurance Claims Representatives
- How to use proper office procedures and records management

How to Get Reimbursed by an Insurance Company

This chapter describes in detail what you must do to establish insurance reimbursement as a financial pillar of your massage/bodytherapy practice. It also covers (with sample forms and letters) the following essential preliminary matters:

1. Verifying Coverage (confirming with the company that the client has insurance, what it covers and that you are eligible for reimbursement)

2. Establishing Payment Policies

3. Types of Insurance

4. Basic Procedures for All Claims

(For detailed billing procedures for the three types of insurance: [Major Medical, Worker's Compensation, and Personal Injury] see Chapters 8-10.)

Prerequisites For Insurance Reimbursement for Massage/Bodytherapy

To be accepted as an effective member of the healthcare team, you must have:

- Solid clinical skills and advanced techniques beyond the basic massage therapy training in your area of speciality.

- A good understanding of medical terminology. Most community colleges and medical assisting schools have courses in this area.

- A thorough knowledge of anatomy and physiology. Take a two-semester course in anatomy and physiology at a junior college or university, since many massage certification programs are inadequate in this area.

- The ability to define what you do and explain it to medical professionals in their language. For example, massage is "soft-tissue mobilization." Trager® or Hellerwork are called "neuromuscular re-education."

- Good communication skills. You must be able to explain to doctors how your skills can help their patients.

- Work experience in a medical/chiropractic setting. A few hours a week in a doctor's office will help you understand how the healthcare delivery and health insurance systems work.

- Accurate, concise progress records on all clients. Record your findings, subjective and objective, along with procedures and recommendations.

- Accurate accounting records on all clients, using a bookkeeping system with receipts, ledger cards and insurance log.

- Supervision from your primary healthcare provider. In many licensed states, practitioners work in their own office with face-to-face and telephone supervision from the doctor, as needed.

In many unlicensed states, supervision means working in the doctor's office at least half the time. Verify supervision requirements with your state agency or professional association.

- Your own professional liability insurance, regardless of the doctor's coverage. See Suggested Readings and Reference Materials after Chapter 17 for names of companies offering liability insurance for practitioners.

- Finally, you must be familiar with reimbursement procedures, and know how to make them work for you, to ensure that you receive timely reimbursements for your services.

Frustrated bodytherapy practitioners often tell me, "Since the doctor's office did all of the billing for me, I felt I did not have to worry about that part. Later, I found that the staff did not know all the procedure codes for my services, and payments for my services were delayed significantly."

If you work in a doctor's office, you can avoid delays by clarifying billing procedures on Day One with the billing staff and your clients.

Verifying Coverage

The first step in filing a claim with an insurance company is to verify coverage, which is usually done by the practitioner or the doctor's front office staff. You must understand how the process works, especially if you are renting space in a doctor's office or in an adjacent office.

When a client first comes to the office, obtain the following information:

The name and telephone number of the insurance company .

The name of his employer/company

The client's insurance group number

The client's insurance identification number, sometimes called subscriber number. Usually it is the person's Social Security number.

When a client is first accepted into an insurance plan, either on his own or through his employer, he receives a membership card which has the information that you need. Usually he will bring it with him to the first appointment. In a doctor's office the secretary will make a photocopy of the card or record this information in the patient's chart during the first visit. (Figure 1 shows an example of an insurance ID card.)

Figure 1

Sample Insurance ID Card

Insurance Company Name & Logo		
Subscriber Name	Effective Date	
S. B. SMITH	**04/ 22/ 96**	
Subscriber Identification	Group Number	
123-45-6789	**111221**	
Type of Contract	Plan Code	Hosp. Code
Ind.	**245**	**X**

To verify coverage: Phone the insurance company and give your name and the doctor's name, as well as the client information. For example, say:

"This is Susan Jones calling from Dr. Smith's office. I would like to verify coverage for Gladys Green, a patient. Her group number is 1223344 and her identification number is 552-02-3112."

At this point the person answering the phone may ask you to wait while the record is called up onto a computer terminal. When you can, give the rest of the information. For example, you might say:

"The doctor's diagnosis is headaches and shoulder muscle spasms. I would like to verify coverage for soft tissue therapy/neuromuscular re-education." (Remember to use the medical terms for massage therapy and bodytherapy recognized by the insurance company.)

The insurance company's claims representative will tell you at what percentage soft tissue therapy/neuromuscular re-education is covered. Most companies cover these procedures at 80%, and there may be a deductible amount which the client must pay before the company will pay anything. The policy may also have limitations and exclusions on these types of procedures. For example, the company may pay for only "x" number of visits per year and the charge for each visit may not exceed "x" amount.

Once you know what percentage of your services are covered and any limitations or exclusions to the coverage, keep the information in the client's file along with the general client information sheet. Many doctors' offices send a written request for verification of coverage to the insurance company in order to document the verbal information.

Establish a Policy on Payment of Fees

You should also prepare a Practitioner Information Sheet (see Appendix B for guidelines) which describes your services to the client, your scope of practice (the skills you have and how you work) and specifically how your work is an important adjunct to the healthcare practice you work in.

On an additional sheet attached to your Practitioner Information Sheet, state your policies regarding insurance reimbursement. (See Practitioner Policy Statement on Insurance Reimbursement on page 44.) This will be affected by the office policies of the doctor you work with.

For example, if the professional practice is primarily for cash, most clients are required to pay in full for services rendered at the time of their visits. They receive a pre-printed billing statement which they attach to their claim form and send to the insurance company. (See Chapter 8.) The front desk assists them in filling in the patient information on their claim forms and attaches a pre-printed billing form. However, patients (not the insurance company), have final responsibility for paying the service provider.

Some offices prefer to collect 20% of the total due (which is called the co-payment, the amount the insurance company will require the client to pay) and then bill the insurance company for the remaining 80%. In this case, the client signs the assignment of benefits section of the claim form stating that benefits are payable to the provider's office.

When benefits are assigned to the provider, the office has significantly more paperwork to complete as well as follow up with insurance companies. The average amount of time for reimbursements from the insurance company to the provider's office is 4 weeks.

You must be clear in your initial meeting with your client about your policy regarding insurance payments. Tell clients at their first visit, both verbally and in writing, that you request full payment at the time of the visit. Also, this policy shall apply unless prior arrangements are made. (In cases of financial hardship, if the client is unable to pay in full, you should ask for payment of 20% of the outstanding balance and get assignment of benefits to your office. See Chapter 10 for an explanation of assignment of benefits.)

If you are working in a doctor's office, you should similarly clarify the payment policies and procedures in your initial business meetings with the doctor and his office staff.

In a cash payment practice the client must understand that he or she is responsible to pay for services received regardless of insurance coverage.

Retain Patients by Educating Them About Your Value

Your first visit with a patient is the time to begin their education about the value of your work with them and the reality of limits on insurance reimbursement. Eventually their insurance will stop covering your services, especially since insurance covers TREATMENT but not ongoing maintenance. To begin establishing your ongoing relationship in the patient's mind, you can easily say something like this:

"I'm here as your ongoing provider. My job is to help you regain your full health and maintain it whether or not you have insurance coverage. My services can still serve as a vital part of your ongoing healthcare program. It's important to understand that and plan and budget for it, so that this important work can continue as long as we both feel you can benefit from it."

Choose the Best Billing Option for Now

The following are four billing options (from most integrated to most independent) in establishing your relationship with a doctor's office. The best billing option for you will change as your practice evolves.

Option A - You work in the doctor's office and the doctor bills for your services. You are paid every 2 weeks for your work regardless of insurance reimbursements received by the office.

Option B - You rent space in the same office as the doctor and do your own billing. You primarily accept cash at the time of the visit and help the client submit claims directly to his own insurance company.

Option C - You work in the doctor's office, which bills the insurance company on your behalf. You receive later payment when the insurance company reimburses the doctor. You may have to wait 4 to 6 weeks before you receive your first payment. When insurance checks begin arriving, you are paid every 2 weeks, retroactively, for services you performed 4 to 6 weeks before.

Option D - You work in your own office and consult regularly with the doctor by telephone and in person. You bill insurance claims from your own office with the doctor's referral letter/prescription form. In licensed states this option is used most frequently, with the practitioner billing the insurance company directly.

The option you choose will depend on the type of statewide regulation for your professional specialty, your working relationship with the doctor, your financial situation and your career goals.

Carefully review the following information to determine which reimbursement system is appropriate for you. Then make sure your practitioner policy statement on insurance reimbursement and practitioner/client agreement on insurance reimbursement are in harmony with your choice. Be sure to discuss and establish these agreements with the client at the time of the first visit when you review the case history. Then include the forms in the file. (See Chapter 4.)

Types of Insurance

Insurance companies pay for major medical, Worker's Compensation, personal injury and Medicare claims.

Major Medical is the term generally used to describe health insurance. This may be a group policy through the employer or an individually purchased policy.

Major medical insurance covers illness or accidents not related to employment. (See Chapter 8.)

Worker's Compensation Insurance is provided by the employer, under state requirements, for work-related injuries and accidents. (See Chapter 9.)

Personal Injury (medical payment or liability) insurance covers injuries from an automobile accident and other accidents. (See Chapter 10.)

Medicare Insurance (as of the Fall of 1996), pays for massage therapy only in Connecticut. To apply for a Medicare Provider Number, contact the Medicare Bureau at (203) 630-4728. Or write to P.O. Box 9000, Meriden CT 06454.

HMOs (Health Maintenance Organizations) and **PPOs** (Preferred Provider Organizations), which are prepaid, pay for services performed by providers who are employed by them (such as medical doctors and registered physical therapists.) Currently, certified massage therapists/bodytherapy practitioners can do this through several managed care networks. See Chapter 15 for more information.

With a referral and appropriate supervision, Worker's Compensation and personal injury insurance companies almost always pay for your services when recommended by a healthcare provider, while major medical coverage generally pays for adjunctive services when they are billed as soft tissue therapy/neuromuscular re-education or soft tissue mobilization.

Which Insurance Type do you Bill for This Client?

Source of Complaint	Insurance Type that Covers	Go to Chapter
Accident (Auto or Other)	Personal Injury	10
Work-Related	Worker's Comp*	9
Other	Major Medical*	8

*NOTE: In states with no statewide licensure for your profession, you must be appropriately supervised in a provider's office in order to bill for Worker's Compensation and Major Medical. You can still bill auto and other accidents from your own office. If you DO have statewide licensure for your profession, you may bill all three types from your own office.

Basic Steps for Submitting an Insurance Claim

Four methods are commonly used to submit insurance claims:

1. Manual submission (Paper forms are filled in by hand and sent in the mail to the insurance company.)

2. Computer Preparation (Forms are completed and printed out on your computer system and submitted in the mail.)

3. Service Bureau (An independent firm uses raw information you provide to prepare and submit claims under contract.) Note that service bureaus may know little about your profession and need "support" (i.e. training from you) to be sure details are handled correctly.

4. Electronic Filing (Claims are submitted by your office or a service bureau as raw data files sent over computer networks to insurance companies.)

Regardless of how the claim is submitted, the practitioner or the doctor's office follows these basic steps in handling an insurance claim:

Basic Steps Common to All Types of Insurance Claims

1. **Client First Presents Form**   The client obtains an insurance claim form and brings it to the office visit. The form is checked to be sure the client has signed the Release of Information statement. The claim form is date stamped and logged into the insurance claims register. (See client insurance record at the end of each forms section.) The insurance company is called to verify coverage. (See above.)

2. **Superbill Attached to Medical Record**   A client service slip is attached to the client's medical record. The slip contains the client's name, date, and, in some cases, the previous balance due.

3. **Diagnostic and Procedure Codes**   The doctor has already given the client a diagnosis at the first visit. After the bodytherapy professional sees the patient, she completes the superbill by checking off the appropriate procedure codes and fees (as previously approved by the doctor's office.) The diagnosis may be entered by the office staff or the practitioner (with doctor's approval.)

4. **Payment Arrangement**   The client takes the superbill to the reception desk and either pays or arranges for future payment. The next appointment may also be scheduled now.

5. **Posting of Payment**   The medical assistant uses a copy of the client service slip to post payment to the patient's ledger card and day sheet.

> **NOTE:** When the patient is expected to submit his own insurance claim, he will be given two copies of the superbill. The patient keeps the pink copy for his records and attaches the yellow copy to the insurance claim form, (see major medical claim form in Chapter 8), and forwards it to the insurance company. The superbill serves as an itemized billing statement with all pertinent information so the patient can bill the insurance company directly.

6. **Physician Review**   The completed insurance form is routed to the physician, who reviews it for accuracy and signs it.

7. **Recordkeeping and Mailing**   A duplicate of the claim is retained in the office pending file in the event payment is not received, requiring follow up. Insurance billed and date submitted are noted on the patient's financial record (ledger card). The claim form is mailed to the insurance carrier.

8. **Processing Received Payment**   Payment from the insurance carrier should arrive in 4 to 8 weeks. When proper payment is received, the duplicate copy of the insurance claim is pulled from the pending file and filed in an annual alphabetical file. Some offices file claim forms at the back of the patient's medical record after payment is received and accepted. The payment is posted (credited) to the patient's ledger card and current day sheet. The check is then endorsed, entered on a bank deposit slip and may be deposited.

   The check from the insurance company should arrive with an "Explanation of Benefits" form. (See sample on page 72.) This form shows the dates and nature of service and the name of the insured, as well as the percentage paid, the deductible (if applicable) and any ineligible amounts.

   If a claim is not paid within 4 to 8 weeks, the doctor's office may send a letter of inquiry (called a tracer) to the insurance company. The letter will summarize the claim and request information on the delayed payment. (See sample on page 74.)

9. **Billing Balance Due**   The patient is billed for the balance due, if any. When insurance claims are sent in monthly, the balance due on the patient's ledger card may differ from the balance due on the insurance claim form. This difference occurs because of the time lag between rendering service and receiving payment from the insurance company.

10. **Payment to Bodytherapy Professional**   The doctor's office pays the bodytherapy professional for services rendered when the check is received by the insurance company or every 2 weeks, depending on the arrangement. The amount paid will be minus a percentage or billing fee due the doctor. The office staff keeps track of money paid to the practitioner and files the appropriate tax documents according to schedules. (For federal taxes, a W-2

form if the practitioner is an employee; a Form 1099 if the practitioner is an independent contractor.)

Claims Procedures for Licensed States

Follow these basic steps in handling an insurance claim from your office:

1. Client obtains blank claims form from insurance company or employer and fills out Insured (subscriber) information.

2. Client signs authorization to release medical information. This appears on all insurance forms (line 12 on standard claim form).

3. Client signs authorization to pay therapist when assignment is taken (line 13 on standard form) and gives insurance form to practitioner.

4. Photocopy client's insurance identification card for your records.

5. Call insurance company to verify coverage (see pages 64–65). Record date and person to whom you talked.

6. Fill in provider information on standard claim form with diagnosis/treatment information obtained from the referring doctor.

7. Fill in date of service/place of service/procedure codes (need to be approved by insurance company when you verify coverage) and charges. (For details on procedure codes, see Chapter 7.)

8. Sign in the box titled "Signature of physician or supplier" and enter your social security number, name, address and telephone.

9. Keep in the client's file one copy of all forms mailed.

10. Keep an insurance log for each client.

11. When payment is received, photocopy the check and put it in the client's file or insurance record.

12. If there is any overpayment, never send a client a check made out to you. Deposit the check you receive and write a check to the client.

13. In the insurance log, note the date and amount paid by the insurance company. Bill the client for their balance (if not already collected on a weekly basis). Show on the statement the amount paid by the insurance company and the balance due, payable to you or your clinic.

Like any industry, insurance has a wide variety of companies, some easy to work with and considerate, others difficult, slow to respond and slow to pay. For example, some companies seem to always want more information and documentation, while others rarely question what is submitted. Your best defense against this is to know in advance that everything will not always go as smoothly as described here.

If you are on solid ground with your documentation and procedures, and call upon the doctor's front office staff to give you the benefit of their experience, you

If you have any questions about this claim, or wish a review of the decision please contact:

WEST POINT GROUP CLAIM
P.O. BOX 1111
SAN MATEO, CA 94402
(415) 123-4567

EXPLANATION OF BENEFITS

Date | DECEMBER 13, 1996

ROLF COMPUTER, INC.

SUSAN SMITH
123 HOME ST.
ANYTOWN, USA 00000

Keep This Statement For Tax Purposes.
No Other Record Will Be Provided.

Batch # 11-23-456-789-A

* If Code Present See Memo Box Below

Nature of Service/Provider	Date of Service		Total Charge	Ineligible		Amount * 100%	Amount * 80%	Amount * 100%	Amount * 80%
	From	To		Amount	*Code				
JONES, D, MD	11/6/96	12/6/96	301.00					301.00	
		Totals	301.00					301.00	

Control No. 10023　　Branch 001

Insured SUSAN SMITH

Less Deductible	
Balance	301.00
Percentage	
Benefit	301.00
Total	301.00

Dependant　　　　Relationship

Identification # 123-22-3345

ROLF COMPUTER, INC.

P20 4685508

Date DECEMBER 18, 1996

Control No. 10011 111 22　　*$301*00*

***THREE HUNDRED ONE DOLLARS AND 00 CENTS

Insured SUSAN SMITH

A CHECK FOR THIS
AMOUNT HAS BEEN SENT
TO: **DR. JONES, M.D.**
145 WAVERLY PLACE
EASTSIDE, NEW JERSEY 12345

Patient No.:

NOT NEGOTIABLE

should have a minimum of unpleasant surprises. The doctors offices that do best at getting paid are those that regularly call to check on the status of their claims. As always, it helps to be patient, persistent and pleasant. A little courtesy and rapport with the insurance company claims staff can go a long way toward making reimbursement easier and faster.

General Office Procedures and Records Management

Establish an Insurance Claims Register to record what you have done, or need to do in the near future, with each case that has been billed. (See page 95 for sample form.)

Date stamp all incoming insurance forms, whether brought in by the patient or received in the mail. This will enable you to remind the patient when you received the form in case the patient's own records are incomplete.

Group together all the ledgers and charts from patients who have the same type of insurance (Major Medical, Worker's Compensation, and Personal Injury) and bill them all at once. This cuts down on errors and makes completing the forms easier.

Your fees must be consistent and the same for clients who have insurance coverage and those who do not. Do not bill one fee to the insurance company and a different fee to the patient.

When you receive an insurance payment, post it on the client's ledger card. Show the date billed, name of insurance company, amount and name of the patient if the ledger shows more than one family member is covered.

Process claims as soon as possible after you render professional services except for clients receiving continuing care. Keep in mind and observe any time limits (from 30 days to 18 months) for filing an insurance claim. The time limit may also vary with the insurance carrier and whether treatment is in response to an illness or an accident. If you file the claim after the deadline, the insurance company can deny payment.

File a copy of each claim in two ways, one by the client's name; the other by the carrier name. Thus, you will be able to respond easily to inquiries from both patients and carriers.

Or record the name of the insurance company on each client's ledger card and keep a file by carrier name only. In the carrier file, record the name of each patient covered by that carrier. Then you will find it easy to inquire about all that company's policyholders in one letter. (It's time consuming, and therefore expensive, to write a different letter about each patient.)

Another good procedure to help you get your claims paid faster is to put all your unpaid claims into a pending or tickler file for each month. When you group them by month, you know immediately which items have "aged" 30, 60 or 90 days. To speed up payment, write a follow-up letter to the insurance company asking for payment, and enclose a copy of the original claim form. Then attach a copy of the follow-up letter to the file copy of the claim form and put it into a tickler file in a folder for 30- to 60-day follow-up.

INSURANCE CLAIM TRACER

Insurance Company Name: _____ Date: _____

Address: _____

Patient Name: _____ Insured: _____

City: _____ Group Name/Number: _____

IRS Number: _____ Insured: _____

Employer Name and Address: _____

Date of Initial Claim Submission: _____ Amount: _____

Dates of Service: From _____ To _____

An inordinate amount of time has passed since submission of our original claim as described above. We have not received a request for additional information and still await payment of this assigned claim. Please review the attached duplicate and process for payment within seven (7) days.

If there is any difficulty with this claim, please check one of these below and return this letter to our office.

Claim pending because: _____

Payment of claim in process: _____

Payment made on claim. Date:_____ To Whom: _____

Claim denied: (Reason) _____

Patient notified: Yes ___ No___

Remarks: _____

_____

Thank you for your assistance in this important matter. Please contact: _____ in our office if you have any questions regarding this claim.

Office of: _____

Address: _____

_____ Telephone Number: _____

Diagnostic and Procedure Codes: A Critical Piece of the Insurance Puzzle

Chapter 7

Quick Summary of Key Points

Diagnostic and Procedure Codes: A Critical Piece of the Insurance Puzzle

- What types of codes are required for reimbursement
- Codes must be consistent with each other
- Diagnostic codes are used only by doctors
- Procedure codes are used only by licensed medical providers or others they supervise
- Procedure codes must be consistent with your scope of practice

Diagnostic and Procedure Codes: A Critical Piece of the Insurance Puzzle

To process an insurance claim, major medical and Worker's Compensation insurance companies require diagnostic and procedure codes.

These numbers, which are used only by doctors and other licensed healthcare providers, identify the diagnosis of a medical condition and the specific procedure done, as well as the length of time. For example, Number 97124 in the Physicians' Current Procedural Terminology (CPT) Codebook refers to massage therapy lasting 15 minutes.

The Diagnostic Codes for licensed healthcare providers are listed in an ICD-9-CM International Classification of Diseases Code Book. These codes are used by physicians when diagnosing and prescribing soft-tissue/bodytherapy for their patients. A listing of the most common codes is included for reference purposes only at the end of this chapter.

> **IMPORTANT:** A massage/bodytherapist may never diagnose and must therefore get these codes from the doctor's office before listing them on a billing form.

Bodytherapy practitioners do not yet have their own procedure codes, so your work is billed using the physical medicine codes for neuromuscular re-education, myofascial release and massage therapy. These codes are in the section on physical medicine in the Physician's Current Procedural Terminology (CPT) Codebook. A new edition is issued each year. The procedure and diagnostic codebooks are listed in Suggested Readings & Reference Materials after Chapter 17. These books are available in medical offices and medical bookstores. Review them to learn the systems currently used in your state.

> **NOTE:** You must be aware of the law and your responsibility in using these codes as an unlicensed practitioner. The codes may only be used under the direct supervision and specific recommendation of a licensed healthcare provider. A bodytherapy professional is not permitted to use these codes when working unsupervised and without a doctor's referral.

This section contains the codes for nationwide CPT and California Worker's Compensation, (as an example,) as well as current reimbursement values (fees paid for specific codes.)

This chapter also contains case examples and illustrates specific billing procedures used by bodytherapy practitioners in a chiropractic office where bodywork is an adjunct to the doctor's treatment program.

INSURANCE PROCEDURE CODING INFORMATION

The following pages contain the two code systems used for insurance company billing. The two systems are:

- Physician's Current Procedural Terminology (CPT)
  (used nationwide)
- Worker's Compensation Fee System
  (Different for each state. California is used in this book as an example.)

Check with the doctor you work with and the insurance company to verify the coding system used in your state. The majority of insurance companies nationwide are using the CPT coding system.

The following are the **NATIONAL CPT** codes used most commonly to bill for bodytherapy procedures, **effective January 1998**.

90060   INITIAL VISIT WITH EVALUATION, 30 DAYS, WITH REPORT*

97110   THERAPEUTIC PROCEDURE, one or more areas, each 15 minutes; THERAPEUTIC EXERCISES TO DEVELOP STRENGTH AND ENDURANCE, RANGE OF MOTION, AND FLEXIBILITY

97112   NEUROMUSCULAR RE-EDUCATION OF MOVEMENT, BALANCE, COORDINATION, KINESTHETIC SENSE, POSTURE AND PROPRIOCEPTION

97116   GAIT TRAINING**

97124   MASSAGE, INCLUDING EFFLEURAGE, PETRISSAGE, AND/OR TAPOTEMENT (STROKING, COMPRESSION, PERCUSSION)

97122   TRACTION MANUAL

97139   UNLISTED THERAPEUTIC PROCEDURE (SUCH AS SHIATSU, FELDENKRAIS, TRAGER, ASTON PATTERNING, HELLERWORK AND OTHER BODYTHERAPY PROCEDURES)

97250   MYOFASCIAL RELEASE/SOFT-TISSUE MOBILIZATION. ONE OR MORE REGIONS

97530   THERAPEUTIC ACTIVITIES, DIRECT 1-ON-1 PATIENT CONTACT BY THE PROVIDER (USE OF DYNAMIC ACTIVITIES TO IMPROVE FUNCTIONAL PERFORMANCE), each 15 minutes

97545   WORK HARDENING/CONDITIONING; INITIAL 2 HRS**

97546   EACH ADDITIONAL HOUR**

95833   TOTAL EVALUATION OF THE BODY (EXCLUDING HANDS)*

95834   TOTAL EVALUATION OF THE BODY (INCLUDING HANDS)*

95831   MUSCLE TESTING*

Coding Definitions

 * Check with your state licensing board to verify if this code is within your scope of practice
** Most commonly used by physical therapists, physical therapy assistants, chiropractors, chiropractic assistants

97799 UNLISTED PHYSICAL MEDICINE/REHABILITATION SERVICE OR PROCEDURE**

99056 SERVICES PROVIDED AT REQUEST OF PATIENT AT A LOCATION OTHER THAN YOUR OFFICE WHICH WOULD NORMALLY BE PROVIDED IN THE OFFICE

99075 MEDICAL TESTIMONY

99080 SPECIAL REPORTS SUCH AS INSURANCE FORMS, INTERIM REPORTS, NARRATIVE REPORTS AND MORE THAN THE INFORMATION COVERED IN THE USUAL MEDICAL COMMUNICATIONS OR STANDARD INSURANCE FORM

99202 NEW CLIENT EXAM WITH REPORT*

99351 ESTABLISHED PATIENT, HOME VISIT

The following are the **CALIFORNIA WORKER'S COMPENSATION** codes used most commonly for neuromuscular re-education, massage therapy and other physical medicine procedures.

97112 NEUROMUSCULAR RE-EDUCATION, each 30 minutes

97124 MASSAGE THERAPY, each 30 minutes

97530 THERAPEUTIC ACTIVITIES, each 30 minutes

97110 THERAPEUTIC PROCEDURE, (RANGE OF MOTION) ONE OR MORE AREAS, THERAPEUTIC EXERCISES, each 30 minutes

97250 MYOFASCIAL RELEASE/SOFT-TISSUE MOBILIZATION, ONE OR MORE REGIONS, each 30 minutes

The following are the average dollar amounts assigned to the CPT codes by insurance companies. Amounts vary by region and state. Check with the doctor's office you work with to find out the prevailing rate in your area.

> **WARNING:** The national standard for billing CPT codes is 15 minutes; not all insurance companies have adopted the industry standard. Be sure to ask specific questions about this when verifying coverage.

CPT CODES

97112	Neuromuscular Re-Education,	$35-45 each 15 minutes
97110	Therapeutic Procedure,	$30-45 each 15 minutes
97124	Massage Therapy,	$25-35 each 15 minutes
97250	Myofascial Release,	$35-45 each 15 minutes
97530	Therapeutic Activities, (Range of motion)	$35-45 each 15 minutes

The following physical medicine codes are taken from the Physicians' Current Procedural Terminology, CPT Procedural Coding Book, 1998

PLEASE NOTE: If you live in a state without statewide licensure of massage therapy, the procedure codes on this page are to be used only when billing from a doctor's office.

PHYSICAL MEDICINE AND REHABILITATION

PHYSICIAN OR THERAPIST REQUIRED TO HAVE DIRECT (ONE-ON-ONE PATIENT CONTACT).

MODALITIES – Any physical agent applied to produce therapeutic changes to biologic tissue; includes but not limited to thermal, acoustic, light, mechanical, or electric energy.

SUPERVISED – The application of a modality that does not require direct (one on one) patient contact by the provider.

97010   Application of a modality to one or more Areas; hot or cold packs

97012   Traction, mechanical**

97014   Electrical stimulation (unattended)*

97016   Vasopneumatic devices**

97018   Paraffin bath

97020   Microwave**

97022   Whirlpool

97024   Diathermy**

97026   Infrared*

97028   Ultraviolet*

97039   Unlisted modality (Any other hydro, helio or other modality)

CONSTANT ATTENDANCE – The application of a modality that requires direct (one-on-one) patient contact by the provider.

97032   Electrical stimulation (manual), each 15 minutes*

97033   Iontophoresis, each 15 minutes*

97034   Contrast baths, each 15 minutes

97035   Ultrasound, 15 minutes*

97036   Hubbard Tank

97039   Unlisted Modality (Any other hydro, helio or other modality)

PROCEDURES

PHYSICIAN OR THERAPIST REQUIRED TO HAVE DIRECT (ONE-ON-ONE) PATIENT CONTACT

97110   Therapeutic Procedures, one or more areas; Therapeutic Exercises to develop strength and endurance, range of motion and flexibility

97112   Neuromuscular Re-Education of Movement, Balance, Coordination

97116   Gait training**

97118   Electrical stimulation (manual)*

97120   Iontophoresis*

97122   Traction, manual

97124   Massage

97126   Contrast baths

97128   Ultrasound*

97139   Unlisted procedure (Any other hydro, helio or other modality)

97250   Myofascial Release/soft-tissue mobilization

97530   Therapeutic Activities (Range of Motion) to improve functional performance

97540   Training in activities of daily living (self-care skills)**

97545   Work hardening**

Physical Medicine

CALIFORNIA WORKER'S COMPENSATION SYSTEM - The following codes and values are to be used for billing Worker's Compensation in California only. This new system has been effective since March 1994.

MODALITIES

(Physical Medicine Treatment to one area)

97010	Hot or Cold Packs	3.0	$18.45
97012	Traction, mechanical**	3.0	$18.45
97014	Elec. stimulation (unattended)*	3.0	$18.45
97016	Vasopneumatic devices**	3.0	$18.45
97018	Paraffin bath	3.0	$18.45
97020	Microwave**	3.0	$18.45
97022	Whirlpool	3.0	$18.45
97024	Diathermy**	3.0	$18.45
97026	Infrared*	3.0	$18.45
97028	Ultraviolet*	3.0	$18.45
97039	Unlisted modality (Specify)	3.0	$18.45

PROCEDURES

(PHYSICAL MEDICINE TREATMENT TO ONE AREA, initial 30 minutes)

97110	Therapeutic Exercises	5.4	$33.21
97112	Neuromuscular Re-Education	5.4	$33.21
97114	Functional Activities**	5.4	$33.21
97116	Gait Training**	4.4	$27.06
97118	Electrical Stimulation (manual)*	3.8	$23.37
97120	Iontopheresis*	4.9	$30.14
97122	Traction (manual)	3.3	$20.30
97124	Massage Therapy	3.6	$22.14
97126	Contrast Baths	3.3	$20.30
97128	Ultrasound*	3.4	$20.90
97139	Unlisted Procedure (specify)	4.9	$30.14
97220	Hubbard Tank; initial 30 minutes	6.0	$36.90
97530	Therapeutic Activities, each 15 min.	5.4	$33.21
97540	Training in Activities of Daily Living**	5.4	$33.21
97541	Each additional 15 minutes**	2.4	$14.76

ATTENTION: Be sure to register for the update service and receive all the new billing codes for next year!

Stay updated in this rapidly changing healthcare field.

Call 1-800-888-1516 to register today or fill out the form on page xiv.

CASE EXAMPLES OF PROCEDURE CODING IN THE DOCTOR'S OFFICE FOR MASSAGE AND BODYTHERAPY PROFESSIONALS

CASE A: PATIENT IS SEEN FOR A 30-MINUTE MASSAGE AND A
CPT   CHIROPRATIC ADJUSTMENT WITH ULTRASOUND AFTER
MASSAGE

Use Codes

90050	Limited office visit	$45
97124	Massage Therapy, initial 30 min.	$35
97128	Ultrasound	$15

CASE B: PATIENT IS A NEW CHIROPRACTIC PATIENT; IS SEEN FOR INITIAL
CPT   VISIT OF 45 MINUTES; CHIROPRACTIC ADJUSTMENT, ULTRASOUND
AND 15-MINUTE MASSAGE

Use Codes

90070	Exam, Comprehensive	$125
97128	Ultrasound	$15
97124	Massage Therapy, initial 30 minutes	$35

CASE C: PATIENT IS SEEN FOR 30 MINUTES TRAGER® BODYTHERAPY,
CPT   CHIROPRACTIC ADJUSTMENT AND ULTRASOUND

Use Codes

90050	Office visit with manipulation	$45
97112	Neuromuscular Re-education initial 30 min.	$45
97128	Ultrasound	$15

CASE D: PATIENT IS SEEN FOR ONE HOUR OF BODYTHERAPY
CPT   INCLUDING NEUROMUSCULAR RE-EDUCATION AND
THERAPEUTIC ACTIVITIES

Use Codes

97112	Neuromuscular Re-education, initial 30 min.	$45
97530	Therapeutic Activities (ROM)	$45

CASE E: PATIENT IS WORKER'S COMPENSATION (INJURY ON THE JOB) AND
CPT   IS SEEN FOR 30-MINUTE MASSAGE TO THE NECK AND BACK

Use Code

97124	Massage therapy, 30 min.	$35

ICD-9 CLASSIFICATION AND CODING

The International Classification of Disease or ICD-9 (9th Revision), Clinical Modification is a numeric code system for diagnoses and procedures. Almost all known diseases, symptoms, and conditions are classified by providing specific identification of the disease using a code number.

> **IMPORTANT:** A massage/bodytherapist may never diagnose. You must get these codes from the doctor's office before listing them on a billing form. Before using these codes, check to see if the code is within the scope of your practice for your state or if it needs to be billed from the doctor's or physical therapists office.

Listed below are a few examples of ICD-9 Codes frequently used by physicians when prescribing massage/soft-tissue therapy. These codes define the client's condition and where it is located in the body. Use this listing for your reference only. For further information, review the ICD-9-CM Code Book, 9th Revised Edition, Clinical Modifications at your local medical bookstore.

728.85	Muscle Spasm	847.4	Coccyx Sprain/Strain
729.1	Fibromyalgia	847.0	Neck Sprain/Strain
729.12	Myofascial Syndrome of the Trapezii muscles	847.1	Thoracic Sprain/Strain
		847.2	Lumbar Sprain/Strain
729.15	Myofascial Syndrome of the Gluteal muscles	847.3	Sacral Sprain/Strain
		848.0	Other and ill defined Sprain/Strain
847.0	Cervical Sprain/Strain		
845.0	Ankle Sprain	354.0	Carpal Tunnel Syndrome
847.1	Thoracic Sprain/Strain	307.81	Tension Headache
847.2	Lumbar Sprain/Strain	784.0	Headache
840.4	Rotator Cuff Sprain	840.6	Supraspinatus Sprain and Strain
840.9	Shoulders/Upper Arm Sprain/Strain		
		840.5	Subscapularis (muscle)
724.3	Sciatica	724.4	Lumbrosacral Riducular (lower extremities)
524.6	Temporomandibular joint disorders		
		346.0	Migraine (Classical)
842.0	Wrist Sprain/Strain	346.1	Migraine (Common)
846.0	Lumbrosacral Sprain/Strain	346.2	Variants of Migraine
847.5	Pelvic Sprain/Strain		

Major Medical Insurance: Claims Procedures and Sample Forms

Chapter 8

Quick Summary of Key Points

- Claims Procedures: Major Medical Insurance
- Major Medical Insurance Billing Procedures
- Forms Required for Major Medical Billing:
    - Health Insurance Claim Form
    - Doctor's Prescription Form
    - Client Insurance Billing Information Log
    - Client Insurance Record

Claims Procedures: Major Medical Insurance

Major Medical insurance covers individuals either alone or as part of a group. Some policies are more comprehensive than others, but all cover claims not specifically limited to work or auto accidents.

This chapter shows how to bill major medical insurance, whether the billing is done from the doctor's office or by the client using a health insurance claim form *or* the practitioner's pre-printed billing form (superbill). Health insurance claim forms (HCFA-1500) with case examples are included, along with examples of the required progress notes.

As discussed in the background section in Chapter 1, in unlicensed states you must provide your services under the doctor's supervision. In licensed states, you may consult with the physician about the patient's care, but you are not required to have direct supervision by the doctor. Be sure to check with the insurance company and your state licensing agency to verify legal requirements.

In some states, such as Florida, you may bill major medical insurance companies from your own office with the doctor's referral letter and prescription form. If the billing is done from the doctor's office, as required in most unlicensed states, follow the procedures outlined below.

The doctor's office:

> **Verifies coverage**
>
> Determines the appropriate **diagnosis** and **procedure** codes
>
> Completes the **claim form** as shown in this chapter

For a patient being seen regularly over weeks or longer, the claim form is sent monthly to the insurance company and reimbursement is expected within 4 to 6 weeks. Most insurance companies require a co-payment of 20%, which is collected by the doctor's office from the patient at each visit. (See the standard health insurance claim form on the following pages.)

The patient:

> **Assigns Benefits** to the doctor by **signing box 12** on the claim form
>
> **Makes co-payments** of 20% of the bill at each office visit

The insurance company sends the reimbursement to the doctor's office in the form of a check with an Explanation of Benefits form. (See example on page 72.) The doctor's office will pay you every two weeks for services rendered or when payment is received, depending on your written agreement with him or her. (See Chapter 3 on drafting a payment agreement.)

Many doctors' offices require their patients to pay in full for services rendered at the time of the visit. This policy is usually stated when the patient first phones for an appointment. In this case the doctor's office assists the patient with filling in the standard health insurance claim form which the patient receives from his insurance company. (See the example later in this chapter.) The patient brings the form to the office, and the receptionist fills in lines 14 through 33. The patient fills in lines 1 through 13, sends in the form to the insurance company and is reimbursed within 4 to 6 weeks.

Many doctors and practitioners have pre-printed billing forms which contain all the physician or supplier information required on a standard claim form. At the time of the visit, the patient receives the superbill, which has three copies. The white copy stays in the patient's file at the doctor's office. The patient receives the yellow and pink copies at the time of the visit. The patient then submits the yellow copy to the insurance carrier, along with a standard claim form with only the patient's information part completed. The pink copy is for the patient's records.

Practitioners may sometimes bill major medical from their own office under the doctor's supervision using the doctor's superbill. This includes weekly telephone and personal supervision by the doctor's office, and the practitioner pays a fee to the doctor's office for the supervision time. (This may vary with state legal requirements and the doctor's discretion.)

In this case, the client pays the practitioner in full at the time of the visit and receives his copies of the doctor's billing form, already signed by the doctor, with the appropriate diagnosis and procedure codes agreed upon by the doctor's office. The patient then submits the necessary forms to the insurance carrier.

Major Medical Insurance Billing Procedures

For major medical insurance reimbursement, if the client has health insurance through his employer, he must obtain an insurance claim form from the employer's insurance division. This claim form must be on file with the provider's office or the office which handles the billing. If the client has an individually purchased policy, he must call the company to obtain a claim form.

A client may be covered by two major medical policies at the same time, because many policies cover spouses and children as part of an employee benefits package. If the client and the spouse are both employed and covered by insurance, the client's insurance company is considered the primary carrier and is billed first. If the client is a dependent on a spouse's insurance policy, the spouse's company is the secondary carrier.

On the major medical form (see page 91) the client fills out the patient and insured (subscriber) information. The referring doctor's office fills in the physician's or supplier information part. (This will vary with state licensing regulations.)

As a bodytherapy practitioner, you fill in the following:

- date of service (Section 24 on the claim form)

- place of service

- procedure code (Must be approved by the physician's office. See Chapter 7 for a sample listing of national CPT codes.)

- description of service

- diagnosis code (from physician information, number 21, and filled out by dotor's office. In a licensed state, the practitioner may use the diagnosis code provided by the physician on the referral letter/prescription and fill in number 21 with that information.)

- charges for your service

In unlicensed states, the supervising physician must sign number 31 as well as fill in his name, address and telephone number in number 33, (as shown on page 91.) In licensed states, (Florida, for example) once you have verified coverage with the insurance company and it has approved your services, you may sign number 33 and fill in your name, address and telephone number in 32. (See sample forms.)

Number 25 on the claim form asks for a Federal Tax ID Number, which in most cases is your Social Security Number. However, if you work as part of a partnership, group or are employed by someone else, it will be the Employer Identification Number (EIN) of that entity.

Forms Required for Major Medical Insurance Billing:

- Health Insurance Claim Form
- Doctor's Prescription Form
- Client Insurance Billing Information Log
- Client Insurance Record

SAMPLE

APPROVED OMB-0938-0008

PLEASE
DO NOT
STAPLE
IN THIS
AREA

HEALTH INSURANCE CLAIM FORM

| | PICA | | PICA | |

1. MEDICARE (Medicare #)   **MEDICAID** (Medicaid #)   **CHAMPUS** (Sponsor's SSN)   **CHAMPVA** (VA File #)   **GROUP HEALTH PLAN** (SSN or ID) [X]   **FECA BLK LUNG** (SSN)   **OTHER** (ID)

1a. INSURED'S I.D. NUMBER (FOR PROGRAM IN ITEM 1)
809-33-3112

2. PATIENT'S NAME (Last Name, First Name, Middle Initial)
Smith, Susan D

3. PATIENT'S BIRTH DATE MM DD YY
01 01 45   **SEX** M □ F [X]

4. INSURED'S NAME (Last Name, First Name, Middle Initial)
Smith, Susan D

5. PATIENT'S ADDRESS (No., Street)
15 Fortuna Street

6. PATIENT RELATIONSHIP TO INSURED
Self [X]   Spouse □   Child □   Other □

7. INSURED'S ADDRESS (No., Street)
15 Fortuna Street

CITY Tampa   **STATE** FL

8. PATIENT STATUS
Single □   Married [X]   Other □

CITY Tampa   **STATE** FL

ZIP CODE 08854   **TELEPHONE** (Include Area Code) (777)123-4567

Employed □   Full-Time Student □   Part-Time Student □

ZIP CODE 08854   **TELEPHONE** (INCLUDE AREA CODE) (777)123-4567

9. OTHER INSURED'S NAME (Last Name, First Name, Middle Initial)
N/A

10. IS PATIENT'S CONDITION RELATED TO:

11. INSURED'S POLICY GROUP OR FECA NUMBER
ABN8975632

a. OTHER INSURED'S POLICY OR GROUP NUMBER
N/A

a. EMPLOYMENT? (CURRENT OR PREVIOUS)
YES □   NO [X]

a. INSURED'S DATE OF BIRTH MM DD YY
01 01 45   **SEX** M □ F [X]

b. OTHER INSURED'S DATE OF BIRTH MM DD YY N/A   **SEX** M □ F □

b. AUTO ACCIDENT?   PLACE (State)
YES □   NO [X]

b. EMPLOYER'S NAME OR SCHOOL NAME
Zebra Corporation

c. EMPLOYER'S NAME OR SCHOOL NAME
Zebra Corporation

c. OTHER ACCIDENT?
YES □   NO [X]

c. INSURANCE PLAN NAME OR PROGRAM NAME
Health Pro Plan

d. INSURANCE PLAN NAME OR PROGRAM NAME
Health Pro Plan

10d. RESERVED FOR LOCAL USE

d. IS THERE ANOTHER HEALTH BENEFIT PLAN?
YES □   NO [X]   If yes, return to and complete item 9 a-d.

READ BACK OF FORM BEFORE COMPLETING & SIGNING THIS FORM.
12. PATIENT'S OR AUTHORIZED PERSON'S SIGNATURE I authorize the release of any medical or other information necessary to process this claim. I also request payment of government benefits either to myself or to the party who accepts assignment below.
SIGNATURE ON FILE   1/20/97
SIGNED ___   DATE ___

13. INSURED'S OR AUTHORIZED PERSON'S SIGNATURE I authorize payment of medical benefits to the undersigned physician or supplier for services described below.
SIGNATURE ON FILE
SIGNED ___

14. DATE OF CURRENT: MM DD YY
12 15 96   ILLNESS (First symptom) OR INJURY (Accident) OR PREGNANCY(LMP)

15. IF PATIENT HAS HAD SAME OR SIMILAR ILLNESS. GIVE FIRST DATE MM DD YY
11 15 95

16. DATES PATIENT UNABLE TO WORK IN CURRENT OCCUPATION MM DD YY
FROM ___ TO ___

17. NAME OF REFERRING PHYSICIAN OR OTHER SOURCE

17a. I.D. NUMBER OF REFERRING PHYSICIAN

18. HOSPITALIZATION DATES RELATED TO CURRENT SERVICES MM DD YY
FROM ___ TO ___

19. RESERVED FOR LOCAL USE

20. OUTSIDE LAB? $ CHARGES
YES □   NO [X]

21. DIAGNOSIS OR NATURE OF ILLNESS OR INJURY. (RELATE ITEMS 1,2,3 OR 4 TO ITEM 24E BY LINE)
1. 750.2 Cervical Rib
2. 729.1 Myofascitis
3. 847.0 Cervical Strain
4. 353.0 Thoracic Outlet

22. MEDICAID RESUBMISSION CODE   ORIGINAL REF. NO.

23. PRIOR AUTHORIZATION NUMBER
A0657892

24. A DATE(S) OF SERVICE		B Place of Service	C Type of Service	D PROCEDURES, SERVICES, OR SUPPLIES (Explain Unusual Circumstances) CPT/HCPCS MODIFIER	E DIAGNOSIS CODE	F $ CHARGES	G DAYS OR UNITS	H EPSDT Family Plan	I EMG	J COB	K RESERVED FOR LOCAL USE
From MM DD YY	To MM DD YY										
01 04 97	01 04 97	11	AE	97124	1234	45 00					
01 08 97	01 08 97	11	AE	97010	1234	15 00					
01 12 97	01 12 97	11	AE	97250	1234	45 00					
01 12 97	01 12 97	11	AE	97110	1234	45 00					
01 15 97	01 15 97	11	AE	97112	1234	45 00					
01 15 97	01 15 97	11	AE	97124	1234	45 00					

25. FEDERAL TAX I.D. NUMBER   SSN EIN
809-33-3112

26. PATIENT'S ACCOUNT NO.
SMIT1199

27. ACCEPT ASSIGNMENT? (For govt. claims, see back)
YES [X]   NO □

28. TOTAL CHARGE
$ 240

29. AMOUNT PAID
$ 0

30. BALANCE DUE
$ 240 00

31. SIGNATURE OF PHYSICIAN OR SUPPLIER INCLUDING DEGREES OR CREDENTIALS (I certify that the statements on the reverse apply to this bill and are made a part thereof.)
Roberta Johnson, L.M.T.
SIGNED ___   DATE ___

32. NAME AND ADDRESS OF FACILITY WHERE SERVICES WERE RENDERED (If other than home or office)

33. PHYSICIAN'S, SUPPLIER'S BILLING NAME, ADDRESS, ZIP CODE & PHONE #
800-232-4441
Roberta Johnson, L.M.T.
1545 Woodsbury Lane
Tampa, Florida   08854
PIN# ___   GRP# ___

(APPROVED BY AMA COUNCIL ON MEDICAL SERVICE 8/88)   **PLEASE PRINT OR TYPE**

FORM HCFA-1500 (12-90)
FORM OWCP-1500   FORM RRB-1500
#29426
Use with Envelope #14145 (gummed) or #14146 (self-seal)

CARRIER

PATIENT AND INSURED INFORMATION

PHYSICIAN OR SUPPLIER INFORMATION

SAMPLE

DOCTOR'S PRESCRIPTION FORM

It is my recommendation that _____ Susan Smith _____
undergo the following adjunctive procedure:

☑ Soft-Tissue Therapy

☑ Neuromuscular Re-education

Sessions to be scheduled:

☑ 3 times per week for ____2____ weeks

☑ 2 times per week for ____4____ weeks

☐ Once per week for _____ weeks

Diagnosis:

_____ Cervical Subluxation, Thoracic Subluxation _____

December 9, 1996 _____
Date

_____
Physician's Signature

CLIENT INSURANCE BILLING INFORMATION LOG

Check one:

☐ Worker's Comp   ☐ Private Pay   ☐ Group Ins.   ☐ Medicare   ☐ Other _____

CLIENT INSURANCE INFORMATION

Date _____ Account/Control No. _____

Client's name _____ Date of birth _____ Soc. Sec. No. _____

Client's address _____

Date of first office visit _____ Home phone _____ Work phone _____

Owner of vehicle _____ **Relation to client** _____

Insurance carrier _____ Whose Ins.? _____

Claims office address _____ Out of State ☐ Yes ☐ No

Policy No. _____ Expiration date _____ Limit $_____ PPO _____

Type of insurance ☐ Auto/Med pay ☐ Health ☐ **Worker's Compensation** ☐ Other _____

AUTO INFORMATION (Check one) ☐ Passenger ☐ Driver ☐ Pedestrian

Date of injury _____ Doctor's release date _____

Attorney _____ Comments _____

Address _____ Phone No. _____

Lien forms (Date sent to Attorney) _____ Date Returned _____

Insurance Company _____

Billing Address _____ Phone No. _____

Assignment form (Date sent to Insurance Company) _____

Insurance verified by _____ How _____

Date verified _____ Verification check list on file ☐ Yes ☐ No

AUTO INSURANCE (Medical Payment)

a. **PRIMARY INSURANCE CARRIER** ((Car client was in) _____

   Insured's name (car owner) _____ Phone No. _____

   Billing address _____

   Policy No. _____ Claim No. _____ Contact _____

   Insured's date of birth _____ Soc. Sec. No. _____

b. **SECONDARY INSURANCE CARRIER** (Client's car or one owned by relative or household member)

   _____ Relation to patient _____

   Insured's name _____ Phone No. _____

   Billing address _____

   Policy No. _____ Claim No. _____ Contact _____

   Insured's date of birth _____ Soc. Sec. No. _____

c. **UNINSURED MOTORIST APPLICATION** (Applies if other car is responsible for accident and other car is either a "hit and run" or is uninsured).

☐ Hit and Run ☐ Adverse care uninsured

Available insurance **(Client's car or insurance from relative or household member)**

Insured's name _____ _____ Date of birth _____

Phone No. _____ Relation to client _____

Insurance Company _____ Phone No. _____

Address _____

Policy No. _____ Claim No. _____ Contact _____

HEALTH INSURANCE INFORMATION

Client's name _____ Date of birth _____

Insurance Carrier _____

☐ Individual (Policy No.) _____ ☐ Group. No. _____ Group name _____

Billing address _____ Phone _____

Deductible (if applies to accident injury) $_____

Policy coverage $_____ X-rays $_____ Office visits $_____

Orthopedic devices $_____ Supports and braces $_____

Exemptions _____ Other limitations _____

ANY OTHER INSURANCE CARRIERS WHICH MAY BE AFFECTED BY THIS CLAIM? _____

_____

_____

_____

Did this accident occur during work hours? **Worker's Compensation**

☐ Yes ☐ No Was employer notified? ☐ Yes ☐ No Date & time notified _____

Client Signature _____ Date _____

ATTACHED: Photocopy of insurance I.D. Card ☐ Yes ☐ No

HCFA #1500 Claim form signed ☐ Yes ☐ No

DATE BILLED	AMOUNT BILLED	SESSION DATES FROM/TO	CLAIM NO.	TO WHOM BILLED CARRIER/OTHER	DATE TRACER SENT	DATE PAYMENT RECEIVED	AMOUNT RECEIVED	BALANCE DUE	POSTED BY	ACTION PENDING	
										YES	NO

INSURANCE COMPANY COMMUNICATION LOG

DATE OF CALL	TIME OF CALL	PERSON CALLING	NAME OF PERSON SPOKEN TO	CONVERSATION	ACTION PENDING YES	NO

INCOMING CORRESPONDENCE LOG

DATE LETTER	LETTER FROM	PERSON SIGNED LETTER	DATE RECEIVED	CLAIM NO.	COMMENTS	ACTION PENDING YES	NO

Chapter 9

Worker's Compensation: Claims Procedures and Sample Forms

Chapter 9

Quick Summary of Key Points

- Claims Procedures: Worker's Compensation
- Worker's Compensation Billing Procedures
- Worker's Compensation Progress Report Guidelines
- Complete List of Worker's Compensation Boards
- Forms Required for Worker's Compensation Billing:

    Doctor's First Report of Occupational Injury or Illness
    Certificate of Disability
    Comprehensive Client Intake Form for Worker's Compensation
    Doctor's Prescription Form
    Worker's Compensation Outpatient Care Certification
    Worker's Compensation Claim Form
    Worker's Compensation Fee Schedule
    Client Insurance Record

Claims Procedures: Worker's Compensation

This chapter shows you how to bill Worker's Compensation insurance, whether the billing is done from the doctor's office or the practitioner's office. It also includes a comprehensive list of all the U.S. Worker's Compensation state boards, as well as examples of all the forms you need.

Worker's Compensation is an insurance program that state governments require employers to join for the benefit of employees. The purpose of the program is to protect employees against industrial accidents and other job-related health problems, including disability.

The details of Worker's Compensation, including the amount and terms of benefits, vary from state to state. Some states cover employees through a state monopoly; some use private insurance companies; and some use a combination of private and public agencies. Some states are liberal with benefits, while others place strict limits on the amount of physical therapy and medical treatment covered. A current California fee schedule is included as an example in this chapter.

For your particular state, call or write your state labor board as well as the covering insurance company. (See complete listing of state labor boards on pages 103-107.)

Because Worker's Compensation requires close supervision and frequent reporting, in most unlicensed states Worker's Compensation claims should be billed from a doctor's office. While some practitioners do accept Worker's Compensation clients in their own offices, they usually have difficulty getting reimbursed because they do not know how to complete the more complex paperwork required. In most cases you will do better to accept a Worker's Compensation client only when the doctor will work closely with you and keep the insurance approval up to date. The doctor's office bills the Worker's Compensation insurance carrier as illustrated in this section. Case examples and forms are also given in this chapter.

This chapter uses California as an example to describe the procedures for Worker's Compensation insurance claims. Carefully study the procedures, case examples and forms provided, but remember that your state may differ from California.

Worker's Compensation Billing Procedures

The doctor's office always files a first report, a pink form of 3 to 4 pages, within one week of the initial visit. (A sample is in the Forms for Worker's Compensation Billing section later in this chapter.) The doctor who sees the patient initially will fill out this form and do the evaluation, referring the patient to the massage therapist or health practitioner.

As part of your client intake, you must get the client's employment and insurance information. Specifically, ask for the client's employer, date of injury, name of supervisor at work, employer's telephone number and doctor's orders (if seen previously). Be sure to get the name, address and telephone number of the Worker's Compensation insurance carrier, name of claims representative and telephone number, as well as the claim identification number.

Use a Comprehensive Client Intake Form (such as the one shown on pages 111–112) to document the type of injury, the percentage of time spent on different physical activities/tasks at work and a hierarchy of symptoms. (Have the client describe in detail their symptoms related to specific muscle groups. Then have them shade in complaint areas on the Body Diagram form and indicate by number most painful #1 to least painful #3. See Appendix D for sample form.) Have the client describe how the injury happened and if tasks at work make the complaints worse. Have them identify specific areas of pain, soreness and achiness.

You can also have the client keep a chart at home to show how their symptoms change day to day and any improvements that occur with your therapy. (Have them use the Body Diagram form found in Appendix D.) In this way you can be sure to document the specific outcome as a result of your therapy. For example, "After 2 weeks of soft-tissue therapy pain in right arm is reduced by 80%." This kind of specific information is what insurance companies look for to justify the medical necessity of your type of therapy as an adjunct to the doctor's treatment plan.

You or the doctor's secretary must call the insurance carrier to verify coverage and request approval for soft-tissue mobilization (the term Worker's Compensation uses for massage therapy) as a required part of the treatment program.

If appropriate, the doctor must sign a Certificate of Disability and include that with the pink form.

When verifying coverage, the doctor's office also must specify how often and for how many weeks the doctor is recommending the bodytherapy. (For example, "Soft-tissue therapy 2 times per week for 2 weeks and then once per week for 3 weeks.")

Then, be sure you or the doctor has received authorization from the insurance company for your services. The company should specifically approve the frequency and type of service you provide. When a claim is approved, it is assigned an authorization code. Record this number in the client's intake record along with their claim identification number. This number must be shown on each bill that the provider submits to the insurance company. Some companies will mail the provider of service an Outpatient Care Certification Form which specifies what is approved and for how long. This certification (see sample form on page 114) is for medical necessity and appropriateness and does not confirm or guarantee insurance coverage.

Fill in the Claim Form as shown on page 115. You fill out the dates of service, place of service, procedure codes, diagnosis codes (provided by the doctor's office) and charges. The codes shown are CPT codes for demonstration purposes. In California, always use CPT procedure codes when you bill. The maximum charge allowed for 30 minutes of neuromuscular re-education is $33. (See Current California Worker's Compensation Fee Schedule later in this chapter.)

Since the amount you can charge per visit and the procedure codes vary from state to state, be sure to call your state Worker's Compensation Department for a listing of current procedure codes for your state and a fee schedule. (See pages 103–107.)

Remember that in some states you may bill the carrier directly, while in others you must bill the doctor, who then bills the insurance company for your services and his, and then pays you. Check with your state labor office and the Worker's Compensation carrier to verify legal requirements for your state. In either case, claims should be sent to the carrier once a month, or every two weeks if visits are frequent.

The carrier should pay within 4 to 6 weeks. If payment has not been received, the doctor's office should call about the status of the claim.

If the carrier has not paid the doctor within 60 days, interest charges can begin to be added at the rate of 1.5% per month. (The interest rate will vary from state to state.)

If the doctor recommends your work for a specific period, (for example, "2 times per week for 30 minutes for 2 weeks, and then 1 time per week for 2 weeks") you or the doctor's office must send progress reports every few weeks with the claim form documenting what happened at each visit.

Each time the client sees the doctor for a follow-up visit, he should get a new order form for your particular services, specifying the number of visits to your office. The carrier must again authorize the number of visits with you and give your or the doctor's office a certification number.

> **IMPORTANT**: Keep accurate chart or progress notes each time you see the client. Worker's Compensation may request your records at any time, and you must send a current status report when you do the billing (generally once or twice a month). The progress notes should contain your subjective observations, an objective description of your services, your assessment of progress and what you plan to do and/or recommend to the patient. (Use the acronym SOAP to help you remember the four categories.)

Worker's Compensation Progress Report Guidelines:

Subjective   Information: How the client is doing and any complaints or symptoms described to you.

Objective   Information: Specify exactly what you are doing. Describe muscles and areas that you worked on. For example, "Soft-tissue mobilization (massage) to the cervical paraspinales, trapezius and rhomboid muscles."

Important Terminology Note: Use "Soft-Tissue Therapy" and, when appropriate, "Neuromuscular Re-Education" instead of "Massage." (Insurance companies understand this better.)

Assessment: Your observation of how the client is doing and progress made as a result of sessions. For example, "Soft-tissue therapy is reducing soft tissue tone (pain) in lumbar paraspinales muscles. After several sessions of soft-tissue therapy, pain is reduced in lower back areas." Include information about any emotional stress factors that may be contributing to the problem.

Plan: Includes what you think is necessary to do during subsequent visits. For example, "Client can benefit from 3 to 4 sessions focusing on soft tissue therapy to further decrease spasms and pain in low back area." or "Train in exercises to improve range of motion and flexibility."

Be specific in your progress notes. Work with the doctor on Assessment and Plan in both licensed and unlicensed states.

Once a month, the doctor's office must send a Worker's Compensation claim form along with the necessary progress notes to the Worker's Compensation insurance carrier.

IMPORTANT: Remember that the law does not allow your profession to diagnose. "Diagnose" means identifying a disease from its symptoms and signs.

Most Worker's Compensation carriers request frequent follow-up letters, medical verifications and very detailed chart notes. Usually the doctor's office staff will phone the carrier and ask for an extension of the bodytherapy services, as needed. The carrier will then verify or decline the extension based on the medical reports submitted and statements of medical necessity.

You must keep accurate progress notes each time you see the client. A copy of these notes must be in the client's chart. Interim status reports and supplemental reports are requested frequently by Worker's Compensation carriers to determine how the client is doing.

Worker's Compensation usually reimburses the doctor's office within 4 to 6 weeks and clients do not pay the doctor until the insurance has paid.

The current Worker's Compensation reimbursement fee schedule is included here, since it varies from other fee schedules. Be sure to contact the appropriate regulatory agency in your state for their current fee schedule.

In Worker's Compensation cases, according to California law, all neuromuscular re-education work must be done on the premises of the referring licensed provider. The doctor's office must call the Worker's Compensation insurance carrier and get authorization for your service from the carrier as a medically necessary adjunctive service. The doctor's office then submits the Worker's Compensation claim forms (see later in this chapter). The insurance carrier requires that the doctor periodically evaluate the referred client and then request authorization for continuation of services for a specified period of time (usually 1-2 months).

For other states, contact the client's Worker's Compensation insurance carrier or the Worker's Compensation Board to determine supervision requirements. Many states which license massage therapists will permit practitioners to work in their own offices and bill Worker's Compensation carriers with a doctor's prescription and/or referral letter. For example, as a result of a new Florida law, Worker's Compensation insurance carriers now recognize massage therapists as providers. Other states may require that the work be done at the doctor's office and be supervised by him at all times.

The following is a list of the contact person in each state for information regarding fee schedules and how to file a Worker's Compensation Claim.

ALABAMA
Scottie Spates, Chief
Worker's Compensation Division
Department of Industrial Relations
649 Monroe St.
Montgomery, AL 36131
(334) 242-2868

ALASKA
Paul Grossi, Director
Division of Worker's Compensation
Department of Labor
1111 W. 8th St., Rm. 307
P.O. Box 25512
Juneau, AK 99802
(907) 465-2790

ARIZONA
Industrial Commission of Arizona
P. O. Box 19070
Phoenix, AZ 85005-9070
(602) 542-4661

ARKANSAS
John Kennedy, Chief Executive Officer
Arkansas Worker's Compensation
Commission
324 Spring Street
Little Rock, AR 72201
(501) 682-3930

CALIFORNIA
California Worker's Compensation Board
P.O. Box 429003
San Francisco, CA 94142
(415) 557-1954

COLORADO
Jacquelin Calvert, Deputy Director
Department of Labor and Employment
Division of Worker's Compensation

1515 Arapahoe St.
Denver, CO 80202-2117
(303) 575-8700

CONNECTICUT
Connecticut Worker's Compensation
Board
700 State Street
New Haven, CT 06511-6500
(203) 789-7512

DELAWARE
John F. Kirk III, Administrator
Office of Worker's Compensation
4425 No. Market St.
Wilmington, DE 19802
(302) 761-8200 or (302) 577-2884

DISTRICT OF COLUMBIA
Worker's Compensation Board
1200 Upshur Street, N.W.
Washington, DC 20011
(202) 576-6265

FLORIDA
Jimmy Ray Glisson, Director
Department of Labor
Division of Worker's Compensation
2728 Centerview Dr., Suite 126
Forrest Bldg.
Tallahassee, FL 32399-0687
(850) 488-2514

GEORGIA
Harrill L. Dawkins, Chairman
State Board of Worker's Compensation
270 Peachtree St., N.W.
Atlanta, GA 30303-1299
(404) 656-2034 or (404) 656-3818

Continued

HAWAII
Gara Hamada, Administrator
Disability Compensation Division
Department of Labor and Industrial
Relations
830 Punchbowl St., Rm. 209
P.O. Box 3769
Honolulu, HI 96812
(808) 586-9161

IDAHO
Idaho Worker's Compensation Board
P. O. Box 83720
Boise, ID 83720-0041
(208) 334-6000

ILLINOIS
lllinois Industrial Commission
100 West Randolph Street
8th Floor, #200
Chicago, IL 60601
(312) 814-6500

INDIANA
Worker's Compensation Board of Indiana
402 West Washington, #W196
Indianapolis, IN 46204
(317) 232-3808

IOWA
Iris Post, Industrial Commissioner
1000 E. Grand Ave.
Des Moines, IA 50319
(515) 281-5934

KANSAS
Philip S. Harness, Director
Division of Worker's Compensation
Department of Human Resources
800 S.W. Jackson St., Suite 600
Topeka, KS 66612-1227
(913) 296-3441

KENTUCKY
Walter W. Turner, Commissioner
Department of Worker's Claimes
Labor Cabinet

1270 Louisville Rd.
Perimeter Park W., Bldg. C
Frankfort, KY 40601
(502) 564-5550

LOUISIANA
Ron Menville, Assistant Secretary
Office of Worker's Compensation
Department of Labor
1001 N. 23rd St.
Baton Rouge, LA 70802
(504) 342-7555

MAINE
Susan Pinette, Chairman
Worker's Compensation Board
Deering Bldg., AMHI Complex
27 State House Station
Augusta, ME 04333
(207) 287-3751

MARYLAND
Worker's Compensation Board of
Maryland
6 North Liberty Street
Baltimore, MD 21201
(410) 767-0900

MASSACHUSETTS
Industrial Accidents Board
H.R.Div.
Industries Drive
P. O. Box 946
Norfolk, Massachusetts 02056
617-727-8877
617-727-0135 X436 Kathy

MICHIGAN
Department of Consumer and Industry
Services
Bureau of Worker's Disability
Compensation
P.O. Box 30016
Lansing, MI 48909
517-322-5433
fee schedule: (517) 322-5433

Continued

MINNESOTA
Gretchen Maglich, Assistant
Commissioner
Worker's Compensation Division
Department of Labor and Industry
443 Lafayette Rd.
St. Paul, MN 55155
(612) 296-6490 or (612) 296-2432
Fax, Records Division: (612) 215-0080

MISSISSIPPI
Claire M. Porter, Chairman
Worker's Compensation Commission
1428 Lakeland Dr.
P.O. Box 5300
Jackson, MS 39296-5300
(601) 987-4252

MISSOURI
Jo-Ann Karll, Director
Division of Worker's Compensation
Department of Labor and Industrial
Relations
3315 W. Truman Blvd.
P.O. Box 58
Jefferson City, MO 65102-0058
(573) 751-4231

MONTANA
Kris Brandt, Medical Benefits Technician
Montana State Compensation Insurance
Fund
5 S. Last Chance Gulch
Helena, MT 59601
1-800-332-6102

NEBRASKA
Laureen Van Norman, Presiding Judge
Nebraska Worker's Compensation Court
P.O. Box 98908
Lincoln, NE 68509-8908
(402) 471-6468
Within Nebraska: 1-800-599-5155

NEVADA
Douglas Dirks, Chief Executive Officer
State Industrial Insurance System
9790 Gateway Drive
Reno, Nevada 89511
(702) 327-2700

NEW HAMPSHIRE
Worker's Compensation Board of New
Hampshire
Spalding Building
95 Pleasant Street
Concord, NH 03301
(603) 271-3176

NEW JERSEY
Paul Kapalko,Director
Dept. of Labor
Division of Worker's Compensation
P. O. Box 381
Trenton, N.J. 08625-0381
(609) 984-2515 or (609) 292-2516

NEW MEXICO
Alex Maestas, Clerk of the Court
New Mexico Worker's Compensation
Administration
P.O. Box 27198
Albuquerque, NM 87125-7198
(505) 841-6000

NEW YORK
Robert Steingut, Chairman
Worker's Compensation Board
180 Livingston Street
Brooklyn, N.Y. 11248
(718) 802-6600

NORTH CAROLINA
J. Howard Bunn, Chairman
North Carolina Industrial Commission
Department of Comerce
Dobbs Bldg.
430 N. Salisbury St.
Raleigh, NC 27611
(919) 733-4820
Fax: (919) 715-0282

Continued

NORTH DAKOTA
Patrick Traynor, Director
Worker's Compensation Bureau
500 E. Front Ave.
Bismarck, ND 58504-5685
(701) 328-3800

OHIO
James Conrad, Administrator
Ohio Bureau of Worker's Compensation
30 W. Spring St.
Columbus, OH 43215
(614) 466-2950

OKLAHOMA
Counselors' Office
Worker's Compensation Court
1915 No. Stiles Ave.
Oklahoma City, OK 73105
(405)522-8630

OREGON
Worker's Compensation Division
350 Winter Street, N.E.
Salem, OR 97310
(503) 947-7585

PENNSYLVANIA
Richard A. Himler, Director
Bureau of Worker's Compensation
Department of Labor and Industry
1171 So. Cameron St., Rm. 103
Harrisburg, PA 17104-2501
(717) 783-5421

RHODE ISLAND
Worker's Compensation Board of Rhode
Island
610 Manton Avenue
Providence, Rhode Island 02909
(401) 457-1800

SOUTH CAROLINA
Worker's Compensation Board of South
Carolina
1612 Marion

Columbia, SC 29201
(803) 737-5700

SOUTH DAKOTA
James E. Marsh, Director
Division of Labor and Management
Department of Labor
Richard F. Kneip Bldg.
700 N. Governor's Drive
Pierre, SD 57501-2291
(605) 773-3681

TENNESSEE
Dina Tobin, Director
Department of Labor
Tennessee Worker's Compensation
Division
710 James Robertson Parkway, 2nd Floor
Andrew Johnson Tower
Nashville, TN 37243-0661
(615) 741-2395

TEXAS
Todd Brown, Executive Director
Texas Worker's Compensation
Commission
4000 S. IH 35
Southfield Bldg.
Austin, TX 78704
(512) 448-7900

UTAH
Lee Ellertson, Chairman
Worker's Compensation Industrial
Commission
Heber M. Wells Bldg.
160 E. 3rd South St.
P.O. Box 146610
Salt Lake City, UT 84114-6610
1-800-530-5090
(801) 530-6800 or (801) 288-8010

VERMONT
Dept. of Labor and Industry
National Life Bldg, Drawer 20
Montpelier, VT 05620-3401
(802) 828-2286

Continued

VIRGINIA
Lou-ann D. Joyner, Clerk of the
Commission
Virginia Worker's Compensation
Commission
1000 DMV Drive
Richmond, VA 23220
(804) 367-8600 or (804) 367-8615
Fax: (804) 367-9740

WASHINGTON
Washington State Department of
Labor & Industries
P. O. Box 44269
Olympia, WA 98504-4269
(360) 902-5800

WEST VIRGINIA
Worker's Compensation Board of
West Virginia
P. O. Box 3151
Charleston, WV 25332
(304) 558-3423

WISCONSIN
Gregory Krohm, Administrator
Worker's Compensation Division
Department of Work Force Development
161 General Executive Facility I
201 E. Washington Ave.
P.O. Box 7901
Madison, WI 53707-7901
(608) 266-1340
Fax: (608) 267-0394

WYOMING
Worker's Compensation Board of
Wyoming
Herschler Building
122 West 25th Street, 2nd Floor
Cheyenne, WY 82002
(307) 777-7441

Forms Required for Worker's Compensation Insurance Billing:

- Doctor's First Report of Occupational Illness or Injury
- Certificate of Disability
- Doctor's Prescription Form
- Comprehensive Client Intake Form
- Worker's Compensation Outpatient Care Certification
- Worker's Compensation Claim Form
- Worker's Compensation Fee Schedule
- Client Insurance Record

FOR PHYSICIANS' AND CHIROPRACTORS' USE ONLY

DOCTOR'S FIRST REPORT OF OCCUPATIONAL INJURY OR ILLNESS
STATE OF CALIFORNIA

Within 5 days of your **initial examination,** for every occupational injury or illness, send **TWO** copies of this report to the **employer's workers' compensation insurance carrier** or th **self-insured employer.** Failure to file a timely doctor's report may result in assessment of a civil penalty. **In the case of diagnosed or suspected pesticide poisoning,** send a cop of this report to Division of Labor Statistics and Research, P.O. Box 420603, San Francisco CA 94142-0603, and notify your local health officer by telephone within 24 hours.

		PLEASE DO NOT USE THIS COLUMN
1. **INSURER NAME AND ADDRESS**		
2. **EMPLOYER NAME**		Case No.
3. Address: No. and Street City Zip		Industry
4. Nature of business (e.g., food manufacturing, building construction, retailer of women's clothes)		County

5. **PATIENT NAME** (First name, middle initial, last name)	6. Sex ☐ Male ☐ Female	7. Date of Mo. Day Yr. Birth	Age
8. Address: No. and Street City Zip	9. Telephone Number ( )		Hazard
10. Occupation (Specific job title)	11. Social Security Number - -		Disease
12. Injured at: No. and Street City County			Hospitalization
13. Date and hour of injury or onset of illness Mo. Day Yr. Hour _____ a.m. _____ p.m.	14. Date last worked Mo. Day Yr.		Occupation
15. Date and hour of first examination or treatment Mo. Day Yr. Hour _____ a.m. _____ p.m.	16. Have you (or your office) previously treated patient? ☐ Yes ☐ No		Return Date/Cod

Patient please complete this portion, if able to do so. Otherwise, doctor please complete immediately. Inability or failure of a patient to complete this portion shall not affect his/her rights to workers' compensation under the California Labor Code.

17. **DESCRIBE HOW THE ACCIDENT OR EXPOSURE HAPPENED** (Give specific object, machinery or chemical. Use reverse side if more space is required.)

18. **SUBJECTIVE COMPLAINTS** (Describe fully. Use reverse side if more space is required.)

> I have not violated Labor Code Section 139.3 and the contents of this report and bill is true and correct to the best of my knowledge. This statement is made under penalty of perjury.
> DATE OF REPORT _____
> Dated this _____ day of _____ 19____
> at _____ County, California.

19. **OBJECTIVE FINDINGS** (Use reverse side if more space is required.)

    A. Physical examination

    B. X-ray and laboratory results (State if none or pending.)

20. **DIAGNOSIS** (if occupational illness, specify etiologic agent and duration of exposure.) Chemical or toxic compounds involved? ☐ Yes ☐No

    ICD-9 Code ___ ___ ___ . ___ ___

21. Are your findings and diagnosis consistent with patient's account of injury or onset of illness? ☐ Yes   ☐ No If "no", please explain.

22. Is there any other current condition that will impede or delay patient's recovery?   ☐ Yes   ☐ No If "yes", please explain.

23. **TREATMENT RENDERED** (Use reverse side if more space is required.)

24. If further treatment required, specify treatment plan / estimated duration.

25. If hospitalized as inpatient, give hospital name and location.   Date admitted   Mo. Day Yr.   Estimated stay

26. **WORK STATUS**   Is patient able to perform usual work? ☐ Yes   ☐ No
    If "no", date patient can return to: Regular work ___/___/___
                             Modified work ___/___/___   Specify restrictions _____

Doctor's Signature _____   Date _____   CA License Number _____
Doctor Name and Degree (Please Type) _____   IRS Number _____
Address _____   Telephone Number (_____) _____

Any person who makes or causes to be made any knowingly false or fraudulent material statement or material representation for the purpose of obtaining or denying workers' compensation benefits or payments is guilty of a felony.

FOR PHYSICIANS' AND CHIROPRACTORS' USE ONLY

CERTIFICATE OF DISABILITY

To Whom it May Concern:

This is to certify that _____ Sue Jones _____
is disabled to perform the duties purtenant to his/her regular employment beginning

____1/15/97_____ Estimated return to work date ____3/1/97_____

_____   2/15/97
PROVIDER'S SIGNATURE   DATE

CERTIFICATE OF DISABILITY

To Whom it May Concern:

This is to certify that _____
is disabled to perform the duties purtenant to his/her regular employment beginning

_____ Estimated return to work date _____

_____   _____
PROVIDER'S SIGNATURE   DATE

COMPREHENSIVE CLIENT INTAKE FORM
FOR WORKER'S COMPENSATION

Name : _____Mary Andrews_____   Claim Number ____09834____

Address:____123 State Street____   Social Security Number__001–003–9562__

City:____Anytown____   Referring Doctor:____Dr. Joe Hancock____

Zip Code: ____90080____   Insurance Co. Name: __The Worker's Comp Trust__

Telephone Number: (800) 666-1282 _____

Date of Injury: ____1/1/97____   Legal Case: Yes

Describe Injury:____Client experienced sharp pain in (R) wrist and elbow as well as

right shoulder while performing her job for several weeks.

Physical Activities at Work: Indicate Percentage (%) of time spent at each of the following activities:

90% Sitting   0% Lifting   90% Typing

10% Standing   0% 10-Key   90% Mousing

0% Twisting   20% Writing   0% Drawing

0% Reaching   0% Carrying   50% Talking

Indicate the percentage of time spent on the telephone per day:

Please circle one: Headset   Yes   (No)

Do you use it   Yes   (No)

Touch Typist   (Yes)   No

Trackball   (Yes)   No

Mouse on left   Yes   (No)

HIERARCHY OF SYMPTOMS: (Please list symptoms from most severe to least severe, describing the specific body area involved and the percentage (%) of time symptoms are present).

LOCATION OF SYMPTOMS:	(% of time present)	Flares with Task
Right elbow	100% of the time	Yes
Right wrist	90% of the time	Yes
Right shoulder	90% of the time	Yes

COMPREHENSIVE CLIENT INTAKE FORM
FOR WORKER'S COMPENSATION (continued)

Do tasks make the symptoms worse?   (Yes)   No

What other therapies have you tried?   Physical therapy 2 x per week for 3 months.

_____

_____

Describe your regular sleep patterns: Awake every 2-3 hours for about 1 hour.

How do you feel when you wake up in the morning? Do the symptoms wake you up at times?

_____ Feel tired upon awakening. Wake up during the night with pain.

_____

_____

Fatigue Level (1-10 where 10 is the most fatigued)

Fatigue level at the beginning of the day: 7

Fatigue level at the end of the day: 10

Stress Level (1-10 where 10 is the highest level of stress)

Indicate stress level at the beginning of the day: 5

Indicate stress level at the end of the day: 10

Do you drink caffeinated beverages? Yes If yes, how often and how many:

_____   2 cups coffee per day

_____
              Yes   Walk 3 times per week

Do you exercise? _____   What type and how often? _____
                        Listen to music

What do you do regularly to relax? _____
                        No

S A M P L E

DOCTOR'S PRESCRIPTION FORM

It is my recommendation that _____ Susan Smith _____
undergo the following adjunctive procedure:

☑ Soft-Tissue Therapy

☑ Neuromuscular Re-education

Sessions to be scheduled:

☑ 3 times per week for _____1_____ weeks

☑ 2 times per week for _____3_____ weeks

☐ Once per week for _____ weeks

Diagnosis:

_____ Cervical Subluxation, Thoracic Subluxation _____

December 9, 1996_____
Date

_____
Physician's Signature

WORKER'S COMPENSATION OUTPATIENT CARE CERTIFICATION

09/30/96

CHRISTINE ROSCHE MA/CERTIFIED MASSAGE THERAPIST
4157 EL CAMINO WAY
SUITE C
PALO ALTO, CA 94306

RE: **PROSPERITY CORPORATION**

EMPLOYEE INFORMATION:

EMPLOYEE NAME: **JOYCE GOLD**
SSN#: **612–48–4499–01**
EMPLOYER: **PROSPERITY CORP.**
DOI: **10/11/96**
CLAIM#: **061072334961**

PROVIDER INFORMATION:

PHYSICIAN: **SUSAN SMITH   595-06-2122**
FACILITY: **CHRISTINE ROSCHE   MA/MASSAGE THERAPY   552043112**

CERTIFICATION RECOMMENDATION: CERTIFICATION NUMBER: 20000–000

TREATMENT DATES: **09/30/96 to 10/30/96**
PRIMARY DIAGNOSIS: 739.1   **CERVICAL JOINT DISFUNCTION**
PRIMARY PROCEDURE: 729.1   **FIBROMYALGIA**
PROCEDURE/SERVICE: **MASSAGE THERAPY 1 x per week for 4 weeks**

**PLEASE NOTE THAT ALL FUTURE MEDICAL TREATMENT
REQUIRES PRE-CERTIFICATION.**

THE PROVIDER HAS INDICATED THAT CHARGES FOR THE NOTED SERVICE (S)
WILL BE: $ 260

THIS CERTIFICATION IS FOR MEDICAL NECESSITY AND APPROPRIATENESS AND
DOES NOT CONFIRM OR GUARANTEE INSURANCE COVERAGE.

UTILIZATION REVIEW NURSE: (800) 881-0291

WORKER'S COMPENSATION CLAIM FORM
(Final or Monthly Report & Bill)

Claim No.

Itemized Bills, in duplicate, are to be submitted at the termination of the case. Monthly statements are positively required on cases under treatment. Services beginning late in month and extending into next month may be itemized together.

1. INSURANCE COMPANY Orion Group	**2.** ADDRESS 15 Shaw Drive, Palo Alto, California 94303
3. EMPLOYER'S NAME Silicon Valley Technical Group	**4.** ADDRESS 2033 Douglas St., San Francisco, California 95110

5. EMPLOYEE'S NAME Ron Smith	**6.** SOCIAL SECURITY NO. 022–985–3112	**7.** PATIENT'S SEX ☑ MALE ☐ FEMALE	**8.** DATE OF BIRTH 4-15-45

9. DATE OF INJURY ACCIDENT 2-1-96	**10.** IF EMERGENCY CHECK HERE ☐

11. DATE PATIENT DISCHARGED FROM CARE 9-1-96	**12.** DATE PATIENT FAILED TO RETURN N/A
13. HAS PATIENT HAD SAME OR SIMILAR SYMPTOMS?	**14.** DATE PATIENT REFUSED TREATMENT

15. NAME AND ADDRESS OF FACILITY WHERE SERVICES RENDERED (IF OTHER THAN HOME OR OFFICE)

16. DATE PATIENT ABLE TO RETURN TO WORK 9-5-96	**17.** DATES OF TOTAL DISABILITY FROM 5-1-96 TO 7-1-96	**18.** DATES OF PARTIAL DISABILITY FROM 7-1-96 TO 9-1-96

19. SERVICES FOR THE MONTH OF	**20.** CONDITION OF PATIENT AT TIME OF LAST VISIT Good

21. DIAGNOSIS OR NATURE OF ILLNESS OR INJURY. RELATE DIAGNOSIS TO PROCEDURE IN COLUMN D BY REFERENCE NUMBERS 1, 2, 3, ETC. OR DX CODE

A. 739.2   Thoracic Segmental Dysfunction
1. 719.9   Myofascitis
2. 847.2   Lumbar Sprain/Strain
3.
4.

22. A. DATE OF SERVICE FROM — TO	B. PLACE OF SERVICE	C. FULLY DESCRIBE PROCEDURES, MEDICAL SERVICES OR SUPPLIES PROCEDURE CODE IDENTITY — FURNISHED FOR EACH DATE GIVEN		D. DIAGNOSIS CODE	E. CHARGES
8-1-96 8-1-96	Office	97112	Neuromuscular Re Education	A, 1, 2	33.21
8-1-96 8-1-96	Office	97250	Myofascial Release	A, 1, 2	40.00
8-8-96 8-8-96	Office	97110	Therapeutic Exercises	A, 1, 2	33.21
8-15-96 8-15-96	Office	97145	Massage Therapy	A, 1, 2	22.14
8-15-96 8-15-96	Office	97145	Additional 15 Min	A, 1, 2	13.53
8-15-96 8-15-96	Office	97145	Additional 15 Min	A, 1, 2	13.53

23. ANY CHARGES SHOWN ABOVE WHICH ARE IN EXCESS OF THE FEE SCHEDULE EXPLAINED BELOW WITH THE NATURE OF SUCH SERVICES AND THE DATE RENDERED	**24.** TOTAL CHARGE $155.62
	25 PREVIOUS BILLING DUE 0
	26. BALANCE DUE $155.62

27. EMPLOYER'S I.D. NO.	**28.** SOCIAL SECURITY NO. 652-05-0011	**29.** PHYSICIAN'S OR SUPPLIER'S NAME, ADDRESS, ZIP & TELEPHONE NO.
30. DATE 8-31-96	**31.** LICENSE NO. A066867	Richard Jackson, M.D. 12345 Tree Lane
33. SIGNATURE OF PHYSICIAN OR SUPPLIER *Richard Jackson, M.D.*		Sacramento, California 91110 919-432-5561

CALIFORNIA WORKER'S COMPENSATION FEE SCHEDULE
EFFECTIVE MARCH 1996

MODALITIES
(Physical medicine treatment to one area)

CODE	DESCRIPTION	RV	FEE
97010	Hot or cold packs	3.0	$18.45
97012	Traction, mechanical	3.0	18.45
97014	Elec. stimulation (unattended)	3.0	18.45
97016	Vasopneumatic devices	3.0	18.45
97018	Paraffin bath	3.0	18.45
97020	Microwave	3.0	18.45
97022	Whirlpool	3.0	18.45
97024	Diathermy	3.0	18.45
97026	Infrared	3.0	18.45
97028	Ultraviolet	3.0	18.45
97039	Unlisted modality (specify)	3.0	18.45

PROCEDURES
(Physical medicine treatment to one area, initial 30 min)

CODE	DESCRIPTION	RV	FEE
97110	Therapeutic exercises	5.4	$33.21
97112	Neuromuscular reeducation	5.4	33.21
97114	Functional activities	5.4	33.21
97116	Gait training	4.4	27.06
97118	Elec. stimulation (manual)	3.8	23.37
97120	Iontophoresis	4.9	30.14
97122	Traction, manual	3.3	20.30
97124	Massage	3.6	22.14
97126	Contrast baths	3.3	20.30
97128	Ultrasound	3.4	20.91
97139	Unlisted procedure (specify)	4.9	30.14
97145	Each additional 15 minutes	2.2	13.53

PATIENT INSURANCE RECORD

PATIENT NO: _____

CLAIM NO: _____

TYPE OF CASE: _____

Patient's Name: _____ Phone: _____

Address: _____ Zip: _____

Insured's Name (If Not Patient): _____ Phone: _____

Policyholder (If Employer): _____ Phone: _____

Address: _____ Zip: _____

Insurance Company: _____ Phone: _____

Address: _____ Zip: _____

Name of Examiner or Agent: _____

Claim No: _____ Policy No. _____ If Accident, Date: _____

Coverage: _____

_____

Attorney's Name: _____ Phone: _____

Address: _____ Zip: _____

Remarks: _____

_____

Date Billed	Amount Billed	Date Paid	Amount Paid	Balance	Comments

Personal Injury: Claims Procedures and Sample Forms

Chapter 10

██████

Quick Summary of Key Points

- Claims Procdures: Personal Injury
- Personal Injury Billing Procedures
- Forms Required for Personal Injury Billing:

    Authorization to Pay Provider

    Assignment and Instructions for Direct Payment

    Practitioner's Lien

    Doctor's Prescription Form

    Practitioner's Billing Statement

    Client Insurance Record

Claims Procedures: Personal Injury

Personal injury claims are those that result from automobile accidents and other injuries such as a fall in a store.

Since automobile insurance companies do not require procedure codes, in both licensed and unlicensed states you may work out of your own office and bill personal injury companies using the statement shown in this chapter along with the doctor's referral/prescription memo. The following pages outline the procedures and the billing forms.

At the time of the first visit, ask the client if he has medical payments coverage on his automobile insurance. In order for you to get paid by the insurance company, the client must sign an Assignment of Benefits form (also called Authorization to Pay Provider) which you then send to the insurance company. This chapter includes samples of these forms. Medical payments coverage (or Med-Pay) will reimburse for your services within 2 to 4 weeks after billing.

The insurance company will not pay anyone other than its insured client unless authorized to do so. **Since your getting paid depends on this form being on file with the insurance company, make sure you send it in rather than relying on the client to do it**.

When the client does not have medical payments coverage from his auto insurance, you may receive payment either from major medical insurance, (see Chapter 8) or from the client directly. Reimbursement to you will depend on the case being settled, either in court or by outside agreement. This process can take from 6 months to 3 years, depending on details of the case and the type of claim.

To assure you get paid for your services when there is no medical payments insurance coverage, you must have what is called "a lien" against the settlement. A lien establishes your right to be paid before the injured person receives the amount of the settlement. In practice, the lien is a written agreement among all the concerned parties, (the client, the doctor, the attorney and the practitioner) that makes sure the interested professionals receive payment for their services when the case is settled. Two different lien forms are in this chapter for your reference.

Remember that personal injury laws and billing requirements vary from state to state. Be sure to call the appropriate attorney in your state and the client's insurance company to verify laws and billing procedures.

Personal Injury Billing Procedures

Verify coverage and ask if the client has medical payment coverage on his auto insurance. Med-Pay on your client's auto or accident insurance policy is preferable because payment can begin immediately following the accident for procedures which are medically necessary and prescribed by the doctor. Again, check your state auto insurance laws to determine coverage for your particular situation.

Med-Pay means that you can get paid within 2-4 weeks after submitting the bill for your services. Once the case is settled, the insurance company of the party at fault has to repay your client. However, the case settlement can take 1 to 2 years, or longer, from the date of the accident.

If the client does not have medical payment coverage on his auto insurance policy, you and the other healthcare providers must wait for payment until the claim is settled.

In some cases, clients can pay with cash or with their medical insurance. If you decide to wait for the settlement in order to receive payment, you should obtain a lien, (see page 127) which is a legal document specifying who will get paid for what type of service during the client's treatment program. It is essential that the lien be filled out properly by the client's attorney and be on file with the insurance company, the referring doctor's office and the attorney's office when you begin working with the client.

Without a lien, your chances of receiving payment for services rendered are reduced significantly. The lien form is available through the doctor's or attorney's offices.

When you file for personal injury claims, you will need a pre-printed business statement (page 129 includes a pre-printed form) showing the name of your business, your name, address, phone number, state license number and National Certification Number (if applicable).

You must state the date of service, description of service, (remember to use soft tissue therapy/neuromuscular re-education) and the amount of the charge. You do not need to use procedure codes when billing for your services.

Total the charges and submit the completed statement (as shown in Chapter 10) every two weeks to the client's insurance company with a copy to the client's attorney.

Be sure to review the Doctor's Prescription Form on page 128. Please note the doctor must fill in the number of times per week for how many weeks the patient must see you, as well as his or her diagnosis. Also note that the type of procedure that you do must be specified, (for example, soft tissue therapy, neuromuscular re-education or myofascial release). If any of this information is incomplete or missing, your payment will be delayed.

For good records management and more accurate follow up, use a client insurance record like the one on page 130 to note the date you billed and the amount.

In personal injury cases, three different types of insurance may cover the client's loss:

1. The client's automobile insurance company under the medical payments coverage of the policy

2. The client's major medical or group insurance company

3. "Third party insurance." If someone else was at fault in the accident, the client may bill the other person's insurance company. This insurance is the only type that will not pay until the client's case is settled, that is, until it has been determined who is at fault and must pay.

You may legally bill all three of the above. Notify each insurance company with a note on the billing statement such as:

Statement also sent to:

Insurance Company Name

Insurance Company Address

Name of Insured

Claim Number

Forms Required for Personal Injury/Accident Claims

Note: If Medical Insurance and Procedure Coding is involved, claims must be billed from the doctor's office in unlicensed states. If auto insurance case only, claims may be billed from your office with a doctor's prescription.

- Authorization to Pay Provider
- Assignment and Instructions for Direct Payment
- Practitioner's Lien
- Doctor's Prescription Form
- Practitioner's Billing Statement
- Client Insurance Record

AUTHORIZATION TO PAY PROVIDER

I hereby authorize the _____Prosperity_____ Insurance

Company to pay by check out and mailed directly to:

> Chris Rosche
> 4157 El Camino Way #C
> Palo Alto, CA 94306

for the health care benefits allowable and otherwise payable to me under my current insurance policy, as payment toward the total charges for Professional Services Rendered. This payment will not exceed my indebtedness to the above mentioned assignee and I have agreed to pay in a current manner, any balance of said Professional Service charges over and above this insurance payment.

A photocopy of this authorization shall be considered as effective and valid as the original.

Date _____2/15/97_____   Name _____Susan Smith_____

This office holds an assignment lien on this case for services rendered.

Any settlement of this claim without honoring this assignment lien will cause you to be responsible to this office for payment.

Street address _____123 Anytown_____

City State & Zip _____Blueridge, CA 94111_____

ASSIGNMENT/INSTRUCTIONS FOR DIRECT PAYMENT

PRIVATE, GROUP, ACCIDENT AND HEALTH INSURANCE

TO: _____
INSURANCE COMPANY

_____

_____

Phone _____

Patient _____

Employer: _____

Claim / Group # _____

Soc. Sec. # / I.D. #_____

I hereby instruct and direct the above Insurance Company to pay by check made out and mailed directly to:

OR

If my current policy prohibits direct payment to practitioner, then I hereby also instruct and direct you to make out the check to me and mail it as follows:

c/o

for professional benefits allowable, and otherwise payable to me under my current insurance policy as payment toward the total charges for professional services rendered. THIS IS A DIRECT ASSIGNMENT OF MY RIGHTS AND BENEFITS UNDER THIS POLICY. This payment will not exceed my indebtedness to the above-mentioned assignee, and I have agreed to pay in a current manner, any balance of said professional service charges over and above this insurance payment.

A photocopy of this Assignment shall be considered as effective and valid as the original.

I also authorize the release of any information pertinent to my case to any insurance company, adjuster or attorney involved in this case.

_____
Signature of Policyholder

Date _____

_____
Signature of Claimant, if other than Policyholder

Witness

ACKNOWLEDGEMENT OF INSURANCE COMPANY

This insurance company hereby acknowledges receipt of the above instruction and agrees to mail payment of medical coverage benefits of the policy directly to the office of and to the order of the practitioner.

Date: _____ Authorized Signature: _____

Please date and sign one copy. Kindly return for the patient's file.

NOTICE OF PRACTITIONER'S LIEN

TO: Attorney _____

_____

_____

| Practitioner: |
| |

RE: Health Care Reports and Practitioner's Lien

I do hereby authorize the above practitioner to furnish you, my attorney, with a full report of his/her evaluation of myself in regard to the accident in which I was involved.

I do hereby authorize and direct you, my attorney, to pay said practitioner such sums as may be due and owing him/her for health care service rendered me by reason of this accident and by reason of any other bills that are due his/her office and to withhold such sums from any settlement, judgement or verdict as may be necessary to adequately protect said doctor. And I hereby further give lien on my case to said practitioner against any and all proceeds of any settlement, judgement or verdict which may be paid to you, my attorney, or myself as the result of the injuries for which I have been treated or injuries in connection therewith.

I fully understand that I am directly and fully resposible to said practitioner for all medical and/or surgical benefits, including major medical, submitted by him/her for service rendered me and that this agreement is made solely for said practitioner's additional protection. I further understand that such payment is not contingent on any settlement, judgement or verdict by which I may eventually recover said fee. If this account is assigned for collection and/or suit, collection costs and/or interest, and/or attorneys fees, and/or court costs will be added to the total amount due.

Date: _____

Dated: _____ Client's Signature: _____

Witness: _____ Address: _____

ACKNOWLEDGEMENT OF ATTORNEY

The undersigned being attorney of record for the above client does hereby agree to observe all the terms of the above and agrees to withhold such sums from any settlement, judgment or verdict as may be necessary to adequately protect said practitioner above named. Any settlement of this claim without honoring this assignment/lien will cause you to be responsible to this office for payment. The prevailing party in any litigation resulting from enforcement of this lien shall be entitled to actual attorney's fees and court costs.

Dated: _____ Attorney's Signature: _____

Attorney: Please date, sign and return one copy to above doctor's office at once.
Reply envelope attached.
Keep one copy for your records.
(Updated)

S A M P L E

DOCTOR'S PRESCRIPTION FORM

It is my recommendation that _____ Susan Smith _____
undergo the following adjunctive procedure:

☑ Soft-Tissue Therapy

☑ Neuromuscular Re-education

Sessions to be scheduled:

☑ 3 times per week for ____1____ weeks

☑ 2 times per week for ____3____ weeks

☐ Once per week for _____ weeks

Diagnosis:

_____ Cervical Subluxation, Thoracic Subluxation _____

December 9, 1996
Date

_____
Physician's Signature

SAMPLE

PRACTIONER'S BILLING STATEMENT

(Business Name or Logo)

Practitioner's Name: Salley Jones
Address: 15 Hayward Court
City, State, Zip: Alfredo, MT 02210
Telephone Number: 415-622-9681

To: Little Giant Insurance Company
     925 Waverley Plaza, Suite 202
     Bigtown, CT 06107

Re: Trudy Dennis
Claim Number: 322-555

DATE	DESCRIPTION	AMOUNT
5-03-96	Neuromuscular Re-education	$35
5-07-96	Neuromuscular Re-education	$35
5-14-96	Neuromuscular Re-education	$35

TOTAL DUE $105

SAMPLE

CLIENT INSURANCE RECORD

EMPLOYER: _____ The Appleton Corporation _____

CLAIM/GROUP NO: _____ 2328125 _____

SOC. SEC. NO./I.D. NO. _____ 111-666-888 _____

Client's Name: _____ Sandra Smith _____   Phone: _____ 212-611-1181 _____

Address: _____ 2 Junction Lane, Yuba _____   State, Zip: _____ CT   11061 _____

Insured's Name (If Not Client): _____   Phone: _____

Policyholder (If Employer): _____ The Appleton Corp. _____   Phone: 601-222-1212

Address: _____ 2 Independence Dr., Yuba _____   State, Zip: _____ CT   11061 _____

Insurance Company: _____ The Fravid Grp _____   Phone: _____ 601-000-2121 _____

Address: _____ 123 Lane, Anytown _____   State, Zip: _____ CT   11061 _____

Name of Examiner or Agent: _____ Fred Jones _____

Claim No. _____ 12345 _____   Policy No. _____ X1681 _____   If Accident Date _____

Coverage: _____

_____

Attorney's Name: _____ Paul Sasson _____   Phone: _____

Address: _____ 1285 Swan Lake, Yuba _____   Zip: _____ CT   11061 _____

Remarks _____

_____

Date Billed	Amount Billed	Date Paid	Amount Paid	Balance	Comments
2/12/96	80	2/20/96	70	10	
2/20/96	80	3/10/96	70	10	
3/5/96	80	3/20/96	70	10	
3/10/96	80	3/27/96	70	10	
3/20/96	80	4/15/96	70	10	

Troubleshooting and Tracing Delinquent Claims

Quick Summary of Key Points

Troubleshooting and tracing delinquent claims

- How to educate insurance companies and their claims representatives
- Finding the solution to reimbursement problems
- Understand what is covered in your client's policy

Types of problems to submit to the Insurance commissioner

Claims management techniques

Typical reimbursement problems and their solutions

Troubleshooting and Tracing Delinquent Claims

Before you learn why reimbursement gets delayed or refused and what to do about it, you must be sure insurance companies and their claims representatives understand the medical value of your services. This groundwork must be in place for you to receive reimbursement.

Many insurance carriers do not know that your services offer clinical, therapeutic benefits in conjunction with a doctor's treatment plan. Instead, they see massage and bodytherapy services as offering only relaxation benefits. Perceiving our profession this way, they think paying such claims would waste money on something of no medical value.

For example, they often deny claims by saying they do not pay for preventive or wellness services. They also reject claims because they require that soft-tissue/massage therapy be done by a registered physical therapist or medical doctor. Also, they disallow claims in states where massage therapists are not licensed, since lack of licensure means to them "not a medical professional." (This suggests another reason for you to work with your state professional association to lobby for state licensure.)

The root of refusal problems is widespread ignorance of the scope and value of our services. While Europe and Asia have traditionally seen the value of massage/bodytherapy and included it in their modern healthcare and hospital systems for medical rehabilitation, U.S. insurance companies and physicians don't recognize its clinical value as an adjunctive treatment.

Preliminary research on massage performed in hospital settings clearly shows its effectiveness. Depending on the study, the patients and the therapy used, noted benefits include increased circulation, range of motion and function, decreased pain, shorter length of hospital stay, and decreased need for medication. These benefits all have cost-saving implications which should appeal to those trying to limit healthcare costs. But more outcome studies are needed, and the results must reach those who can make decisions in our favor.

Therefore, you can help both yourself and your profession by educating insurers and their claims representatives to the efficacy and cost-effectiveness of your services. For example, you can pave the way for reimbursement by sending insurance carriers a well-written, professional letter describing your services along with copies of doctors' testimonial letters and reputable outcome studies demonstrating the significant clinical benefits of massage/bodytherapy. Further, you may even consider giving a 15-20-minute free demonstration massage on a claims representative. This can be a highly effective way to show the value of your services. (See Touch Therapy Research in the Appendix.)

You should also point out that massage/bodytherapists have an average of 500-1000 hours of training in soft-tissue therapy/massage therapy. This contrasts with physical therapists, who usually receive only 15-30 hours training in massage therapy.

Further, explain to claims representatives that massage therapists are uniquely qualified to perform these services, and their fees are significantly lower than a medical doctor's for the same services. For example, a massage therapist will spend 45-60 minutes with a patient and charge only $65, while a physician may charge at least $200 for a service not commonly part of his practice.

In brief, you can write that massage therapy has specific clinical therapeutic value, we specialize in it, we have far more training than any other profession, and we charge two-thirds less than physicians. The sooner you establish these facts with insurance company executives, the sooner you will begin to receive reimbursement.

Finding the Solution to Reimbursement Problems

When you have difficulty getting paid by an insurance company (claims are delayed, reduced or rejected) you will find the solution in one of four places:

1. **Your Office:**

    Correct errors in your paperwork and office procedures.

2. **The Doctor's Office:**

    Have them give timely, accurate and complete information on patient, diagnosis and procedure.

3. **The Insurance Company:**

    Insist it meet its payment obligations (time and amount) under the patient's policy and state laws.

4. **Your State Insurance Commissioner:**

    Ask for an investigation of reimbursement problems.

Claims Provisions in Health Insurance Policies

Many details on what's covered and who may be reimbursed are spelled out in the detailed language of the client's policy. To make the insurance reimbursement system work for you in building your practice, you must understand and follow these crucial details. Remember, an insurance policy is nothing more than a contract between a company and a person or group. Essentially, the insurance company agrees to pay money, IF you and the patient meet specific requirements.

Time, or when things must occur, is a key requirement in all policies. For example, individual health insurance policies require the company to pay benefits promptly after they receive a claim. However, how quickly they must pay varies from one company to another.

In addition, the person making the claim must notify the insurance company of a loss within a certain time period, or the insurer may deny benefits. If the insured disagrees with the company on the amount it paid for the claim, he can begin a lawsuit only within 3 years after submitting the claim.

Another common provision says an insured cannot bring legal action against the insurance company until 60 days after submitting a claim. If a payment problem develops and the insurance company ignores, denies or is too slow to pay a claim, you or the insured may ask the state insurance commissioner to intervene on your behalf.

The insurance commissioner does not have the power to force a company to pay a claim, but his authority does include the following:

1. Hold a hearing to determine whether licensed insurers, brokers and agents have complied with state laws.

2. Review a policy's provisions to determine if the insurer's denial of the claim has violated its obligations under the insurance contract.

3. Advise the patient whether the company has violated the law. (This may pave the way for the client to sue the insurance company.)

Types of Problems to Submit to the State Insurance Commissioner

1. Improper denial of a claim

2. Settlement for a lesser amount than the policy provides

3. Unreasonable delay in settling a claim

4. Illegal cancellation or termination of an insurance policy

5. Problems about premium rates

Submit requests to the insurance commissioner in writing. See page 257 for a sample. Include the following information:

1. The inquiring person's name, address and telephone number

2. The policyholder's name and address

3. The name and address of the insurance company, agent or broker

4. The policy period

5. The policy or claim number

6. The dates of loss or services

7. A statement of the complaint including, if possible, a copy of the policy, medical bills, unpaid medical insurance claims, canceled checks, and any correspondence from the company about the claim

NOTE: Since the commissioner's responsibility is to the client (the consumer), not the doctor or provider of service, any letters must include the client's signature, address and telephone number.

If an insurance company pays the patient directly, even though the provider (doctor or massage/bodytherapist) has sent in an Assignment of Benefits form with the claim, file a complaint with the state insurance commissioner. After receiving this complaint, the commissioner will write to the insurance company and request a review of the claim. If an Assignment of Benefits was on file with the insurance company, it must pay the therapist within 2 to 3 weeks and honor the assignment even before it recovers its money from the patient.

> **NOTE:** If the company is chronically slow to pay, you can speed up payment by including the following wording in a letter with your claim: "IF THIS CLAIM IS NOT PAID OR DENIED WITHIN 30 DAYS, A FORMAL WRITTEN COMPLAINT WILL BE FILED WITH THE STATE INSURANCE COMMISSIONER."

Because the insurance commissioner's duties include monitoring how well the public is served, carriers usually want to keep complaints to a minimum. The above wording, and your commitment to follow through on a complaint, will help improve insurance company performance.

To contact your state insurance commissioner for assistance, please see listing on pages 143–146.

CLAIMS MANAGEMENT TECHNIQUES

Insurance Claims Register

In Chapter 6 you learned to establish a follow-up procedure for insurance claims by logging the claims completed onto an Insurance Claims Register. (See sample on Pages 95 and 117.)

Use a loose-leaf notebook indexed by insurance company name. Place a copy of the insurance claim in the pending file labeled for each month of service so that you can easily retrieve the unpaid claims for follow-up.

When referring to this register, you can quickly locate delinquent claims by simply looking through the book under the Date Claims Paid column. If that column is blank, check the Date Claims Submitted column. You can request a tracer on a claim when no payment has been received from the insurance company.

When you receive a payment, with one or more Explanation of Benefits forms, pull out the copies of claims that correspond with the payments and discard them.

Recall from Chapter 6 that the EOB form explains the company's response to a claim, how much, if any, of a claim they are paying, as well as the amounts applied to annual deductible and ineligible amounts. Often the EOB gives simple numeric codes to explain why the company denied or discounted the claimed amount. Be sure you understand the meaning of these brief statements of denial or discount. To receive full payment for future claims, make sure you correct whatever error or deficiency the company is finding.

Post payments to the client's ledger card and deposit the check in the proper account. When all claims on a page have been paid, draw a diagonal line across the page. Retain the pages for future reference.

Tickler File

A tickler file, also called a suspense or follow-up file, helps you keep track of submitted, pending or resubmitted insurance claims. You can also set up tickler files in a computer system.

To begin using this system, print two completed HCFA-1500 Health Insurance Claim Forms. Send the original to the payer and file a copy in the tickler file.

After you receive the Explanation of Benefits form (see sample on page 72) and payment check from the insurance company, post the payment on the financial record and pull all claims noted on the EOB from the tickler file.

Compare the charges paid on each claim to the payments listed on the EOB form. Then attach a copy of the EOB to the claim and put it in a paid file.

Copies of the claims remaining in the tickler file exceeding the time limits for manual or electronic submission should be re-submitted to the insurance company for reconsideration. Keep copies of the documents in the tickler file and enter the date of the second submission. Write "second request" on the copies.

TYPICAL PAYMENT PROBLEMS

In order to fully understand this section, be sure to read or review Chapter 6, especially types of insurance and basic procedures for all claims.

Typical problems include payments that are denied, delinquent or insufficient, down coding and processing delays. These problems require some type of follow-up action by you. (One advantage of submitting claims electronically: follow-up inquiries are fast and easy.)

Denied Claims

"Denied" means they totally reject the claim for some reason, such as provider does not meet licensure requirements or policy does not cover this service. Insurance companies save dollars when they deny a claim. Also, from experience they know that only a small percentage of individuals follow up on denied claims.

Claims denials fall into two categories: Technical Errors and Medical Policy Coverage Issues.

Technical Errors consist of missing or incorrect information and are found via computer audits and screening processes. Medical Policy Coverage Issues, such as medical necessity, time period of coverage and the credentials of the provider, are more variable.

Common Technical Reasons Why Claims Are Denied

1. Incorrect or Incompatible Professional Service Codes: The procedure and its code must correspond with your profession's scope of practice and be consistent with the doctor's diagnosis. For example, a skeletal procedure such as "traction" would not be reimbursed as a service provided by a massage therapist, whose practice is muscular.

2. Inconsistent Diagnosis and Procedure Codes: Whatever the doctor's diagnosis, his prescribed treatment must be established with the insurance company as medically necessary.

The diagnosis must correspond to the appropriate procedure code given on the billing form. For example, the services of bodytherapy professionals are billed under physical medicine procedure codes, such as myofascial release and massage therapy. These procedure codes must be billed with the related diagnostic code given by the doctor from the physical medicine diagnostic code book, such as "cervical joint dysfunction," "fibromyalgia," or "myofascial syndrome of trapezius muscle."

These diagnostic groups refer to the physical body. Some physicians make the mistake of giving a mental health diagnosis, such as "tension state" or "anxiety," followed by a physical medicine procedure code such as "neuromuscular re-education." Insurance companies will not pay for such physical-mental combinations. A mental health diagnosis (which you may not legally make in any case) must be accompanied by an appropriate procedure code such as "stress counseling" or "office visit." Insurance companies do not recognize bodytherapy services for anxiety or tension state, while they do allow them for back pain, neck muscle spasm and other neuromuscular disorders.

3. Missing, Incorrect, Non-Standard or Incomplete Diagnosis: The diagnosis must be clear, consistent with established medical practices and follow the terminology of medical diagnostic coding books.

4. Fees Higher than Usual, Reasonable and Customary (known as "UCR").

5. Therapist has Dual Fee Schedule (charges insurance a higher fee than uninsured patients).

6. Missing Patient Information: Make sure the patient answers all questions on his or her portion of the form.

7. Incorrect or Duplicate Dates of Service: Make certain all dates are listed and accurate.

8. Blank Fee Column: Fill in the fee column and total the charges for each claim.

9. Incorrect Dates.

10. Incorrect Patient Account Number.

11. Transposed Numbers.

12. Multiple Same-Day Visits: Normally a bill will not show two or more visits on the same day without explanation. For example, a bill may be rejected because it shows a chiropractic adjustment, an office visit with the doctor and an hour of massage therapy on the same date. Some insurance companies consider this excessive services in one day or excessive charges.

Partial Payment

"Partial payment" means you receive a check with an Explanation of Benefits form showing that the company is paying only a portion of the amount you submitted and the reason why. Reasons for not paying the full amount include:

1. Too many visits for the indicated diagnosis. For example, "shoulder muscle spasm" does not justify 30 visits in one year.

2. The claim asked for payment for more visits than the policy may allow for that condition. Physical medicine procedures may allow only 12 visits per year, for example.

3. "Down coding." When the claim has insufficient diagnostic information or when the coding system you used does not match the one used by the insurance carrier, the company converts the code you submitted to the nearest it recognizes. This code may pay at a lower amount than you submitted.

Pending Payments

"Pending" or "suspense" means the company wants more information. Most often for bodytherapy or massage, the company will ask:

1. Are you licensed in your state?
   (This is the crucial question. Insurers pay for services only from state licensed providers.)

2. Who is providing the services?

3. Can you demonstrate medical necessity? ("Medical necessity" means the patient needs this treatment to recover or be rehabilitated from an illness or an injury.)

Sometimes the insurance company will send a letter requesting more information from the doctor before it will consider paying the claim. It may request diagnosis, prognosis and progress reports and ask the doctor to state why the service is medically necessary and how long the doctor expects the procedures to continue. As a way to reduce costs, many insurance companies routinely ask for more information on any claim that continues beyond a certain length (usually 1 to 3 months from the beginning of treatment). The time frame will vary considerably with each insurance company.

Some companies also document the number of claims a provider submits for specific procedures. If they think a provider is billing excessively for certain services, they will request more information and carefully review the claim to determine if the service billed is medically necessary. In a licensed state, if you work in your own office, the doctor may ask you to assist with the letter of medical necessity.

When you need to contact an insurance company about a delinquent claim, use the form shown on Page 142.

Remember that state laws require insurance companies to notify the insured of a denial with an explanation.

The time limit for receiving insurance reimbursement can vary depending on the insurance carrier or program. It is reasonable to expect payment as follows:

Program	From Date Claim was Manually Submitted	From Date Claim was Electronically Submitted
Private Insurance Companies	4 to 6 weeks by mail	2 weeks or less
Blue Cross/Blue Shield	4 to 6 weeks by mail	2 weeks or less
CHAMPUS	8 to 12 weeks by mail	2 weeks or less
Medicare	4 to 6 weeks by mail	2-4 weeks or less
Worker's Compensation	4 to 8 weeks by mail	2 weeks or less

SOLUTIONS TO REIMBURSEMENT PROBLEMS

IMPORTANT: Be sure to remind your clients to read their insurance policies carefully to determine deductible, benefits and any restrictions or limitations. While they are responsible to know the extent of their contract with the insurance company, it is your income that is affected.

If a claim is not paid within a reasonable amount of time (4 to 10 weeks depending on the insurance company and the type of claim) the doctor's office or the practitioner may send an inquiry letter to the insurance company (also called an insurance tracer). The purpose of the tracer is to determine the status of a claim to find out why something is missing. An example is on page 142. With your tracer, include a copy of your detailed progress notes and any other documentation to support the medical necessity of your services.

If a claim is not paid within 30 days, the provider can also re-bill both the insurance company and the patient. Be sure your re-bill includes language to the insurance company stating that if unpaid within 30 days you will file a written complaint with the state insurance commissioner. It also helps to call the claims representative within a week to say, "I want to verify you have received a re-bill for this unpaid claim." When you re-bill the patient, remind them that they are responsible for any amounts unpaid by their insurance.

When a claim is denied, notify the patient by mail or telephone as soon as possible to keep them informed. Always retain the correspondence from the insurance company so you can retrieve it quickly for patient inquiries.

When a claim is denied or inadequately paid, the recourse is to appeal, which is a request for more payment by asking for a written review. Usually appeals carry time limits, so it is important for you to read and understand the Explanation of Benefits form.

If you establish an ongoing rapport with a claims representative, you can significantly shorten these kinds of delays. You can also speed up your collection times by establishing regular office procedures and claims management techniques (i.e., insurance claims register, tickler file, etc.) These support systems enable you to follow up quickly and correctly. They can even allow you to recover payment after a claim has been denied in whole or part.

By following the above suggestions and staying in touch with the claims representatives, you can get paid promptly and in full.

INSURANCE CLAIM TRACER

Insurance Company Name: _____ Date: _____

Address: _____

Patient Name: _____ Insured: _____

City: _____ Group Name/Number: _____

IRS Number: _____ Insured: _____

Employer Name and Address: _____

Date of Initial Claim Submission: _____ Amount: _____

Dates of Service: From _____ To _____

An inordinate amount of time has passed since submission of our original claim as described above. We have not received a request for additional information and still await payment of this assigned claim. Please review the attached duplicate and process for payment within seven (7) days.

If there is any difficulty with this claim, please check one of these below and return this letter to our office.

Claim pending because: _____

Payment of claim in process: _____

Payment made on claim. Date:_____ To Whom: _____

Claim denied: (Reason) _____

Patient notified: Yes ____   No____

Remarks: _____

_____

Thank you for your assistance in this important matter. Please contact: _____ in our office if you have any questions regarding this claim.

Office of: _____

Address: _____

_____ Telephone Number: _____

INSURANCE COMMISSIONERS

Mail to the insurance commissioner should be addressed to:
CONSUMER SERVICES, INSURANCE DEPARTMENT.

ALABAMA
P.O. Box 303351
Montgomery, AL 36130-3351
(334) 269-3550
(334) 269-3213

ALASKA
3601 C Street, #1324
Anchorage, AK 99503-5948
(907) 269-7900
(907) 269-7910 FAX

ARIZONA
2910 N. 44th Street, #210
Phoenix, AZ 85018
(602) 912-8400
(602) 912-8421 FAX

ARKANSAS
1123 S. University, #400
University Tower Building
Little Rock, AR 72204-1699
(501) 686-2900
(501) 686-2913 FAX

CALIFORNIA
300 S. Spring Street
Los Angeles, CA 90013
(213) 897-8921
1-800-927-4357

COLORADO
1560 Broadway, #850
Denver, CO 80202
(303) 894-7499

CONNECTICUT
P.O. Box 816
Hartford, CT 06142-0816
(203) 297-3900

DELAWARE
841 Silver Lake Boulevard
P.O. Box 7007
Dover, DE 19903-1507
(302) 739-4251

DISTRICT OF COLUMBIA
441 North Street N.W., 8th Floor
Washington, DC 20001
(202) 727-7424

FLORIDA
Larson Building
200 E. Gaines Street
Tallahassee, FL 32399-0300
(904) 922-3132
1-800-342-2762

GEORGIA
2 Martin Luther King Jr. Drive
Floyd Bldg., 7th Floor, West Tower
Atlanta, GA 30334
(404) 656-2056
(404) 656-0874 FAX

HAWAII
P.O. Box 3614
Honolulu, HI 96811
(808) 586-2790

IDAHO
P.O. Box 83720
700 W. State Street
Boise, ID 83720-0043
(208) 334-2250
(208) 334-4398 FAX

ILLINOIS
320 W. Washington Street
Springfield, IL 62767-0001
(217) 782-4515
(217) 782-5020 FAX

INDIANA
311 W. Washington Street #300
Indianapolis, IN 46204-2787
(317) 232- 2385

IOWA
Lucas Bldg.
Des Moines, IA 50319
(515) 281-5705
(515) 281-3059 FAX

KANSAS
420 S.W. 9th Street
Topeka, KS 66612-1678
(913) 296-3071
1-800-432-2484

KENTUCKY
P.O. Box 517
Frankfort, KY 40602
(502) 564-6027

LOUISIANA
P.O. Box 94214
Baton Rouge, LA 70804-9214
(504) 342-5900
(504) 342-3078 FAX

MAINE
State House Station #34
Augusta, ME 04333
(207) 624-8475
(207)624-8599 FAX

MARYLAND
501 St. Paul Place, 7th Floor
Baltimore, MD 21202
(410) 333-6300
1-800-492-6116

MASSACHUSETTS
470 Atlantic Avenue
Boston, MA 02210-2223
(617) 521-7794

MICHIGAN
P.O. Box 30220
Lansing, MI 48909
(517) 373-0240

MINNESOTA
133 E. 7th Street
St. Paul, MN 55101
(612) 296-4026
(612) 296-4328 FAX

MISSISSIPPI
P.O. Box 79
Jackson, MS 39205
(601) 359-3569
(601) 359-2474 FAX

MISSOURI
301 W. High Street, #630
P.O. Box 690
Jefferson City, MO 65102
(314) 751-4126
(314) 751-1165 FAX
1-800-726-7390

MONTANA
P.O. Box 4009
Helena, MT 59604-4009
(406) 444-2040
(406) 444-3497 FAX
1-800-332-6148

NEBRASKA
941 O Street #400
Lincoln, NE 68508
(402) 471-2201
(402) 471-4610 FAX

NEVADA
1665 Hot Springs Road, #152
Carson City, NV 89710
(702) 687-4270
(702) 687-3937 FAX
1-800-992-0900

NEW HAMPSHIRE
169 Manchester Street
Concord, NH 03301
(603) 271-2261
(603) 271-1406 FAX
1-800-852-3416

NEW JERSEY
20 W. State Street, CN325
Trenton, NJ 08625
(609) 292-5360
(609) 292-5865 FAX

NEW MEXICO
P.O. Drawer 1269
Santa Fe, NM 87504-1269
(505) 827-4500
(505) 827-4023 FAX

NEW YORK
160 W. Broadway
New York, NY 10013
(212) 602-0434
(212) 602-8872 FAX

NORTH CAROLINA
P.O. Box 26387
Raleigh, NC 27611
(919) 733-2004
(919) 733-0085 FAX
1-800-662-7777 NC

NORTH DAKOTA
600 East Boulevard, 5th Floor
Bismarck, ND 58505
(701) 328-2440
(701) 328-4880 FAX
1-800-247-0560

OHIO
2100 Stella Court
Columbus, OH 43215-1067
(614) 644-2658
(614) 644-3744 FAX
1-800-686-1526

OKLAHOMA
P.O. Box 53408
Oklahoma City, OK 73152-3408
(405) 521-2828
(405) 521-6652 FAX
1-800-522-0071

OREGON
350 Winter Street, N.E.
Salem, OR 97310
(503) 378-4271

PENNSYLVANIA
1321 Strawberry Square
Harrisburg, PA 17120
(717) 787-2317
(717) 785-8585 FAX

RHODE ISLAND
233 Richmond Street #233
Providence, RI 02903-4233
(401) 277-2223
(401) 751-4887 FAX

SOUTH CAROLINA
P.O. Box 100105
Columbia, SC 29202-3105
(803) 737-6160
(803) 737-6205 FAX
1-800-768-3467

SOUTH DAKOTA
500 E. Capital Avenue
Pierre, SD 57501
(605) 773-3563
(605) 773-5369 FAX

TENNESSEE
500 James Robertson Pkwy
Nashville, TN 37243-0565
(615) 741-2241
(615) 741-4000 FAX
1-800-342-4029

TEXAS
333 Guadalupe, P.O. Box 149104
Austin, TX 78714-9104
(512) 463-6169
(512) 475-2005 FAX
1-800-252-3439

UTAH
3110 State Office Building
Salt Lake City, UT 84114
(801) 538-3800
(801) 538-3829 FAX
1-800-439-3805

VERMONT
89 Main Street, Drawer 20
Montpelier, VT 05620-3101
(802) 828-3301
(802) 828-3306 FAX

VIRGINIA
P.O. Box 1157
Richmond, VA 23218
(804) 371-9741
1-800-552-7945

WASHINGTON
P.O. Box 40256
Olympia, WA 98504-0256
(360) 753-7300
1-800-562-6900

WEST VIRGINIA
1124 Smith Street
Charleston, WV 25301
(304) 558-2094
(304) 558-0412 FAX

WISCONSIN
P.O. Box 7873
Madison, WI 53707-7873
(608) 266-3585
1-800-236-8517

WYOMING
122 W. 25th Street, 3rd Floor East
Cheyenne, WY 82002
(307) 777-7401
1-800-438-5768

Chapter 12

Electronic Billing

Quick Summary of Key Points

- Benefits of electronic billing
- Making electronic billing work for you
- What to look for in electronic billing software

Electronic Billing

Even a few of the tools of the information/technology revolution can add real power and efficiency to your billing once you understand and use them. Electronic billing for insurance reimbursement will also speed up your business growth.

Professionals of every kind, including massage and bodytherapists, have adopted these tools because they remove hassles and save money (sometimes a lot of money), at every step of billing and collection.

Sometimes the savings are direct and immediate (less than a penny to send a claim form hundreds of miles over a telephone line or by satellite in seconds versus 32 cents in U.S. postage in 1-2 days.) Sometimes the savings are slower but much larger. For example, electronic claims are nearly 100 percent accurate, which means you don't have to spend money for staff time (or your own time) to tediously follow up what are usually *clerical* errors.

Here's the best reason for learning to use electronic billing: accurate claims get processed and paid much faster. For your income growth, that means much less waiting while "the check is in the mail." Because of what's called "the time value of money," a check you receive in 2 weeks is worth more to your business than one you wait 3 months to receive.

Thus, whatever anxiety or hesitation you may have about the electronic revolution, your ability to collect insurance claims promptly will more than pay for your time and effort to learn how to use these new tools.

Fortunately, putting the technology at your service doesn't mean you have to *understand* electronics and the workings of a computer, any more than driving a car means you have to understand electronic fuel injection or compression ratios. To drive a car, you learn the rules of the road, get a driver's license and a car owner's manual. To use electronic billing, you obtain (or get the use of) the right kind of computer, the right computer program (also called "software") and some brief training in how to use it for record keeping, billing and follow up. Or, you hire someone to do it for you.

Electronic Billing Briefly Explained

Electronic billing (a form of electronic data interchange), dates from the late 1960s. In simplest terms, two computers talk back and forth by wires inside a building, outside telephone lines or by radio waves.

An electronic claim is one you submit to the insurance carrier using no paper. Instead the claim is in digital form (1s and 0s) and sent directly (computer to computer), on a magnetic medium (such as a tape or diskette) or as a digital fax.

To standardize the process (and save more money), in 1981 eleven major insurance companies formed the National Electronic Information Corporation (NEIC). This industry group provides a national network and clearinghouse to electronically receive, process, edit, sort and transmit claims to insurers for payment in two weeks or less. By comparison, claims submitted the traditional way by first class mail are usually paid within four to six weeks.

The NEIC system benefits physicians and healthcare providers by letting them use *one* version of software to communicate with a variety of insurers. (Imagine the headache of having to learn and use 11 different electronic billing programs.) You can submit claims directly to NEIC for routing to your client's insurance company.

Or you can do your billing through a network of independent software companies, clearinghouses and billing centers. A clearinghouse, also called a "third-party administrator" (or TPA), receives claims, (you don't have to submit them one at a time, but can batch them together), separates them and sends each to the correct insurance payer. All this information is sent as fast as electricity flows and requires little or no intervention by error-prone, human operators.

Nearly 90 percent of all insurance companies use electronic claims submission to drastically lower their costs in staff salaries and office space. Electronic claims require no signing or stamping, searching for an insurance carrier's address, postage or trips to the post office, or filing and storing of paper forms. Also, electronic records leave an audit trail, which means you can track when and where the data went, when received, by whom and who may have altered it.

The benefits are many and dramatic:

- Better cash flow

- More time for patient education

- More time for collection efforts

- Lower labor costs

- Much higher accuracy rates

- Fewer disputes of the "We never received the claim, please resubmit it" variety, because proof of receipt is generated at the insurer's end.

- Faster problem resolution. The office is notified of rejected claims faster, allowing quicker follow-up with corrected data.

How to Make Electronic Billing Work for You

To begin using electronic billing, contact your major insurers for a list of vendors approved to handle electronic claims processing. The carriers know which systems meet their criteria and work with their special electronic billing requirements.

If you cannot link your system with the insurance carrier, use a clearinghouse, which forwards a batch of claims to insurers. Some clearinghouses offer other services, such as mailing claims to carriers that are not on-line. For your benefit, this means you can send every claim electronically rather than having to fall back on a paper system for some of them. Clearinghouses charge a flat fee per claim or a percentage of the dollar volume.

In addition to electronic billing, computer programs can provide similar help with your internal billing. If you properly choose, install and use it, a computerized office billing system will save you enormous amounts of time. Plus your records will be easily and quickly accessible in one place. Some systems even offer formats for patient notes, bookkeeping and follow-up progress reports.

What to Look for in Buying Billing Software

The most important components to look for in shopping for the best computerized insurance billing system are:

- Electronic Billing (enabling you to send a HCFA 1500 form to an insurance clearing house over telephone lines via modem)
- Networking (providing the program's functions to more than one computer in the same office)
- Superbill receipts for invoicing
- HCFA 1500 insurance form
- Single or batch printing
- Adjustable state tax rates
- Label and envelope printing
- Changeable welcome, thank you, no show, attorney & custom letters
- Reports: daily, monthly, master, patient totals & accounts receivable
- Modifiable diagnostic and procedure codes
- Comments screen to record SOAP and collection notes
- Instructional video

According to Marla Kopriva, developer of the billing program Ea$y Billing™, you should look to buy from a company offering tech support (prompt help with questions and problems) after the sale. Watch out for hidden costs, since many companies sell bare, modular programs that require additional (and costly) pieces to add the features you need. For example, the ability to change the CPT codes manually as the industry updates them, rather than having to buy an expensive update, can save you a significant amount.

Also investigate the charges and limitations for submitting claims to a clearinghouse. Ultimately, the program must create the forms you need for electronic filing from your database and be easy to use. For more information on Ea$y Billing™, write: Marla Productions, 524 Don Gaspar, Santa Fe, NM 87501. Tel.: (505) 982-5321.

See the Appendix for a listing of computerized billing programs.

Documentation: A Powerful Tool for Proving That Hands Heal

by Diana Thompson, LMT

Chapter 13

Quick Summary of Key Points

- The Proof is in the SOAP Chart
- Motivation for Documentation
- Use of Case Studies as Research
- Subjective Information
- Pain Questionnaires
- Personal Status Reports
- SOAP Charting
- Objective Information

Documentation: A Powerful Tool for Proving That Hands Heal

Documentation of patient information is a valuable tool for validating not only the progress of the patient, but the curative nature of bodytherapy and movement therapies. This information is easily gathered through subjective and objective findings using Pain Questionnaires, Personal Status Reports and SOAP Charting. Utilization of these methods not only aids in the setting and attainment of goals and documenting progress, but contributes to the success of the patient/practitioner relationship as well.

Motivation for Documentation

Documentation validates our profession as well as the relationship we have with our patients. Most health care providers are motivated to document because of external sources. Insurance companies refuse to pay for services without it; referring Primary Providers seek professional practitioners who can inform/communicate with it; attorneys expect it, as no case can be won without it; and state and provincial law may require it. The external motivations are numerous. However, the impetus for documentation should come from the most important source, which is the patient/practitioner relationship. This relationship should serve as the *internal motivation*.

The motivation for being bodytherapists and movement therapists comes from the nurturing of the special and spiritual healing relationship forged between patient and practitioner. This connection needs to serve as the primary motivation for documenting our sessions, not the external demand of insurance companies, primary providers and attorneys. What better way to record the healing properties of our profession? Documentation provides a tool which can strengthen the relationship with our patients by showing proof of goal attainment, of progress, and of the power of the body to heal itself.

Internal motivation is ultimately necessary for us to document well, consistently, and in a way that serves us and our patients, not just those we are externally bonded with. By developing the inspiration to document, we create tools of communication which ultimately reinforce our desire to be health care providers. What better incentive does a healer need than to have documentation that proves progress? And do we owe it to our clients to show them their progress? Historical documentation provides a framework, a time line in which to discuss progress–no matter how subtle or exaggerated.

In addition to developing our patient/practitioner relationship, documentation serves as witness to the validation of our field. We all have a list of cases where peoples' lives were transformed, miraculous recoveries made, memories surfaced and chronic problems resolved. But lip service to our skills and the power of the body to heal itself is not what is needed by our profession. To prove to skeptics that what we do and how we choose to do it is valid and curative, we need documentable evidence.

A friend of mine serves on an advisory panel to an insurance company that now includes massage therapy as a 100% reimbursable treatment modality in prescribed situations. The medical doctor leading the "alternative therapies" advisory panel meeting cited two cases already reported to the adjusters. In these cases, people who had never received massage therapy before and who considered themselves individuals who never would have sought that form of treatment, experienced amazing recovery from very serious conditions. One woman was thrown from a moving vehicle in a car accident, the other had a severe reaction to a surgical procedure which left her crippled. They were expecting to be confined to bedrest for several weeks; both regained function within three weeks as a result of bodytherapy. Although the results in these cases were dramatic, the documentation provided an objective written record which can only serve to validate the healing powers of the body as facilitated by a patient/practitioner team approach inherent in bodytherapy and movement therapies.

Use of Case Studies as Research

The major excuse for ignorance of the benefits of touch therapies and the reason touted for not referring to these modalities is the lack of concrete evidence, such as research in the medical model, proving the benefits of the treatments. We are lucky to have such people as Dr. Tiffany Field from the University of Miami's Touch Research Institute providing us with research that fits the medical model. We must, however, begin creating our own validation of our successes. Because we are not a traditional drug-based therapy, we need to find alternative ways of doing this. It is difficult, for example, to do a double blind study with massage. How would you set up the placebo group? Case studies are an excellent answer to document evidence of the curative nature of bodytherapy and movement therapies. We all have the tools necessary to use each one of our clients as a case study.

What is required by all practitioners is to regard documentation as a tool to prove progress. Our biggest thrill in this profession of touch is watching our patients recover, find their own path to health, and create and maintain a relationship with their body. When our patients achieve desired results, and more, as an expression of our teamwork together, we become excited. We can't bottle it and sell it, nor do we want to. Enhancing health through touch is a function of time, relationship, and growth. Only then is progress obtained.

Often, during the process of healing, there is doubt, frustration, and regression. Charting is an excellent tool for recording the process and documenting the progress that has taken time to exhibit. This article demonstrates how to effectively and efficiently document advancement as a result of bodytherapy and movement techniques. The progress recorded benefits both the practitioner and the client, and ultimately, our profession as well.

Subjective Information

There are many aspects of documentation that demonstrate the ability to show change. First let us explore the subjective realm. Subjective information is usually recorded in the client's own words or in the client's own handwriting. For the purpose of this article, we will concentrate on information that expresses current experience. This includes the patient's presenting symptoms and their ability to function day to day. It does not include a client's past medical history.

Pain Questionnaires

There are a few methods of recording the client's ability to function in daily living. Client journals are an in depth and personal means of documenting daily aspects of the patient's life in the course of their health and how it affects their everyday function. This is ideal but not always realistic. Pain Questionnaires are a more effective method, and only take a minute or two to fill out and can address a fairly complete record of function in daily life. (see pages 163 and 164.)

Pain Questionnaires are completed weekly, daily, or at regular intervals, depending on the stage of recovery. In the acute stage, change occurs rapidly and warrants a daily account of function. In the chronic stage weekly will suffice. Pain Questionnaires comprehensively demonstrate the rise and fall of function, and over the long term, with appropriate treatment, they demonstrate steady progress. (See Figure 1.)

The answers can be rated on a one through six scale of function or can be modified to fit a mild, moderate, and severe grading scale. This information is useful to

---

NECK PAIN AND DISABILITY INDEX (Vernon-Mior)

Name: _____   Date: _____

This questionnaire has been designed to give the health care provider information as to how your neck pain has affected your ability to manage everyday life. Please answer every section and mark in each section only the **ONE** box which applies to you. We realize you may consider that two of the statements in any one section relate to you, but please just mark the box which most closely describes your problem today.

SECTION 1- PAIN INTENSITY
- ☐ I have no pain at the moment.
- ☐ The pain is very mild at the moment.
- ☒ The pain is moderate at the moment.
- ☐ The pain is fairly severe at the moment.
- ☐ The pain is very severe at the moment.
- ☐ The pain is the worst imaginable at the moment.

SECTION 2- PERSONAL CARE (washing, dressing etc.)
- ☐ I can look after myself normally without causing pain.
- ☒ I can look after myself normally but it causes extra pain.
- ☐ It is painful to look after myself and I am slow and careful

SECTION 6- CONCENTRATION
- ☐ I can concentrate fully when I want to with no difficulty.
- ☒ I can concentrate fully when I want to with slight difficulty.
- ☐ I have a fair degree of difficulty in concentrating when I want to.
- ☐ I have a great deal of difficulty in concentrating when I want to.
- ☐ I cannot concentrate at all.

SECTION 7- WORK
- ☐ I can do as much work as I want to.
- ☐ I can do my usual work but no more.
- ☒ I can do most of my usual work but no more.
- ☐ I cannot do my usual work

Figure 1

Note: May rate answers on a scale of one to six, numbering from top to bottom, increasing in severity; or may cluster in two's rating the first two mild, second two moderate, third two severe.

gather prior to a treatment session, and then again immediately following the session to demonstrate the client's response to treatment. By *rating* function as opposed to recording function, one can note progress on more subtle levels. Rarely do we see dysfunction being present before a session and then absent after a session. Most often it progresses, for example, from a moderate dysfunction to a mild dysfunction.

The use of Pain Questionnaires is an efficient use of time, as it does not take away from the treatment time. It provides information useful for the initial and follow-up interview. Your line of questions can be taken directly from the dysfunctions identified, and a treatment plan can be easily designed. It is also a widely accepted method of recording information. Insurance companies in particular are interested in subjective information and in function. Often the information is used to determine the status of a claim.

Personal Status Reports

The second way to utilize documentation in the client's own words is the use of personal (subjective) status reports. This provides an opportunity before each session for the patient to record their presenting symptoms by drawing on figures. Symbols are drawn on the figures and notations of the level of severity attached which clearly demonstrate the client's condition at the moment. At the end of the session, the task may be repeated to document change as a result of the session. (See Figure 2.)

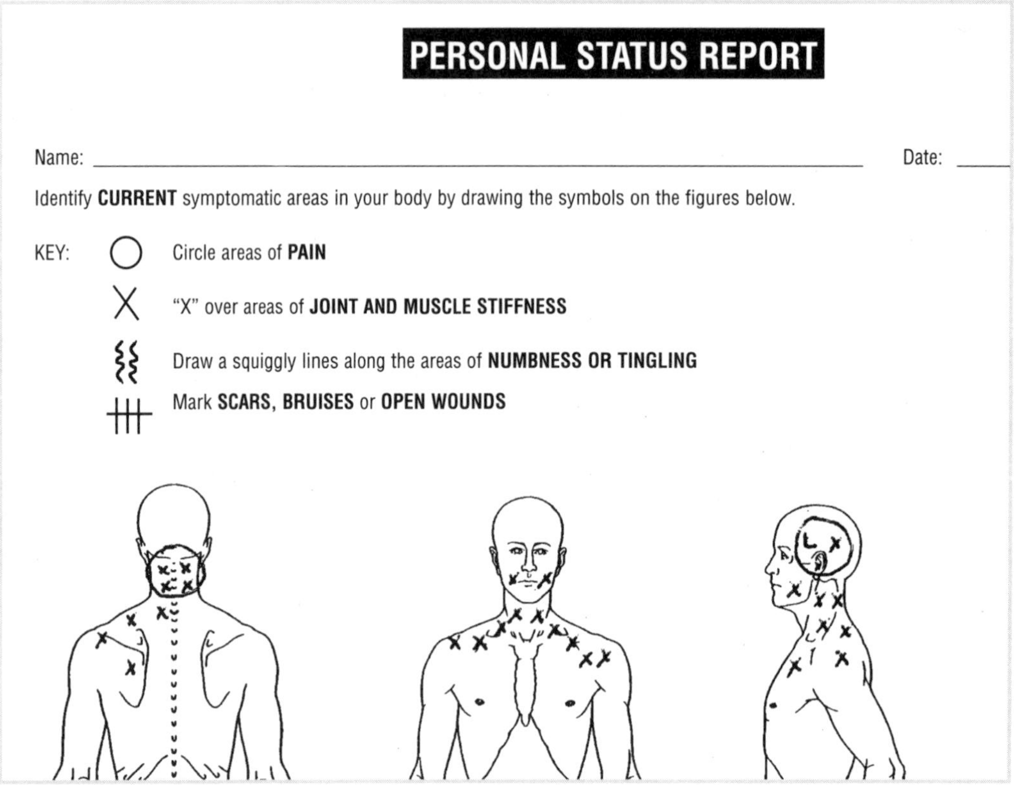
PERSONAL STATUS REPORT

Name: ______ Date: ______

Identify **CURRENT** symptomatic areas in your body by drawing the symbols on the figures below.

KEY: ○ Circle areas of **PAIN**

X "X" over areas of **JOINT AND MUSCLE STIFFNESS**

Draw a squiggly lines along the areas of **NUMBNESS OR TINGLING**

Mark **SCARS, BRUISES** or **OPEN WOUNDS**

Figure 2

Note: Areas of pain and tension are identified by the patient

Personal Status Reports provide another resource for pre-session interview questions. This streamlines the interview process and allows for more treatment time. For clients who are maintaining health or only occasionally seeking therapy, this made be done less frequently, monthly or semiannually.

Having documentation in the client's own handwriting can support the client in maintaining some perspective of their healing process. Too often when we are experiencing our body daily, we lose sight of the big picture. We too easily forget where we came from, and what it took to get us where we are today.

A peer relayed this interesting story. A client came to her and asked for a referral for another practitioner utilizing a different modality because massage therapy wasn't working for her. The practitioner pulled out the client's file and displayed the personal status reports that the client had filled out before each session. When seeing in her own handwriting her progress over ten sessions she was astounded. It was really quite dramatic! The client realized that she had been therapist "surfing" for years and the results of her sessions had never really been apparent. The client and practitioner continue to have a productive relationship, set regular goals, and have regular evaluations of their progress together.

SOAP Charting

We have examined two ways for clients to provide proof of the curative nature of bodytherapy and movement therapies. One addresses the client's ability to function in daily living. The other documents symptoms. The next approach further explores the documentation of symptoms and identifies a method of recording the subjective information gathered by the therapist. This is done on the SOAP (Subjective, Objective, Assessment, Plan) chart.

In order to demonstrate change, we need to qualify the data we gather. To simply note that the client presents with a headache will only give us the ability to note when the headache is no longer present. Without qualification it would be difficult to differentiate the client's status from session to session. Listed below are several identifying factors for further defining symptoms, such as, location, intensity, duration, frequency and description of onset that provide sufficient information for noting progress.

Location of a symptom can aid in clear documentation and efficient treatment of the symptom. The location of the dysfunction may shift as treatment progresses, making the compensational relationships easy to identify. The client isn't led to believe that their condition is worsening as headache pain turns into neck pain, turns into shoulder pain, etc. Instead, we have documented adequate information to track the progress of a condition and show causal relationships. The client experiences the shifts in his/her body and can look back at the charts to see change instead of dwelling on the fact that he/she still experiences discomfort.

Intensity of a symptom can be qualified on a simple three-point scale using mild, moderate or severe as the descriptive words. This allows us to identify gradations of progress without the need for an "all or nothing." This three-point scale can easily be transformed into a nine-point scale by simply adding a plus or a minus to each when slight changes are important to note.

Duration denotes how long the symptom lasts when it occurs. This may be described using seconds, minutes, hours, days, months or years. Progress can be noted when a symptom changes from a headache lasting from 2:00 in the afternoon until bedtime, to lasting only a couple of hours and is relieved after the workday ends.

Frequency describes how often the symptom occurs. Standard adjectives used to describe how often include: seldom, intermittent, frequent and constant. Or, you might use more specific descriptions like twice a week, three times a day, hourly, monthly etc.

Description of onset defines the biomechanics or events that occurred to cause the condition, and when it occurred. This description is important to note but does not contribute to documenting change, only identifying origin.

By qualifying symptoms in this manner, we enable ourselves to show progress on many levels. The presence or absence of a headache is very basic and helpful, but not very realistic if we want to demonstrate progress on a daily basis. Most people do not leap from dysfunction to health in a single session. It becomes imperative to utilize descriptions that demonstrate the subtle changes as well as the dramatic. The use of location (symptom), intensity, duration, frequency, and description of onset provide us the specific information necessary to document change.

For example: Left Parietal, Headache, Moderate, 4-5 times Weekly, 6-7 Hours, Beginning late afternoons at the office is easy to distinguish from next sessions symptoms: **Left Parietal, Headache, Mild, 2 times this week, 3-4 Hours, Beginning late afternoons at the office**. Both of these are a far cry from charting: **Headache** one session and: **Headache** the next session. (See Figure 3.)

S CLIENT GOALS / UPDATE	NAME _____
	DATE _____
LOCATION / SYMPTOMS / INTENSITY / FREQUENCY / DURATION / ONSET	CURRENT MEDS _____
(L)Pariet./ HA / m /4-5 x wk/6-7 hrs/ pm. office	

Figure 3

Example of qualifying subjective information on a SOAP chart

Objective Information

Charting objective data is also useful in noting the progress of a client. This information includes your findings regarding the client's health. Visual and palpable observations and test results are among the options for this category. This information is recorded in the objective section of the SOAP chart and reflects information gathered in each session from the perspective of the practitioner.

Objective information is noted in the moment and does not require the same set of descriptive terms to qualify the data as the subjective information required. Identifying the location and the intensity of the finding is still important; however, each type of finding may have its own set of qualifying descriptions.

For example, when analyzing movement, the end range, quality of movement, level of comfort, and involvement of surrounding structures may all need to be addressed. This, for example, is comparatively different from assessing the breath, where we might address the rhythm, rate, length, depth, and sound quality of breath.

What is key here is the specificity of our data. Without it we cannot note variations subtle or dramatic. Moderate spasm of the right sternocleidomastoid, with moderate pain upon digital pressure, resulting in a mild left cervical rotation and right lateral flexion postural adaptation provides more information with which to identify change than right neck spasm does. (See Figure 4.)

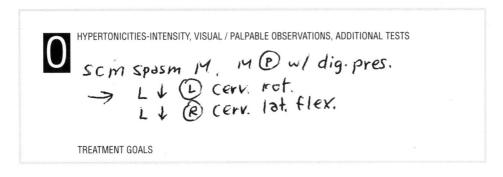

Figure 4

Example of qualifying objective information on a SOAP chart

Summary

Subjective and Objective information is one aspect of documenting the progress of a patient and demonstrating the curative nature of bodytherapy and movement therapies. The use of Pain Questionnaires, Personal Status Reports, and specific qualification of the symptoms and findings under the Subjective and Objective categories of the SOAP chart give us the additional information necessary to sufficiently show patient progress as a result of our teamwork together.

Gathering the data improves patient/practitioner communication. Interviews are more direct and to the point. Key areas to address are easily identified which supports the creation of a more effective and efficient treatment plan.

Discussion with the patient about their changes should happen on a regular basis. This encourages setting short term and long term goals. Patients can stay abreast of their progress, maintain a clear perspective and a healthy attitude regarding their healing process.

Complete documentation on all of our clients provides valuable information not only for ourselves and our patients, but also for referring primary care providers. By educating the health care providers, we increase our referral base, expand recognition of our profession, and create easier access to our services for patients.

The creation of case study documentation is crucial to the promotion of our profession as a viable treatment choice in the health care field. And finally, it is another resource to attain validation and receive vital feedback about the treatment team's abilities. Documentation not only validates the client's ability to heal, but the practitioner's ability to facilitate the healing process.

Diana L. Thompson LMP is the author of **Hands Heal: Documentation for Massage Therapy. A Guide to SOAP Charting**, and the **Instructor's Manual: A Curriculum for Teaching Documentation of Massage Therapy and Bodywork**. Her books and documentation forms are available for purchase. Call 1-800-989-4743 ext. 7, or write to: Diana at Healing Arts Studio, 916 NE 64th, Seattle WA 98115 for a brochure.

LOW BACK PAIN AND DISABILITY QUESTIONNAIRE (revised Oswestry)

Name: _____   Date: _____

This questionnaire has been designed to give the health care provider information as to how your back pain has affected your ability to manage everyday life. Please answer every section and mark in each section only the **ONE** box which applies to you. We realize you may consider that two of the statements in any one section relate to you, but please just mark the box which most closely describes your problem today.

SECTION 1- PAIN INTENSITY
- ☐ The pain comes and goes and is very mild.
- ☐ The pain is mild and does not vary much.
- ☐ The pain comes and goes and is moderate.
- ☐ The pain is moderate and does not vary much.
- ☐ The pain comes and goes and is very severe.
- ☐ The pain is severe and does not vary much.

SECTION 2- PERSONAL CARE
- ☐ I would not have to change my way of washing or dressing in order to avoid pain.
- ☐ I do not normally change my way of washing and dressing even though it causes some pain.
- ☐ Washing and dressing increase the pain but I manage not to change my way of doing it.
- ☐ Washing and dressing increase the pain and I find it necessary to change my way of doing it.
- ☐ Because of the pain I am unable to do some washing and dressing.
- ☐ Because of the pain I am unable to do any washing and dressing without help.

SECTION 3- LIFTING
- ☐ I can lift heavy weights without extra pain.
- ☐ I can lift heavy weights but it causes extra pain.
- ☐ Pain prevents me from lifting heavy weights off the floor.
- ☐ Pain prevents me from lifting heavy weights off the floor, but I manage if they are conveniently positioned (e.g. on a table).
- ☐ Pain prevents me from lifting heavy weights but I can manage light to medium weights if they are conveniently positioned.
- ☐ I can only lift very light weights at the most.

SECTION 4- WALKING
- ☐ I have no pain on walking.
- ☐ I have some pain on walking but it does not increase with distance.
- ☐ I cannot walk more than one mile without increasing pain.
- ☐ I cannot walk more than 1/2 mile without increasing pain.
- ☐ I cannot walk more than 1/4 mile without increasing pain.
- ☐ I cannot walk at all without increasing pain.

SECTION 5- SITTING
- ☐ I can sit in any chair as long as I like.
- ☐ I can only sit in my favorite chair as long as I like.
- ☐ Pain prevents me from sitting more than one hour.
- ☐ Pain prevents me from sitting more than 1/2 hour.
- ☐ Pain prevents me from sitting more than 10 minutes.
- ☐ I avoid sitting because it increases my pain immediately.

SECTION 6- STANDING
- ☐ I can stand as long as I want without pain.
- ☐ I have some pain on standing but it does not increase with time.
- ☐ I cannot stand for longer than one hour without increasing pain.
- ☐ I cannot stand for longer than 1/2 hour without increasing pain.
- ☐ I cannot stand for longer than 10 minutes without increasing pain.
- ☐ I avoid standing because it increases the pain immediately.

SECTION 7- SLEEPING
- ☐ I get no pain in bed.
- ☐ I get pain in bed but it does not prevent me from sleeping well.
- ☐ Because of pain my normal night's sleep is reduced by less than 1/4.
- ☐ Because of pain my normal night's sleep is reduced by less than 1/2.
- ☐ Because of pain my normal night's sleep is reduced by less than 3/4.
- ☐ Pain prevents me from sleeping at all.

SECTION 8- SOCIAL LIFE
- ☐ My social life is normal and gives me no pain.
- ☐ My social life is normal but increases the degree of pain.
- ☐ Pain has no significant effect on my social life apart from limiting my more energetic interests, e.g. dancing, etc.
- ☐ Pain has restricted my social life and I do not go out very often.
- ☐ Pain has restricted my social life to my home.
- ☐ I have hardly any social life because of the pain.

SECTION 9- TRAVELING
- ☐ I get no pain while traveling.
- ☐ I get some pain while traveling but none of my usual forms of travel make it any worse.
- ☐ I get extra pain while traveling but it does not compel me to seek alternate forms of travel.
- ☐ I get extra pain while traveling which compels me to seek alternative forms of travel.
- ☐ Pain restricts all forms of travel.
- ☐ Pain prevents all forms of travel except that done lying down.

SECTION 10- CHANGING DEGREE OF PAIN
- ☐ My pain is rapidly getting better.
- ☐ My pain fluctuates but overall is definitely getting better.
- ☐ My pain seems to be getting better but improvement is slow at present.
- ☐ My pain is neither getting better or worse.
- ☐ My pain is gradually worsening.
- ☐ My pain is rapidly worsening.

NECK PAIN AND DISABILITY INDEX (Vernon-Mior)

Name: _____ Date: _____

This questionnaire has been designed to give the health care provider information as to how your neck pain has affected your ability to manage everyday life. Please answer every section and mark in each section only the **ONE** box which applies to you. We realize you may consider that two of the statements in any one section relate to you, but please just mark the box which most closely describes your problem today.

SECTION 1- PAIN INTENSITY
- ☐ I have no pain at the moment.
- ☐ The pain is very mild at the moment.
- ☐ The pain is moderate at the moment.
- ☐ The pain is fairly severe at the moment.
- ☐ The pain is very severe at the moment.
- ☐ The pain is the worst imaginable at the moment.

SECTION 2- PERSONAL CARE (washing, dressing etc.)
- ☐ I can look after myself normally without causing pain.
- ☐ I can look after myself normally but it causes extra pain.
- ☐ It is painful to look after myself and I am slow and careful.
- ☐ I need some help but manage most of my personal care.
- ☐ I need help every day in most aspects of self care.
- ☐ I do not get dressed, I wash with difficulty and I stay in bed.

SECTION 3- LIFTING
- ☐ I can lift heavy weights without extra pain.
- ☐ I can lift heavy weights but it gives extra pain.
- ☐ Pain prevents me from lifting heavy weights off the floor, but I can manage if they are conveniently positioned, for example on a table.
- ☐ Pain prevents me from lifting heavy weights, but I can manage light to medium weights if they are conveniently positioned.
- ☐ I can lift very light weights.
- ☐ I cannot lift or carry anything at all.

SECTION 4- READING
- ☐ I can read as much as I want to with no pain in my neck.
- ☐ I can read as much as I want to with slight pain in my neck.
- ☐ I can read as much as I want to with moderate pain in my neck.
- ☐ I can't read as much as I want because of moderate pain in my neck.
- ☐ I can hardly read at all because of severe pain in my neck.
- ☐ I cannot read at all.

SECTION 5- HEADACHES
- ☐ I have no headaches at all.
- ☐ I have slight headaches which come infrequently.
- ☐ I have moderate headaches which come infrequently.
- ☐ I have moderate headaches which come frequently.
- ☐ I have severe headaches which come frequently.
- ☐ I have headaches almost all of the time.

SECTION 6- CONCENTRATION
- ☐ I can concentrate fully when I want to with no difficulty.
- ☐ I can concentrate fully when I want to with slight difficulty.
- ☐ I have a fair degree of difficulty in concentrating when I want to.
- ☐ I have a great deal of difficulty in concentrating when I want to.
- ☐ I cannot concentrate at all.

SECTION 7- WORK
- ☐ I can do as much work as I want to.
- ☐ I can do my usual work but no more.
- ☐ I can do most of my usual work but no more.
- ☐ I cannot do my usual work.
- ☐ I can hardly do any work at all.
- ☐ I can't do any work at all.

SECTION 8- DRIVING
- ☐ I can drive my car without any neck pain.
- ☐ I can drive my car as long as I want with slight pain in my neck.
- ☐ I can drive my car as long as I want with moderate pain in my neck.
- ☐ I can't drive my car as long as I want because of moderate pain in my neck.
- ☐ I can hardly drive at all because of severe pain in my neck.
- ☐ I can't drive my car at all.

SECTION 9- SLEEPING
- ☐ I have no trouble sleeping.
- ☐ My sleep is slightly disturbed (less than one hour sleepless).
- ☐ My sleep is mildly disturbed (1-2 hrs. sleepless).
- ☐ My sleep is moderately disturbed (2-3 hrs. sleepless).
- ☐ My sleep is greatly disturbed (3-5 hrs. sleepless).
- ☐ My sleep is completely disturbed (5-7 hrs. sleepless).

SECTION 10- RECREATION.
- ☐ I am able to engage in all my recreation activities with no neck pain at all.
- ☐ I am able to engage in all my recreation activities, with some pain in my neck.
- ☐ I am able to engage in most, but not all of my usual recreation activities because of pain in my neck.
- ☐ I am able to engage in a few of my usual recreation activities because of pain in my neck.
- ☐ I hardly do any recreation activities because of pain in my neck.
- ☐ I can't do recreation activities at all.

Research Information Documenting the Benefits of Massage Therapy

Chapter 14

Quick Summary of Key Points

- Value of documented research to establish credibility with insurance companies and providers

- A summary of the major research studies and where to find them

Research Information Documenting the Benefits of Massage Therapy

As we emphasized in Chapters 6-10 on establishing reimbursement as a financial pillar of your practice, you must show to insurance companies and medical providers that the value of your services is supported by documented research. This chapter gives you an overview and samples of the latest research supporting the safety and clinical effectiveness of massage and bodytherapy. You will need this information to gain credibility as a healthcare provider who deserves access to insurance reimbursement.

Before the advent of pharmaceutical medicine early in this century, references to massage therapy and research were common in mainstream literature. Such journals as the *Journal of the American Medical Association, British Medical Journal* and others carried more than 600 articles on the uses of massage from 1813-1939. Research was also conducted widely in Eastern Bloc countries and China. In the U.S. after World War I, however, focus in this field greatly declined as drugs and other alopathic interventions became dominant in medical practice.

As interest in natural forms of treatment grows in our day, research activity in massage and bodytherapy has gained momentum. Studies have documented benefits in cases of amputation, arthritis, cerebral palsy, cerebral vascular accident, fibrositis syndrome, menstrual cramps, paraplegia/quadriplegia, scoliosis, acute and chronic pain, acute and chronic inflammation, chronic lymphedema, nausea, muscle spasm, soft tissue dysfunctions, grand mal epileptic seizures, anxiety, depression, insomnia and psychoemotional stress.

The following studies are excerpted from the book, **The American Holistic Health Association Complete Guide to Alternative Medicine** by William Collinge, MPH, Phd., by Warner Books, Inc., 1996, and references to the source of each study can be found in Chapter 9:

Massage in the Elderly: A controlled study showed massage therapy produced relaxation in 18 elderly subjects. This study demonstrated physiological signs of relaxation via decreased blood pressure and heart rate and increased skin temperature.

Spinal Pain: A study of the combination of various types of massage in 52 patients with traumatically induced spinal pain led to significant reduction in acute and chronic pain and increased muscle flexibility and tone. This study also found massage to be extremely cost-effective compared to other pain therapies, with cost savings of 15 to 50 percent.

Pain Control: Massage has been shown to stimulate the body's ability to control pain naturally. One study showed that massage stimulates the brain to produce endorphins, chemicals that control pain.

Lymphedema: Lymph drainage massage has been found to be more effective than mechanized methods or diuretic drugs to control lymphedema (a form of swelling) caused by radical mastectomy. Using massage to control lymphedema is expected to significantly lower treatment costs, based on a study comparing massage with the use of sleeve-like pressure cuffs often worn by women with lymphedema.

Inflammatory Bowel Disease: A study found that massage therapy can have a powerful effect on psychoemotional distress in patients with chronic inflammatory bowel diseases such as ulcerative colitis and Crohn's disease. Stress can worsen the symptoms of these conditions, which can lead to great pain, bleeding and hospitalization or death. Massage therapy was effective in reducing the frequency of episodes of pain and disability in these patients.

Therapeutic Touch and Wound Healing: A controlled trial examined the effects of therapeutic touch on healing identical surgically-inflicted minor wounds in the shoulders of 44 male college students. Twenty-three received therapeutic touch treatments and 21 did not. Neither group was aware of the purpose of the experiment, and those treated were not aware they were being treated. After 8 days, the treated group's wounds had shrunk an average of 93.5 percent compared to 67.3 percent for those untreated. After 16 days the figures were 99.3 percent and 90.3 percent.

Reflexology and PMS: A controlled clinical study of 38 women with premenstrual syndrome examined the effects of a 30-minute reflexology treatment weekly for 8 weeks. Those receiving the treatment were treated by ear, hand and foot reflexology. Those in the control group were given placebo or sham reflexology. Based on a daily diary that monitored the severity of 39 premenstrual symptoms, the treated group had a 46% reduction compared to a 19% reduction for the control group.

Unlike often-used hormone-altering and anti-depressant medications, the treatment produced no side effects. The researchers concluded that reflexology might work by softening adrenocortical reactivity to stress, which is known to exacerbate symptoms of PMS.

Touch Research Institute

The most comprehensive program of massage-related research is the University of Miami's Touch Research Institute. Created in 1991 by the School of Medicine, it is the world's first center for basic and applied research in using touch and human development. Its primary aim is to advance knowledge of the biology of touch in health and development and its role in medicine and the treatment of disease. Directed by Tiffany Field, Ph.D., a professor of psychology, pediatrics and psychiatry, the TRI has a multi-disciplinary staff of 40 scientists from the fields of medicine, biology and psychology and another 30 visiting scientists from other universities participating in collaborative studies.

Dr. Fields' credentials include 20 years of research experience, over 200 published credits and membership in over a dozen professional associations.

Many studies have demonstrated impressive benefits for integrating massage therapy into medical care. For example, one study of premature infants treated with daily massage therapy found a gain of 47% more weight per day and shorter hospital stays (by 6 days) than those not massaged. Approximately $3,000 per infant were saved through therapeutic massage.

A second study at the Touch Research Institute reported that massage therapy helps increase immune function in HIV-infected patients. (The results were published in the February, 1996 issue of *The International Journal of Neuroscience.*) As part of the study, 29 men received daily massages. After 4 weeks of massage (45 minutes a day, 5 days a week), researchers found a stronger immune system response as measured by several variables. These measures included natural killer cell number, natural killer cell cytotoxicity and the cytotoxic subset of CD8 cells. They also reported that after being massaged, the subjects felt less anxious and had lower stress hormones (cortisol levels). "These immune measures may be especially important in protecting health in HIV-positive people, since HIV destroys CD4 cells," said Gail Ironson, MD., Ph.D., principal investigator of the study.

A third study looked at massage therapy with 52 hospitalized depressed and adjustment-disordered children and adolescents. After 12 weeks, those receiving massage therapy were less depressed and anxious and had lower saliva cortisol levels, which is an indicator of less depression, compared to a separate control group who only viewed relaxation videotapes.

Current research projects at the institute include:

Children: Newborns of Cocaine Addicted Mothers, Infants of Depressed Mothers, Infant Colic, Infant Sleep Disorders, Infants with Cancer, Burns, Cystic Fibrosis, Dermatitis/Psoriasis, Attention Deficit Disorder, Pediatric Skin Disorders, Asthma, Rheumatoid Arthritis, Diabetes and Pediatric Oncology.

Adolescents: Anorexia, Depression and Sports Massage

Adults: Breast Cancer, Post Burns, Labor and Childbirth, Migraine, Hypertension, Eating Disorders, Spinal Cord Injuries, Headaches, Pregnancy, Rape, Spouse Abuse, Smoking Cessation, Job Performance/Stress, Fibromyalgia Syndrome, Chronic Fatigue Syndrome

The Touch Therapy Research Institute is also setting up workshops for bodytherapists to visit the TRI and do research for 3 days each month. To receive the Touch Research Institute Newsletter and get copies of Research Outcome Results, write to:

Touchpoints **(Send $10 for a one-year subscription to the newsletter)**
Touch Research Institute
Department of Pediatrics (D-820)
University Of Miami School of Medicine
P. O. Box 016820-MM
Miami, FL 33101
or call the Touch Research Institute at (305)-243-6781

Important Research Resources and References

Adriane Fugh-Berman's 1996 book, **Alternative Medicine: What Works — A Comprehensive, Easy-to-Read Review of the Scientific Evidence, Pro and Con**, is an excellent reference guide for examples you can cite for providers or insurance companies. The following studies are summarized from her book and look at the effects of massage on specific conditions.

Anxiety: In a 5-day study of child and adolescent psychiatric patients, daily 30-minute back massage reduced anxiety and depression more effectively than a relaxing videotape. Another study of cancer patients found that therapeutic massage reduced anxiety by an average of 24% (and pain perception by an average of 60%). Back massage also reduced anxiety in elderly institutionalized subjects.

Circulation: According to several studies, slow, stroking massage has various positive effects on heart rate and blood pressure. Massage of the lymphatic system increases urine output and changes the levels of neurohormones excreted in the urine, a marker for decreased stress.

Massage also appears to thin the blood. Regular massage of the legs may improve the circulation enough to prevent blood clots from developing. (Massage would have to occur several times a day.) Future research will investigate this possibility further.

Edema: In one study of 60 post-mastectomy subjects with arm edema (swelling) due to blocked lymphatic vessels, massaging the lymphatic system (the area around the lymph nodes under the arm) 3 times a week for 4 weeks resulted in a significant reduction in edema. This effect lasted at least 3 months.

Frozen Shoulder: In a study of 235 subjects with frozen shoulder (limited mobility of the shoulder joint), 205 (87%) who were treated with gradual stretching and massage showed improvement, and 71% recovered completely. Of the other 30, who had their joints forcefully manipulated while under anesthesia, only 33% improved and only 10% recovered completely.

Pain: In one study, 21 of 26 patients with muscle pain (80%) gained some relief through massage. In 13 subjects with soft-tissue injuries, a few minutes of friction massage relieved pain for periods ranging from 18 seconds to 48 hours (the mean time was 26 hours). An uncontrolled study of 14 patients with inflammatory bowel disease found that massage, combined with deep-breathing exercises, increased the ability to sleep and sense of control over the pain.

In a pair of studies, ice applied to massage acupuncture points on the hand or arm reduced dental pain by half. In another study, ice massage relieved lower back pain as effectively as an electrical stimulation device.

Premature Infants: Several studies suggest that massage may facilitate the growth and development of premature infants. While most healthy infants receive more than adequate touch from parents and family members, preemies in plastic incubators may receive only minimal handling as part of intubation, injections and routine cleaning.

One study compared 6 pre-term babies who were stroked and had their arms and legs flexed for an hour a day with 6 infants who received only normal nursery care. The stroked babies ate more, gained weight faster and weighed more at the end of the study than those who received normal care.

In the best study of prematurity, 20 infants who were stroked for 10 minutes 3 times per day for 10 days gained an average of 47% more weight per day, were more active and alert, showed more mature behaviors and left the hospital an average of 6 days sooner than 20 other premature babies.

In another 10-day study of 30 cocaine-exposed premature newborns, those receiving three 15-minute massages per day gained an average of 28% more weight daily than the untreated babies—without eating more food. The massaged group also had fewer medical complications and showed more mature motor skills.

Respiratory Function: Massaging patients who have chronic bronchitis—especially tapping their back and chest—helps remove mucus, thus improving breathing. Called "chest physical therapy," this type of massage is also often used for hospitalized pneumonia patients.

Another important resource for research information on massage therapy and other forms of complementary health care is the Office of Alternative Medicine (OAM) at the National Institutes of Health. The office is located on the National Institutes of Health's campus in Bethesda, Maryland.

In March 1996, this office approved an $850,000 funding program for eight specialty research centers nationwide. Each has been assigned to study alternative/complementary medical practices in one of eight health fields, including AIDS/HIV, cancer, chronic pain, immunological conditions, neurological disorders and addictions, and women's health issues. Research results will be published in scientific publications.

To receive OAM's Newsletter, as well as results on studies, contact the Office of Alternative Medicine:

National Institutes of Health
9000 Rockville Pike
Building 31, Room 5B-38, Mail Stop 2182
Bethesda, MD 20892
(301) 402-2466

Important Research Resources

One of the most thorough compilations or bibiliographies of clinical research in bodytherapy from 1705 though today is available from the Bodywork Research Institute, 123 E 8th Street, Suite 121, Frederick, MD 21701. You may contact the institute by phone at 301-698-0932 or via the internet at www.fibronet.com. The studies total 300 clinical trials using massage or touch therapy to address conditions from nausea to inflamed bowels to migraines to vein embolisms to pulmonary embolism, etc. The compilation of the research printed in its entirety is over 1000 pages and there is a bibliography, without abstracts, that you can order as well as copies of specific articles.

Most of the research is from Great Britain and the United States. Other top contributors include countries once colonized by England, such as Canada, Australia and New Zealand.

Richard Van Why of the Bodywork Research Institute began this collection in 1988, and keeps it up to date by searching MEDLINE, MEDICA, BIOSIS, SPORTDISCUS and other national and international published materials indexes monthly and yearly.

The collection of research on massage and touch therapies is just a portion of the Bodywork Knowledgebase, which is the Bodywork Research Institute's complete up-to-date library on medical massage. This library consists of over 5000 articles and 500 monographs (books, pamphlets, etc.) dated from 1705 through the present. Complete and partial copies of this library are available at various massage therapy schools throughout the country. Edited versions of 43 volumes on the most pertinent knowledge chosen by the collector are available. Each volume addresses a different topic in medical massage.

Another research resource is Medline, the well-known medical literature search and it is now available to you personally through the internet for $150 per year. Contact MEDLINE. Get their e-mail address from a local university library.

Many important sources of information on research studies on massage are in the book, **A Physician's Guide to Therapeutic Massage**, published by the The Massage Therapists Association of D.C. (See Suggested Readings and Reference Materials.)

I also recommend subscribing to the following journals:

Alternative Therapies in Health and Medicine, published by InnoVision Communications, a division of the American Association of Critical-Care Nurses (AACN), 101 Columbia, Aliso Viejo, California 92656.
Telephone: (800) 899-1712

Alternative and Complementary Therapies, published by Mary Ann Liebert, Inc., 2 Madison Avenue, Larchmont, NY 10538
Telephone: (800) -M-LIEBERT

Journal of Soft-Tissue Manipulation
Focuses on research issues and developments in massage therapy, contraindications and precautions in treatment, technique papers and philosophical inquiries.
Published by Ontario Massage Therapy Association, 324 Oakdale Avenue, Ottawa, Canada K1Y 0E4, Telephone: (613)722-8588

Soft-Tissue Review (previously the *BodyMind Journal*)
This journal's focus is the review of current medical literature addressing soft-tissue.
Write to: 722 36th Avenue, NE, Olympia, Washington 98506
Telephone: 360-956-7238

The *Hospital-Based Massage Network Newsletter*, includes excellent resources and research references. Contact: Laura Koch, CMT, Hospital-Based Massage Network, c/o Rocky Mountain Therapeutics, 5 Old Town Square, Suite 205, Fort Collins, Colorado, 80524; Telephone Number: 970-407-9232

Managed Care and Massage/Bodytherapy: A Model of Integrating Complementary Therapies and Managed Care

Quick Summary of Key Points

- Growing acceptance of "alternative therapies"

- What is the difference between an HMO and a PPO?

- Examples of managed care companies adding massage/bodytherapy as covered services

- How to take advantage of the managed care opportunity

Managed Care and Massage/Bodytherapy: A Model of Integrating Complementary Therapies and Managed Care

An exciting new trend in healthcare in general, and insurance in particular, is the growing acceptance of so-called "alternative therapies." As massage and bodytherapy prove their effectiveness and cost-saving value, insurers under managed care are more open to including your profession in their preferred provider groups (PPOs) and health maintenance organizations (HMOs).

Why should you care about being on a list of providers? Depending on the state where you practice, it can increase by 10 or 20 times the number of people who can see you with insurance coverage, IF you are willing to accept a 20 percent discount below your regular fees. Also, your burden of paperwork and recordkeeping is greatly reduced.

What are HMOs and PPOs?

A health maintenance organization (HMO) is a prepaid group practice sponsored and operated by an insurance company, clinic or hospital/medical plan. "Prepaid" means the healthcare provider agrees to treat all the covered illnesses of everyone in the group for a year at a fixed total price.

Like any business, if the provider spends less than it takes in, it shows a surplus or profit. If it spends more to deliver its services (expenses) than it takes in (revenues), it runs a deficit or a loss. Insurance companies have supported creating HMOs because this form of organization forces the providers to maintain their profits or minimize their losses by holding down their expenses. Providers reduce their expenses by delivering fewer services and/or less expensive services.

A preferred provider organization (PPO) contracts with a group of "preferred" providers to deliver care to members. Unlike HMO members, PPO members are free to choose any physician or hospital for services, but they receive more benefits (or pay less of the cost themselves "out of pocket") if they choose a preferred provider. A PPO plan usually requires filing claims and paying deductibles and co-payments. HMOs largely eliminate this paperwork.

The Good News for Massage and Bodytherapy Professionals

As of September 1996, several managed care companies have added massage and bodytherapy as covered services. Many more are considering adding them to their pool of providers.

For example, Steve Gorman of Alternative Health Insurance Services, Inc. (AHIS) of Thousand Oaks, CA., (800-966-8467), says his company is developing a network of holistic, complementary/alternative healthcare providers, including massage/bodytherapists, on behalf of a number of insurance companies. Similar to a conventional PPO, the network (AHIS) contracts with providers who offer reduced fees to network subscribers (clients who buy their insurance plan) in return for exposure to many new patients. Because the requirements for providers are still being formed and will vary from company to company, you should call them directly to get the latest information as it applies to your specific situation.

Another example, (with more details available), is Harvard Vanguard Medical Associates, a multispecialty physician group comprising the 14 health centers of Harvard Pilgrim Health Care. They have launched a program in complimentary therapies that will include massage therapy, chiropractic and acupuncture. The group is allowing insureds to access specialists directly, without referrals, For additional information, contact Harvard Pilgrim Health Care at (800) 742-8326.

Insurers in the Denver, Minnesota and Pacific Northwest are adding coverage for alternative therapies to their health plans.

Denver's largest managed care organization, Sloans Lake Managed Care, has begun offering an alternative medicine rider to its PPO and HMO plans that will cover such therapies as acupuncture, herbal medicine, massage therapy and bodytherapies, homeopathy, naturopathy, traditional Chines medicine and Ayurvedic medicine. For additional information and to join the provider panels contact Sloans Lake at (303)691-2200.

In the Pacific Northwest two plans have expanded their provider network, to include more Alternative Medicine providers and the companies, based in Portland, Oregon may be reached at (503) 203-8333.

Axis Health Care, also based in Portland, Oregon, has added naturopaths, acupuncturists and massage therapists to its panel of providers and you may contact them at (503)295-2983.

Minnesota's Health Partners has instituted a pilot program to expand its alternative therapies coverage to additional clinics within its network. Therapies now covered include chiropractic, acupuncture, massage therapies and nutritional counseling, including herbal therapies. For more information, contact them at (800)883-2177.

Alternare of Washington State also offers coverage in many complimentary therapies including massage and bodytherapies. To become a provider, you may contact them at (800)500-0997.

In California several managed care companies have recently added massage/bodytherapies to their list of covered benefits and are currently recruiting massage/bodytherapists to join their provider pool.

These include **Blue Shield of California Consensus Health Plan** (you may contact them at 609 Mission Street, 3rd Floor, San Francisco, California 94105 - (650) 777-0334, **AlternaNet, LLC** at 343 Soquel Avenue, Suite 61, Santa Cruz, California 95062 (1-888- ALT-7576), **HHC Health** (1-888-314-4632) and **Common Well, Inc.**, at 4153-B El Camino Way, Palo Alto, California 94306.

Another new HMO worth investigating is Oxford Health Plans Inc., a highly profitable HMO in the Northeast. Oxford has a strong marketing reputation and has the most extensive program to date, covering massage/bodytherapy for wellness care and prevention as well as illness care for a diagnosed disease or injury.

As of Autumn 1996, Oxford Health Plan is signing provider contracts with massage therapists in New Jersey, New York and Connecticut, with more states to be added in the years 1998–2000.

As with other HMOs, Oxford prefers therapists who are licensed by their state or nationally certified (another reason to take the National Certification Exam), have at least 2 years experience, and are graduates of schools with the highest educational standards in the field. Also, they require continuing education hours each year. Ask for specific educational and experience requirements when you contact them. For more information on becoming a provider, write to:

Kerry MacKenzie
Oxford Health Plans, Inc.
800 Connecticut Ave.
Norwalk, CT 06854

Think of how much fuller your appointment schedule will become as larger numbers of clients can receive reimbursement for your services. Becoming a preferred provider and/or joining an HMO is a practice-building opportunity you should pursue with all your energy, IF you are willing to accept lower hourly fees in exchange for many more clients becoming available to you.

The driving motive behind insurance companies accepting alternative practitioners is—what else?—money. A study of one 15-month period (January 1995 through March 1996) looked at the percentage of premiums collected by the Alliance for Alternatives in Health care it paid out to members. For every dollar collected in premiums, it paid out only 59 cents in claims. The remaining 41 cents it kept to pay expenses and return profits to its owners. This "59% claims ratio" is better than average for the insurance industry and tends to encourage other companies to follow along.

Remember, insurance companies make their profits by paying out less in claims than they collect in premiums. Not only do they profit when they pay less; they also profit when they delay payment even for a month. Why? The answer lies in a concept called "the time value of money." To banks, large companies, governments or anyone else with large amounts of money, a dollar today is worth more than a dollar in the future. As individuals, we usually do not notice this because the amounts involved are small. The company owes you $225. What difference does it make if you wait one month or two?

But imagine the insurance company owing $225. to 1,000 practitioners spread out over your state. That $225,000 it holds for a month can be "put to work" earning interest or helping to pay for some other profit-making aspect of its business, especially since the insurance company does not owe you interest on unpaid or delayed claims, even when it causes the delay.

On the other hand, and for your long-term benefit, companies have a strong incentive to pay for therapies that reduce their higher-cost claims. For back pain, for example, an effective therapeutic massage and exercise program may cost 1/50 the price of prescription drugs and back surgery.

Outcome studies showing the difference in cost and effectiveness between alternative therapies and traditional medical approaches make a strong case for including massage and bodytherapy for coverage. When you write to an HMO or PPO, educate them on the cost effectiveness of your profession with articles or citations documenting the results. Such letters help make the larger case for all insurance companies offering lower cost and preventative services. (See the Research Chapter for a sample letter.)

Insurance companies are also more open to covering increasingly popular "alternative therapies" (including massage and bodytherapy) because they see financial loss to themselves if they don't catch up with consumer demand. As many as one in three Americans now use some type of non-traditional treatment, according to a 1993 survey published by Harvard Medical School. And the spending on non-physician, non-prescription treatments is huge: $14 billion compared to $1 trillion on conventional healthcare. (A trillion is 1,000 billion.)

The point for our profession is that when insurance executives see consumers turning toward alternatives not covered by insurance, they see the threat of losing policyholders who opt out of their coverage and pay for these services themselves. The companies want to prevent losing the potential revenue and profits by including these services in their coverage.

"Consumers are already voting with their out-of-pocket expenditures that these services work," says Alan Kittner, a consultant who helps HMOs set up alternative providers.

Not only do favorable profit figures show that insurance companies can benefit significantly when they include alternative/complementary therapies. Studies also show that when alternative therapies are available, members use fewer healthcare services and make fewer claims. As more companies use massage and bodytherapy and realize lower overall healthcare costs, more managed care companies will want qualified therapists to join their provider pools.

How to Take Advantage of the Managed Care Opportunity

The first step is to write to your local HMO or PPO and ask for information on joining. Specific requirements may differ among companies, but in general you must maintain the highest standards of education in your field, document your clinical experience, and have national certification and state licensure where available. You can also improve your acceptability through national certification in your specialty. Further, you can help everyone in your profession by joining and supporting professional associations that lobby for state licensure and insurance acceptance.

> **PLEASE NOTE:** Insurance is a rapidly changing, highly political area. To stay on top of the latest developments affecting you and your practice, be sure to fill out the form that was shipped with this book, to register for the annual Bodytherapy Business Institute update. Also, telephone consultation is available by calling 1-800-888-1516.

A Portrait of the Current Field of Hospital-Based Massage Therapy: Growth & Growing Pains

by Laura Koch, LMT

Chapter 16

Quick Summary of Key Points

- The history of hospital-based massage therapy programs
- Current insurance coverage: challenges and successes
- How to create a hospital-based massage therapy program
- Interviews with program directors throughout the United States
- Listing of resources

A PORTRAIT OF THE CURRENT FIELD OF HOSPITAL-BASED MASSAGE THERAPY: GROWTH & GROWING PAINS

Massage therapists were interviewed to get an idea of what is happening throughout the field of hospital-based massage therapy and bodywork in the United States. Those who began this field, such as Marian Williams and Karen Gibson, started the integration of massage therapy into the hospitals, and hospital-based massage is currently in a state of growth and expansion. It is estimated that 100 to 150 hospitals currently have massage therapy programs. As the integration of the traditional medical field and complementary medicine (previously known as "alternative" medicine) is taken forth, there are, of course, growing pains. Along with the excitement of growth, these growing pains are discussed so that we may understand and learn from them.

Our Foremothers, a Couple of the Trailblazers of Hospital-Based Massage

Marian Williams

Marian Williams was the coordinator of a massage therapy program and internship at California Pacific Medical Center (CPMC) in San Francisco. Through this program thousands of patients and staff have been helped with massage therapy. Many massage therapists have been taught how to work in hospitals and currently use their training. Many in the medical community have been educated as to the benefits of massage therapy for patients and staff, and Planetree (an organization that aids hospitals in becoming more holistic and patient-centered) now recommends a touch therapy program to all of their member hospitals. Based upon Williams' work, a few graduates of the CPMC Massage Internship are presently hired as independent contractors through the hospital.

Begun as a volunteer program by Tedi Dunn in 1985, the massage program was created on a Planetree Unit at CPMC. In 1990, Williams was hired as coordinator of a hospital-wide massage therapy program and developed the first hospital massage therapy internship in the country. As a whole, the program grew and thrived for 10 years, yet was cut from the hospital in October 1995 due to down-sizing, merging, and the managed care environment which desires to cut costs. Due to the hospital's support of the program during its existence, Williams has no doubt that a program may re-emerge later.

Williams points out that a program needs to be revenue-sustaining or otherwise affordable to the hospital (such as through grants) in order to survive. Williams' advice to other hospital-based massage therapists is to not over-extend themselves in the demanding work of pioneering a new field. "Take time to regroup." This will help prevent burnout and injuries. Williams stresses that supporting research on touch therapies is of vital importance right now in order to achieve widespread acceptance of touch therapies in the medical field. The Touch Research Institute is a primary research group on touch therapies in the United States. Additionally, the National Institutes of Health Office of Alternative Medicine is funding six current massage therapy research projects. Williams suggests that hospital-based massage therapists continue to share their progress, through networking and on-going dialogue, in order to further the development of the field. She recommends such support groups as the Bay Area's Hospital Massage Consortium, which acts as forums for communication.

Williams notes that hospitals are integrating more complementary health care into hospitals as more people in administration, or their loved ones, personally experience healing from complementary medicine. "Hospitals really do want to help people," states Williams, and it just takes the administration being educated as to how complementary health care methods help people heal. As the populace increasingly uses complementary methods for their own health care, hospitals may even use complementary health care as a marketing point, which, due to current financial challenges in the health care industry, may be of use to the hospitals.

Williams further addresses the difficulty of starting any new non-revenue-generating program in a hospital right now. Growing HMO (managed care) insurance companies are challenging hospitals to work on minimal costs. This is where the costs saved through an enriched healing process utilizing touch therapy should be stressed. It should be demonstrated that patients who receive touch therapy in the hospital are aided in achieving fuller, more complete, and speedier recoveries, and that this, in turn, reduces costs from complications or other difficulties. The health benefits of touch therapy are partly viewed in the light of hospital costs and must be addressed from here. Simultaneously, the increasing intangible values placed upon wellness and prevention should lead to massage therapy becoming fully integrated into hospitals.

Currently, Marian Williams is a consultant and faculty member of the Planetree Institute, aiding hospitals in creating touch therapy programs and educating massage therapists on how to work in a health care setting. Williams will continue to offer weekend workshops on Massage in Health Care Settings, through Planetree or Alive & Well. Williams is available for private consultations and teaching, and is available to travel for such work.

Having forged the beginnings of the field of hospital-based massage therapy, educating massage therapists and the medical community to work together, Williams looks positively towards the future.

Marian Williams may be contacted with questions about consultation services at 510/527-3934.

Karen Gibson

Karen Gibson, founder and prior head of the massage therapy program and internship at Boulder Community Hospital (BCH), in Boulder, CO, is another well-known pioneer. While the volunteer massage program and internship, consisting of Boulder School of Massage students, are still running, Gibson resigned from her position at

BCH to take a year off from the "front lines." Like Williams, Gibson is regrouping from having held a massage coordination position while simultaneously spending countless hours advising others on creating hospital massage programs. Through the hard work of these two pioneers, hospital massage programs nationwide were created with the help of Gibson's and Williams' shared knowledge and experience.

Gibson is noticing an increased number of hospital authorities desiring massage in their hospitals through their own first-hand experience of massage therapy. More massage therapy schools are offering workshops on hospital massage, and "the demand for teachers is going up." Medical schools are incorporating complementary medicine education into their curriculums, and hospitals are incorporating complementary medicine to satisfy the increased use of such health care. Gibson states, "Hospitals are scrambling to incorporate the best of these [complementary] therapies because of all the positive anecdotal evidence. If we can state our arguments clearly, we've got good evidence [that massage therapy helps patients heal.]"

Gibson continues to see hospital massage programs blossoming. However, she has also seen several successful massage therapy programs be eliminated due to their failure to be revenue-sustaining during this time of hospital downsizing. Hospitals are having to cut back and reduce to basic services. To put it simply, "You don't even think of eliminating the emergency room."

Gibson stresses that the medical community now needs to see facts and figures as to what tangible results are seen from massage, such as fuller and speedier therapy. It needs to be shown through studies and research that massage therapy eases pain and aids patients to breathe easier and relax so that the healing process can take hold. Gibson suggests that studies might later be done to show whether massage therapy has a positive effect on public relations, employee retention, and customer satisfaction as well.

As hospital massage grows, credentialing standards may develop to show who is trained and qualified. Hospital massage therapists' credentials may then grow from knowing how to work safely on hospital patients to also having mastery of the application of various treatment techniques to various conditions and illnesses. Gibson notes there may be much to learn in this area from other countries that have allowed implementing massage in hospitals for countless years.

Gibson is available for consultation, and continues to offer her Hospital-Based Massage Manual, which she plans on updating to include her additional experience and knowledge. She wants to consult, teach, write, and "do the work" in the future, and is looking into hospital massage possibilities in the Glenwood Springs area with a previous student from the BCH internship. Karen Gibson may be reached by phone at 970/945-3060 or by FAX: 970/945-2546.

Current Insurance-Coverage: Challenges & Successes

Vermont

Cara Smiley, co-founder of the Hospital-Based Massage Network, is the founder of a small massage therapy program at Randolf, Vermont's Gifford Medical Center.

Gifford's massage program has been revenue-producing for two years. However, Medicare, Medicaid, and Blue Cross/Blue Shield, which had been covering massage therapy at the hospital during the last 10 years, decided six months ago to withdraw coverage. The insurance companies claim that coverage was withdrawn due to their discovery that the massage therapists are not licensed and the lack of clinical studies substantiating the efficacy of massage therapy. However, there is no licensing procedure in Vermont, and Smiley cites the fact that these same insurance companies do not cover massage in several states where massage therapists are licensed.

Although the massage therapy program was originally challenged by the withdrawal of insurance coverage, the program and the hospital that supports it are adapting well. With insurance coverage reduced by two thirds, the hospital has been putting more effort into general outreach to the public regarding their massage therapy service, including advertising the program in a community newspaper. The massage program's wellness care clientele (patients who come in once a month), have jumped up to 50% of the overall clientele.

Gifford Medical Center now offers a cash discount for patients who pay on the same day of service, a brand new billing procedure for the hospital. Unfortunately, many still cannot afford massage therapy out of their own pockets.

Through massage therapy and acupuncture, the hospital is expanding its focus to include acute care as well as wellness care and preventive medicine. With insurance coverage revoked, referrals to massage therapy from physicians have declined, and most people cannot afford massage therapy as often as the insurance companies had been covering. Thus, the massage therapy program is shifting its focus to increasingly stress home self-care in order to accommodate clients with chronic and acute needs who can only come in once or twice a month. Amidst all these changes, the program continues to be revenue-generating.

Smiley is part of a group of massage therapists investigating the desire to regulate Vermont Massage therapists. Called the Vermont Massage & Bodywork Standards Committee (VMBSC), they have distributed a questionnaire on standards, code of ethics, and regulation to all the Vermont massage therapists they could locate. If 50% or more respondents want certain regulations, the VMBSC hopes to submit a bill by August 1 in accordance with the desires of the massage therapists of Vermont.

Smiley believes that the standards of practice ensured by licensure is a step towards more nationwide insurance coverage. She is in favor of a two-tier system which would enable everyone who practices a form of bodywork to continue doing so freely, while simultaneously credentialing those who want to work with insurance companies and hospitals. Smiley still wonders about the importance of pushing for licensure and standardization. "There is not enough research out there [supporting the validity of massage therapy] and licensed massage therapists in other states are not covered." Only time will tell.

Anyone interested in obtaining results from the survey of Vermont massage therapists can contact Gifford Medical Center; Attn: Cara Smiley, Massage Therapy, P.O. Box 2000, Randolph, VT 05060. Phone: 802/728-2360. Fax: 802/728-4986.

Ohio

Although Tina Nobile, in Ohio, has difficulty with insurance cutbacks as well, she is using an excellent working model for obtaining insurance coverage for massage therapy. Nobile is currently an independent contractor for Meridia Southpointe Hospital in Warrensville Heights (a suburb of Cleveland). She works under the supervision of a physical therapist as part of a team called the Comprehensive Pain Management Program, which focuses on the management of chronic pain. The team assigned to each patient includes a physical therapist, massotherapist, occupational therapist, exercise physiologist, pharmacist, psychologist, tai chi instructor, psychiatrist, physician of patient record, clinical nurse, dietitian, and speech/hearing therapist. The work she does is prescribed by and authorized by the physical therapist, who signs the SOAP notes. Nobile's role is to assist the physical therapist in reaching the team's goals, and the massage therapy is billed to insurance companies under physical therapy. The hospital billing department handles all billing procedures. She submits a bill to the corporate office for the treatment time she has worked in order to be reimbursed.

Nobile's assignment with each patient after a physical therapy evaluation is to provide a plan of treatment and set goals to achieve with the team during a 4- to 6-week outpatient program. Team meetings are held weekly to discuss patient progress and to continue appropriate therapies. Nobile uses a combination of myofascial release, craniosacral therapy, and soft tissue mobilization. She also teaches progressive relaxation and imagery in group sessions in the Stress Management Department.

Just recently the treatment lengths and the number of treatments of massage therapy that Medicare/Medicaid has agreed to cover has decreased to two half-hour (rather than full-hour) sessions per week for 4 to 6 weeks. Worker's Compensation in the area has similarly cut back their coverage to a total of 10 to 12 half-hour treatments. If both the doctor and the insurance company believe that a patient has made significant progress, yet is not fully recovered, coverage is continued for a similar number of treatments. Due to these changes, Nobile has partially reduced her availability at the hospital and offers advice from her own experience. "Keep private work going." She shares her great frustration in attempting to make progress with patients she sees for only half-hour blocks. Half-hours are scheduled back-to-back, meaning that around 10 minutes out of every 30-minute block is spent in evaluating progress, dressing and undressing, which leaves about 20 minutes for actual treatment time. Though most patients at the hospital are unable to afford massage therapy at their own expense, the hospital is not averse to Nobile letting patients know where she can be reached outside of the hospital after insurance coverage has stopped.

Although there are some present difficulties with the insurance companies, the fact that massage therapy is a vital part of a hospital health care team and is simultaneously covered by insurance is extremely exciting.

Colorado

Suzanne Wilner, massage therapy coordinator of Denver's University of Colorado Health Sciences Center, expresses concern over current trends in health care. Wilner states that managed care is not necessarily the answer to fixing the health care system's financial problems, as managed care's tendency is to overstress saving money, to the possible detriment of more personalized human caring for their patients.

Wilner states that the current system may be pushing patients out of the hospital too soon for financial reasons as well. Ironically, these cases may cost insurance companies more money in the long-run if they have to pay for further hospitalizations due to complications from incomplete recovery. Wilner asserts that massage therapists can help patients recover more fully by giving them personalized care through bodywork. Based on the current anecdotal evidence of the effects of massage therapy on patients, Wilner stresses the importance of massage therapy in acute care settings. She encourages massage therapists nationwide to show insurance companies and hospitals how massage therapy can help patients heal more fully by the time they are expected to leave the hospital and reduce the risk of later complications. Wilner views massage therapists as helping hospitals remember the importance of human caring and challenging them to not forget it in the midst of a high tech health care milieu.

In conjunction with others, Wilner has been doing hospital-based research to help provide evidence on the efficacy of massage therapy with hospital patients since 1992, the publication of which is forthcoming in the *Journal of Nursing Research*. She hopes others are prioritizing documentation of the effects of massage to demonstrate its efficacy as well.

Oklahoma

Xerlan Geiser, owner of the Massage Therapy Institute of Oklahoma, who is also involved in some Oklahoma hospitals, spent much of her time at last year's first International Congress on Alternative & Complementary Medicine educating physicians. Many of the physicians with whom she spoke thought that massage was "just a rub" until Geiser educated them about various techniques such as craniosacral, myofascial, and sports massage.

By the end of the conference, many of these doctors were educated to the point that they wished she worked in the same building or next door to them. Eight of the physicians she spoke with returned home from the conference to schedule massage therapy appointments, and one of these physicians has hired a massage therapist to work with the physical therapists she has on staff.

Xerlan's point is that doctors just need to be educated. We just have to let them know what we do and that we want to work with them. Xerlan agrees that once the physicians and hospital executives know the value of having massage therapists on staff, hospitals and physicians themselves will be pushing insurance companies to cover massage therapy, and this is how fuller insurance, in the end, will be obtained.

Washington

Dale Perry of the Hospital Massage Training & Internship of the Brenneke School of Massage in Seattle, WA, states that insurance companies in the state of Washington are now required by law to cover massage therapy. This was implemented on January 1, 1996.

California

In California, many insurance companies are health maintenance organizations (HMOs), which currently do not cover massage therapy.

Portrait of a Success Story

Jeanne Wagner, RN, BSN, CMT, is the coordinator and owner of a massage therapy business which is contracted by four hospitals, including Elmbrook Memorial Hospital, St. Michael's Health Center, St. Francis Hospital, and St. Joseph's Hospital, in the Covenant Health Care System in Wisconsin. Wagner has four massage therapists under her supervision to meet the needs of these hospitals. The primary clientele are pregnant women and massage therapy is available to outpatients and the general public. Couples massage and infant massage classes are also offered. The massage therapy program is incredibly supported by the hospital for three main reasons. (1) The hospitals of the Covenant Health Care System are shifting their focus towards more preventive medicine, and thus strongly support and promote the program. Information on massage therapy is included in patient packets as well as in hospital mailings to prior patients. The physical therapists are also supportive. Additionally, both the hospitals and Wagner encourage massage for employee wellness, Wagner reducing the fees for employees and the hospitals reducing the monetary percentage employees paid for massages. (2) Wagner's business is independently contracted by the hospitals, meaning that the hospitals are putting absolutely no money or energy into paying for the massage therapy coordinator (as they would if the massage program were run by a massage therapy coordinator hired with a salary within the hospital system), and thus their costs for supporting the program are significantly reduced. (3) The program is revenue-generating to the hospital, because a percentage of what is paid to the massage therapy business is paid to the hospital.

The massage therapy sessions are paid by the patients themselves. Because members of the public are comfortably paying for their treatments, insurance coverage has not been an issue.

Wagner's advice to anyone starting a hospital massage business or program is to be patient. "We had slow, steady progress for two years and just now [in October 1995], it blossomed into needing four additional employees. Do lots of promotion and marketing on-site to each department and have another part-time job to begin with for needed income. I'm lucky because you really need to find a strong advocate (the hospital's current philosophy and mission statement, focusing on wellness and stress reduction), and a trailblazer (someone prior to Wagner was responsible for first introducing massage to the hospital). Demonstrate the work that you do. Know what you are talking about and have your proposal completely ready and professional. Know the answers to their questions, educate them."

Wagner's hospital massage business is an example of being successful by being revenue-generating. Wagner's success also introduces the possibility of fully avoiding some of the difficulties of creating a program directly under the hospital administration by creating a business which can be brought into the hospital through independent contracting.

Some Opinions from People Heading Organizations of Hospital-Based Massage Therapists

Andy Bernay-Roman, Nurse's Touch

Andy Bernay-Roman, editor of the National Association of Nurse Massage Therapists (NANMT) publication, *Nurse's Touch*, has seen some trends in what works to bring massage therapy into hospitals.

One Method that Bernay-Roman notes as effective in introducing massage therapy to hospitals is for a massage therapy school to make a liaison effort with a hospital to provide volunteer massage therapy from their students. This would be an exchange where hospitals would show the students how to work in this type of medical setting. When the person organizing this liaison is the massage school owner, and especially if the owner is a nurse, this arrangement is usually successful.

After the massage students begin doing massage in the hospital, nurses will begin to see the beneficial effects on the patients. As a result, many nurses and other staff members have pursued careers in massage therapy. This has helped touch therapies to become an integrated part of hospital care.

Bernay-Roman notes that a significant factor as to whether or not massage becomes integrated into a hospital is whether hospital executives and surgeons use massage therapy as part of their health care program.

Bernay-Roman again confirms that hospitals are indeed, businesses. As businesses, they look for ways to compete and they are realizing that a public image of caring for their patients through offering touch therapies is one crucial factor.

Almost humorously, Bernay-Roman mentions that patients who see massage therapists during their stay at a hospital may be less likely to file lawsuits, feel more cared for, and thus less angry about any perceived wrong from the hospital.

Wendy Arnold, Head of the San Francisco Bay Area's
Hospital Massage Consortium

Wendy Arnold states that hospitals in her area want to accept massage therapy only if it is done on a volunteer basis. The hospitals do not want to pay. Arnold states that hospitals still need to be educated as to why they would even want massage therapy available to their patients.

Arnold mentions a hospital represented in the Consortium at which the massage therapists are paid by the patients, yet no percentage of the income goes to the hospital, because the amount paid is seen as lower than it should be. Currently this hospital is not aiding in promotion of the massage therapy, not even including information on massage with patient admission packets. The amount massage therapists should be paid cannot be covered by the patients, the insurance companies are not helping, and the hospital wants the massage program but cannot help much when it has no income from the massage to put into promoting it.

Arnold supports increased consistency of standards among hospital-based massage therapists via more cohesive communication amongst themselves.

A Prediction

While much of this field is still in the explorational and educational phases of both massage therapists and the medical field, the author would like to entertain the following long-term ideas.

What we are currently seeing in the field of hospital-based massage therapy is the beginning of a shift from primarily volunteer programs to programs with paid massage therapists. The original massage therapy programs, in conjunction with current U.S. healthcare trends, are laying the groundwork for massage therapy programs of the future. Many of the original hospital massage programs that consisted of volunteer massage therapists and a paid coordinator were eventually eliminated because they were not revenue-sustaining nor revenue-generating. In this arrangement, the hospital was paying for the program via the coordinator, promotion and miscellaneous expenses, yet the hospital was taking in no revenue from the program. These original hospital massage programs taught the medical community and massage therapists themselves of the validity and function of massage for hospital patients, yet could not survive.

Hospital administrators, executives, physicians, and their loved ones are increasingly experiencing healing through complementary healthcare methods such as massage, and are thus wanting to offer such healing to their patients. Additionally, the medical community is trying to satisfy the general public, and attract them through offering the increasingly desired complementary health care methods such as massage therapy.

As massage therapy increases in popularity, more people who can afford it are willing to pay for it. Simultaneously, as more insurance consumers (the patients themselves) and more hospital administrators, physicians, and staff want massage therapy covered by insurance, they will increasingly push insurance companies to do so, and thus insurance coverage of massage therapy will increase. This trend has already been seen in Washington State, and by the fact that insurance companies now cover some massage therapy, when there was a time when they did not cover it at all. If hospital massage programs are originally set up to be revenue-sustaining to help prevent being cut later, such programs should become revenue-generating as they grow. These theories indicate that hospital massage therapy will gradually become a common, paid career, especially as the public increasingly desires massage therapy. As Marian Williams so aptly puts it, "Massage therapists should be paid for the work they do. They provide an important service as part of the healthcare team and should be reimbursed for their services, just as any other professional.

"As we are already seeing at CPMC, older programs are being cut to make way for new programs where massage therapists are paid for their work. We shall see where we go from here."

We are so grateful and indebted to Marian Williams and Karen Gibson for their hard work. Without them, we would not yet be at a point where we are today.

Laura Koch, CMT, Editor in Chief, journalist, owner of the *Hospital-Based Massage Network Newsletter*, **can be reached at 5 Old Town Square, Suite 205, Fort Collins, CO 80524. (970) 407-9232. FAX (970) 225-9217. Membership: $20.00 per year, includes member directory and quarterly newsletter.**

ADDITIONAL RESOURCES

- California Bay Area Hospital Massage Consortium, Wendy Arnold, at 415/476-6613.

- Marian Williams, Massage in Medical Settings workshop, contact Alive & Well! Institute of Conscious Bodywork, San Anselmo, CA, at 415/258-0402.

- Upcoming workshops at the Boulder School of Massage Therapy in conjunction with Boulder Community Hospital, Boulder, CO. Contact Peggy Mauro at 303/443-5131.

- For internship information contact: Brenneke School of Massage, Seattle, WA. Contact Dale Perry at 206/282-1233.

- Jeanne Wagner, at 414/789-8189.

Chapter 17

Answers to Frequently Asked Questions

Answers to Frequently Asked Questions

Many readers and colleagues ask similar questions. Over the past 10 years, whether on the telephone, in letters or face-to-face after workshops, I have seen many common concerns emerge. Below are grouped the most common questions and problems by general subject area. For help with specific billing questions or marketing/practice management issues not answered here, please call for an individual consultation: 1-800-888-1516.

Billing

Q: I recently submitted a bill to an insurance company, but it came back unpaid, marked: "No CPT procedure codes." What is a procedure code?
A: CPT stands for Current Procedural Terminology. These terms are listed in a book published by the American Medical Association: "Physicians Current Procedural Terminology." The codebook is a systematic listing of procedures and services performed by physicians and healthcare providers. Each procedure or service is identified by a five-digit code. For example, in the Physical Medicine Section, "Massage Therapy (15 minutes)" is assigned number 97124. Insurance companies require these codes to define what service was done and for how long. (See pages 78–83).

Q: How do I get information on the codes and how to use them?
A: You may order the book directly from the American Medical Association, Department of Coding and Nomenclature, 515 North State Street, Chicago, IL 60610 or call 1-800-621-8335. You must follow strict guidelines for using the codes. These are described in Chapter 7 of this manual.

Q: I have been using the CPT codes for billing massage therapy for several years. How do I find out about changes in the codes and how they affect massage therapists?
A: To update yourself on all the changes, subscribe to the update service from Bodytherapy Business Institute. Call 1-800-888-1516 to get the latest information.

Q: I practice in a state with no statewide regulation (licensing) of massage therapists. Other massage therapists show me billing forms they use to bill an insurance company. Their printed forms includes the name of the referring doctor and all the procedure codes to bill health insurance. They submit the form with their signature and have very few problems getting reimbursed. Is this a legal way to bill in an unlicensed state?
A: No. Our attorneys advise us that a massage/bodytherapy professional in an unlicensed state may use the national CPT codes ONLY when working under the direct supervision (on the premises) of the licensed healthcare provider prescribing the bodytherapy. A bodytherapy professional not licensed by his or her state is not permitted to use these codes on the billing form when working unsupervised (without a doctor on the premises) and without a doctor's referral. In a licensed state, practi-

tioners use these codes from their own offices with a doctor's referral letter after they verify coverage and confirm the company covers their service.

Q: What is a diagnostic code? My chiropractor mentioned an ICD-9CM code book. Do I list this code on my billing form?

A: Yes, you include it on your bill. A diagnostic code identifies a disease from its signs and symptoms and assigns it a number for easy reference on a claim form. The ICD-9 stands for the International Classification of Diseases, which is revised frequently and contains 10,000 diagnostic codes used by doctors and licensed healthcare providers. As a bodytherapy professional, you receive the diagnostic code from the doctor's office for your billing. Remember that the diagnostic code is assigned only by a doctor or other licensed, treating provider.

Q: Our busy medical office provides massage therapy to many clients covered by Worker's Compensation insurance. We have problems getting reimbursed by the insurance company for the full amount that I bill for 1-hour sessions. Many claims are rejected or only partially paid. What can we do to increase our collections?

A: Check with the Worker's Compensation Board in your state for the prevailing fee schedule and guidelines for your service, which varies from state to state and company to company. Usually the carrier will pay ONLY for sessions addressing the work-related injured area, which rarely last more than 30-45 minutes.

When you verify coverage, ask the claims representative for any limitations or restrictions on your type of service. Most Worker's Compensation carriers will reimburse for massage therapy that is medically necessary, but the billing envelope must include letters from the physician ordering the work under his/her supervision.

Q: I have several clients (in a state with no statewide regulation) who are over age 65 and have Medicare insurance. They can only afford to see me with insurance coverage. Can I bill Medicare as a massage therapist?

A: Not yet, except in Connecticut, which is the only state (as of January 1997), that accepts massage therapists as Medicare-approved providers. To bill Medicare, (a federal health insurance program for patients 65 or older plus certain disabled people), your state Medicare Board must issue you a Medicare provider number. Medicare providers must meet all state licensing requirements and be certified by Medicare. Other states may accept massage therapy for Medicare patients in the future.

Q: Our physical therapy office employs several massage/bodytherapists. The Worker's Compensation Board in our state says they pay $22.14 for each 30 minutes of massage therapy. Our usual fee is $32.50. Can we bill Worker's Compensation patients $22.14 for 30 minutes while billing our health insurance customers $32.50? Can we charge different clients different fees for the same service ?

A: No. It is illegal to charge two different fees for the same service, according to insurance attorneys we consult. You must bill the Worker's Compensation carrier at the same rate as you bill other insurance carriers. When they reimburse you, they will adjust your submitted amount (if too high) to reflect their prevailing fee schedule in your state. You may, however, charge different fees for different types of services. For example, many offices employ several bodytherapists who practice different modalities, such as Trager, Feldenkrais and Rolfing, which command different fees.

Q: I would like to do massage therapy in a hospital setting. How can I get more information about hospital-based massage therapy programs?
A: Hospital-based massage is expanding, with up to 150 hospitals offering massage therapy programs. For example, The Brenneke School of Massage in Seattle, WA at (206) 282-1233 (ask for Dale Perry) offers internships in their hospital-based massage therapy program.

For national information on hospital-based massage and to subscribe to a quarterly newsletter, write to The Hospital-Based Massage Network, c/o Rocky Mountain Therapeutics, 5 Old Town Square, Suite 205, Fort Collins, CO 80524.

Q: I work as a massage therapist in a rehabilitation center hospital. I want to expand this pilot program to serve more patients but am having difficulty getting support from hospital administrators. What do you suggest I do?
A: To expand the pilot program you need to get administrative support by showing how this program will help more patients while reducing healthcare costs. Hospital administrators, who are held responsible for the consequences of their financial decisions, need solid proof before they feel comfortable with such a change.

The best support is documentary evidence that over time your work is effective. First, contact the Hospital-Based Massage Therapy Network for a listing of other hospital-based massage programs in the U.S. and examples of how other program directors have documented their cost-effectiveness. In your own hospital, establish a solid database to document your results and cost-effectiveness. Meet frequently with your executives and staff to educate them on research and clinical results. Also, show them positive progress and outcomes with your own patients.

You can also use in-services, lectures and written materials. Consider distributing copies of **A Physician's Guide to Therapeutic Massage** by John Yates. It's available through The Massage Therapists' Association of British Columbia, Third Floor, 34 East 12th Avenue, Vancouver, B.C. V5T 2G5 CANADA.

Q: I recently submitted a claim to an insurance company. They sent it back saying massage therapy has no therapeutic value and is used only for relaxation purposes, which they do not pay for. What can I do?
A: Commit to the time and effort to educate them. Recognize that you must do this to establish reimbursement as part of your practice. Many companies and their claims representatives know little or nothing about the efficacy and therapeutic value of your work.

For example, inform the company, in writing, that the client was referred for a specific, diagnosed health condition. Also, significant outcome studies are available that clearly demonstrate the therapeutic value and benefits of clinical massage therapy. Many of those have been done through the Touch Research Institute and the Office of Alternative Medicine at the National Institutes of Health. Send insurers, and doctors, copies of studies that show research and outcome studies on the condition(s) related to your claims. For a listing of studies and examples of research results, see Chapter 14.

Q: My chiropractor has written a prescription for my clients who have car insurance and Worker's Compensation insurance. The insurance companies returned our claims with a letter asking for more information from the doctor. What should a prescription contain and what's the correct wording?

A: The doctor's prescription should contain the following information: the date, patient's name, diagnosis, the procedure the doctor recommends and how many times per week over how many weeks the procedure is prescribed. For example: "I recommend that Susan Smith receive Clinical Massage Therapy 2 times per week for 4 weeks and then 1 time per week for 2 weeks for the treatment of Whiplash Injury. Patient will be evaluated by the doctor weekly."

Q: A client came to my office last week just after being injured in an automobile accident. She wanted to see me before she saw any doctors, since she felt uncomfortable with her doctor. I referred her to the doctor I work with but she refused to go. What is the best action in this situation?

A: You did the right thing. It is imperative that you inform any injured patient who walks into your office or calls you after an accident that they MUST be seen by a licensed physician, chiropractor or other provider first for a diagnosis and initial evaluation. Only licensed providers can determine the extent and type of massage or bodytherapy they need.

Many patients feel that massage or bodytherapy will help them immediately after an accident and they often prefer to start those treatments first. Yet, I have seen several cases where the patient was seriously injured and unaware of the need for prompt medical attention. You may begin your treatments only after you have spoken with their doctor about the extent of the injury or condition and received the doctor's recommendations.

> **WARNING:** This is also for your protection. You would make yourself vulnerable to liability and an injury lawsuit if you advised or touched an injured person without a doctor's diagnosis and prescription.

Q: I work with a chiropractor who bills for some patient visits in advance (before the patient actually had the service done at the office). She charges one fee for cash patients and $15 more for insurance patients. Please clarify the purpose of these business practices.

A: According to several experts in insurance law, providers must bill at the time of service, not in advance. They must also charge the same fee to insurance patients as they charge their cash patients. They may not charge different fees for the same service. For further information, contact the appropriate legal professional in your state.

Practice Management

Q: Is it necessary to keep S.O.A.P. notes on each of my clients?

A: Yes. If you are billing insurance companies, you must keep detailed progress reports on each client in this format. For non-insurance clients, you must still have this kind of information, but the format can be more flexible.

S.O.A.P. stands for Subjective Findings, Objective Findings, Assessment and Plan. In your notes, record the date of the visit, what you observed, what the patient states and the procedures you performed. Also note any referrals and recommendations you made to the client. All types of insurance carriers request records frequently to document "medical necessity" for continued care when the claim is reviewed. If you work in an unlicensed state, the physician or supervising provider must review your notes and sign them as approved by him or her. For further information, refer to **Hands-Heal** by Diana Thompson, LMP., as well as Chapter 13.

Q: The insurance company returned my bill unpaid, stating that massage therapy has no demonstrable results for the diagnosis on the form. When I phoned them, they asked for outcome studies of my work. What is an outcome study? Where can I find information on how to show that my work is effective?

A: Begin by consulting these excellent resources. The Touch Research Institute in Miami, Florida, (305) 243-6781, offers a newsletter and reprints of studies done with infants, children, adolescents and adults. The Office of Alternative Medicine of the National Institutes of Health in Bethesda, Maryland, (see Chapter 14) does a wide variety of studies in your field and publishes a newsletter and reports of studies.

Several excellent reference books list and describe many outcome studies. See **A Physician's Guide to Therapeutic Massage** by John Yates, PhD, **Alternative Medicine: What Works** by Adriane Fugh-Berman, MD, and **The American Holistic Health Association Complete Guide to Alternative Medicine** by William Collinge, MPH, PhD.

Before the advent of pharmaceutical medicine early in this century, references to massage/bodytherapy and research were common in mainstream literature. Research was also conducted widely in Eastern Bloc countries, Europe and China. Fortunately, after many years of not being recognized, massage and bodytherapy are again the subjects of research activity and journal references.

Q: I have heard and read a lot about HMOs and PPOs. What are they? Can I join as a massage/bodytherapist and bill them for my services?

A: HMO stands for health maintenance organization. It's a prepaid group practice sponsored and operated by an insurance company, clinic or hospital/medical plan.

"Prepaid" means the healthcare provider agrees to treat all the covered illnesses of everyone in the group for a year for a fixed total price.

PPO stands for preferred provider organization. It contracts with a group of "preferred" providers to deliver care to members. Unlike HMO members, PPO-insured patients may choose any physician or hospital for services, but they receive more generous reimbursement if they see a preferred provider.

As of 1996, several managed care companies have added massage and bodytherapists to their pool of providers. WellTouch Corporation of Dallas, Texas, is negotiating managed care contracts with some of America's largest corporations. These contracts will enable nearly 6 million people to receive treatments from contracting massage therapists. For more information, call 1-800-WELLTOUCH.

Also, Oxford Health Plans in the Northwest and Alternative Health Insurance Services are including massage therapy in their benefits packages. For more information, see Chapter 15.

Q: I work in a chiropractic office 30 hours per week as an independent contractor. Do I need to carry my own professional liability insurance, or am I covered under the doctor's insurance?

A: In all cases, yes, you must have your own professional liability insurance. When you work on the doctor's premises under his or her license, the doctor is liable for any injury to a patient. However, the doctor's liability insurance may or may not include coverage for your services. In most cases, the doctor will require you to carry your own insurance policy.

General Business Practices

Q: I just bought a computer for my office. How do I get started if I want to bill insurance companies from my computer?

A: Several excellent software programs can do your billing and allow you to link your system to a clearing house that accepts claims electronically, (i.e., your computer sends the claim over telephone lines.) Electronic billing saves time and makes your records easy to review in one place. (Make sure you create daily backup copies of your records on a separate diskette in case of computer failure or loss.)

Many systems offer formats for patient notes, bookkeeping and follow-up progress reports. Electronic records also leave an audit trail, which means you can track when and where the data went, when received, by whom and who may have altered it.

To get started, contact a software company and ask for a demonstration disk. Try out the software to see if it is easy to use and has all the functions you need. Then contact a sales representative to discuss your specific business and billing needs.

For a list of recommended software programs, see pages 213-214 of this manual or call Bodytherapy Business Institute at 1-800-888-1516.

Q: What kinds of automobile and home office deductions can I take as a massage therapist? Do you have any suggestions on how to do my taxes in less time?

A: Two excellent resource guides to help you figure your taxes and deductions and determine your business status is **Tax Tips for the Self-Employed Bodyworker** by Paul A. Kirchhoff, MA, LMT, and Paul Harold, MBA, CPA and **Business Mastery, A Business and Planning Guide for Creating a Fulfilling, Thriving Business and Keeping it Successful,** by Cherie Sohnen-Moe.

Q: I live in California and just received my license to practice massage therapy. I am designing my business cards with my title "licensed massage therapist." Is that the correct way to refer to myself in public?

A: No. Only someone with a license from a state professional board or regulatory agency may call themselves a "licensed massage therapist." In a state with no statewide regulation of your profession, you may call yourself a certified massage/bodytherapist (as appropriate to the school certificate you received). But do not deceive or mislead the public by confusing a business license with a professional license.

The word "license" causes a lot of confusion among both professionals and the public. Many practitioners living in states with no statewide regulation of massage/bodytherapy, are surprised to find that while the school issues a certificate of completion and is "licensed by the state" to teach, their graduates are not "licensed by the state" to practice their profession.

Here's why: Your educational or training certificate only verifies in writing that you completed the curriculum. It's not a license, or official permission to do something. Also, the "license" you obtain from your city to open your doors and provide a service is a business license for that city. It, too, is not a professional massage license.

If you do have a state's professional license, you should frame it and proudly display it. It designates you a licensed professional who has met high professional standards and passed examinations to demonstrate competence.

Q: I work full time with a chiropractor who has been training me over the past year to do trigger-point therapy. I get paid for my services every two weeks, regardless of money received from the patient. He has asked me to work additional hours for the past week and has specified which days he wants me to work. We have no written contract regarding our working relationship. Given these conditions, do I still qualify to work for him as an independent contractor, or am I now an employee?

A: You are probably his employee for tax purposes, but determining that can be complex. (The IRS has a list of 20 criteria it looks at to determine this.) Here are a few general guidelines. If you set your own hours, fees and method of working, provide your own equipment and supplies, and work for several different people, you are probably an independent contractor. If you work for only one provider, on the doctor's premises, following terms and conditions he sets (fees, hours and how you must perform the work) you are probably his employee.

If you are his employee, (which is the real area of concern for independent professionals), he is required by law to withhold money from your wages and pay it to the government for state and federal income taxes, as well as Social Security and unemployment benefits. For more information, check with your tax advisor or attorney and get a copy of Publication 539 from the Internal Revenue Service.

Q: I have been offered a job as an employee in a chiropractor's office at $15. for each hour I work. His staff told me he bills the insurance company $125 per hour for my services. Is this a fair arrangement?

A: No. This is an excessive charge for your services. An insurance company would probably notice it and view it, and the providers, with suspicion. Find another doctor who will make a fair, reasonable professional agreement with you.

Also, the customary rate at which you should be paid is 50% of what the doctor bills, minus any employee benefits such as health, dental and Worker's Compensation insurance that the doctor pays for you.

Unfortunately, many chiropractic offices across the country get greedy and exploit massage/bodytherapists by hiring them at low rates while billing insurance for them at high rates. Often, these doctors bill excessively high amounts and for too many procedures at once. This practice hurts all other providers and professionals by making it more difficult to establish professional credibility.

Q: I have recently seen some of the electrical stimulator devices sold at massage therapy conventions. They appear to be effective. May I use them in my office and bill the insurance company for them?

A: Yes, but in all cases you must be licensed by your state to use these devices in your office. Study your state's massage practice act carefully (if you live in a licensed state) and consult with an appropriate legal professional.

In unlicensed states, you may use the device only if you are working under the direct supervision of a licensed provider such as a physical therapist or chiropractor. Whether or not you can bill the insurance company depends on your licensure status, scope of practice and medical necessity. (Does the patient really need this to get better?) Call the insurance company when you verify coverage for your clients and ask if they pay for using such devices. In most cases, the procedure has to be recommended and supervised by the doctor.

Q: I just moved to a new community. How do I market my services?

A: Try a variety of strategies and apply them consistently. Attend professional associations and networking groups. Send letters of introduction, your brochure and a portfolio of letters of reference from previous employers and clients to a variety of doctors and chiropractors. Tell everyone you meet about your practice. Offer short demonstrations to businesses and friends. Post fliers around community bulletin boards and set up speaking engagements at health clubs, community events and other places where people gather.

Also, give and get support from others like you. Set up a support group to meet weekly and discuss shared goals. Set both short- and long-term goals and find a buddy to talk with and be accountable to for daily, weekly or monthly targets.

Finally, be patient. As much as anything else, it takes time to establish a strong, profitable practice. An Excellent resource guide is **Business Mastery** by Cherie Sohnen-Moe.

Q: I just moved to a new city and am interested in working with doctors and dentists. How do I locate someone who would be interested in working with me?
A: Get to know other bodytherapy practitioners who practice where you live. Go to massage and bodytherapy centers to get names and addresses. Ask them if they know of any healthcare providers interested in working with bodytherapists. Also, attend meetings of your professional association in your city and ask for referrals to healthcare providers who use bodytherapy as part of their practice. Also, when you visit your dentist or any other healthcare provider, tell them about your work and that you are interested in meeting other health professionals.

Q: I am considering working for doctors or physical therapists to have a more stable practice. What is the difference between the job classifications "massage technician" and "massage therapist"? What is the starting salary or entry level rate of pay?
A: A massage technician generally has an average of 100 hours of education (the minimum requirement in most unlicensed states) and works under the direct supervision of the doctor or physical therapist carrying out the treatment program. Massage technicians usually gain experience by working in the field and sometimes begin by working as employees.

A massage therapist, on the other hand, generally has an average of 500 hours of education (the minimum requirement in many licensed states) and often has 500-1,000 hours of additional training in such modalities as clinical massage, accupressure, trigger point therapy and neuromuscular therapy. Massage therapists, depending on the scope of practice and the laws in their state, may work more independently as part of a group of doctors or chiropractors. They may assess the client's condition and along with the treating doctor determine the appropriate course of treatment.

The starting rate of pay in physical therapy for entry level employees is $10-15 per hour, varying with the type of practice and area of the country. The starting rate of pay for the massage therapist as an employee is generally a bit higher than $15-20 per hour.

Working as an independent contractor (without the benefits of an employee) the massage technician rate of pay would start at $25-35, while the massage therapist would start at $35-45. (less deductions taken by the medical office).

Q: What is the difference between "clinical massage" and "relaxation massage"?
A: The differences lie in the provider, setting, approach and intended result or outcome. Clinical massage services are delivered by a highly-trained health professional in a hospital or the office of a doctor, physical therapist or massage/bodytherapist.

The purpose is to improve or relieve a specific health condition via a known therapeutic effect. By contrast, relaxation massage is usually done by a person who may have training and experience only in that specialty. Also, they work in non-medical settings such as a spa, health club, salon or private home. Usually, the purpose is body/mind relaxation.

Insurance Coverage

Q: I am a massage therapist in an unlicensed state working with my husband, who is a chiropractor. I have my own private clients who want to receive insurance coverage for my work. Does my husband have to see my private clients as patients before they can receive reimbursement by their insurance company?

A: Yes, by him or some other licensed provider. In order to receive reimbursement, your clients have to have a diagnosis by the doctor who is billing for and supervising the treatments. If your husband is providing the forms for billing, then he must see and diagnose your clients first, before they can be reimbursed. In addition, you or the front office staff must verify coverage before starting any treatment. This involves calling the insurance company to verify that they cover chiropractic treatment, as well as massage therapy, done under the supervision of the doctor. Ask if there is a limit to the number of visits and what percentage they pay for.

Q: What about home visits? I work with a medical doctor, and several clients need to be seen in their homes. Will these visits be covered by the insurance company?

A: Most companies pay for home visits if the patient is unable to travel to the office. Check with the specific insurance carrier. Often, a company will pay for home visits if the doctor sends a letter stating the client's diagnosis, prognosis, duration of treatment and that the procedures must be done in the patient's home because the patient is unable to travel to the office.

Suggested Readings
&
Reference Materials

Important Books for the Bodytherapy Professional

Alternative Medicine, A Definitive Guide by Burton Goldberg
Future Medicine Publishing, Inc.
21 1/2 Main Street
Tiburon, CA 94920
1-800-513-4325

Alternative Medicine: What Works–A Comprehensive, Easy-to-Read Review of the Scientific Evidence, Pro and Con by Adriane Fugh-Berman, M.D., 1996
Odonian Press
Box 32375
Tucson, AZ 85751
(520) 296-0936

A Physician's Guide to Therapeutic Massage
The Massage Therapist's Association of British Columbia, B.C.
34 East 12th Avenue
Vancouver, B.C. V5T2G5
(604) 873-4467

Business Mastery, A Business and Planning Guide for Creating a Fulfilling, Thriving Business and Keeping it Successful, by Cherie Sohnen-Moe
Sohnen-Moe Associates, Inc.
3906 W. Ina Road, #200-348
Tucson, AZ 88741-2295
(520) 743-3936
1-800-786-4774

Deep Bodywork and Personal Development by Jack W. Painter
Bodymind Book
Mill Valley, CA 94941

Discovering the Body's Wisdom by Mirka Knaster
Bantam
1540 Broadway
New York, NY 10036
(212) 354-6500

Electronic Data Interchange: The Physician's Guide
American Medical Association
515 North State Street
Chicago, IL 60610
1-800-621-8335

Essentials of Managed Care by Peter R. Kongstvedt, M.D.
Aspen Publishers, Inc.
Gaithersburg, MD 20870
(301) 417-7500

Fundamentals of Therapeutic Massage by Sandy Cochran Fritz
C.V. Mosby Publishing
11830 Westline Industrial Drive
St. Louis, MO 63146
(314) 872-8370

Handbook of Shen by Richard Rainbow Pavek
The Shen Therapy Institute
No. 20 YFH Gate Six Road
Sausalito, CA 94965
(415) 332-2593

Hands-Heal: Documentation for Massage Therapy; A Guide to SOAP Charting
by Diana Thompson, L.M.P.
Healing Arts Studio
916 N.E. 64th Street
Seattle, WA 98115
1-800-989-4743-7

Healing Massage Techniques by Frances Tappan
Appleton and Lange Publishers
Box 120041
Stamford, CT 06912
1-800-423-1359

Job's Body by Deane Juhan
Distributed by: The Talman Company
150 Fifth Avenue
New York, NY 10011

Living the Therapeutic Touch by Dolores Krieger
Dodd, Mead and Co.
1440 Paddock Drive
Northbrook, IL 60062

Marketing Without Advertising by M. Phillips and S. Rasberry
Nolo Press
950 Parker Street
Berkely, CA 94710
(510) 549-1976

Massage, A Career at Your Fingertips by Martin Ashley, J.D., L.M.T.
Enterprise Publishing
P. O. Box 167
Mahopac Falls, NY 10542

Reimbursement Strategies
Medicode
5220 Wiley Post Way, Suite 500
Salt Lake City, UT 84116

Save Your Hands: Injury Prevention for Massage Therapists by Laurienne Greene
Infinity Press
3254 MW 61st Street
Seattle, WA 98017
(206) 706-1999

Step by Step Medical Coding by Carol J. Buck
W. B. Saunders Company
The Curtis Center
Independence Square West
Philadelpia, PA 19106
(215) 238-7800

Tax Tips for the Self-Employed Bodyworker by Paul A. Kirchhoff, M.A., L.M.T. and
Paul Harold, M.B.A., C.P.A.
Health Management Group
2263 N.W. 2nd Avenue, Suite 107
Boca Raton, FL 33431
(888) 362-7724

The 1997 Insurance Directory
Medicode
5225 Wiley Post Way, Suite 500
Salt Lake City, UT 84116

The American Holistic Health Association Complete Guide to Alternative Medicine
by William Collinge, M.P.H., Ph.D.
Warner Books, Inc.
1271 Avenue of the Americas
New York, NY 10020
(212) 522-7200

The Body Electric by Robert O. Becker, M.D., and Gary Selden
Quill Paperbacks/William Morrow & Company, Inc.
1350 Avenue of the Americas
New York, NY 10019
(212) 261-6500

The Bodywork Book edited by Nevill Drury
Prism Alpha
San Leandro, CA

The Bodywork Entrepreneur edited by David Palmer
Thumb Press
San Francisco, CA

The Encyclopedia of Bodywork by Elaine Stillerman
Facts on File, Inc.
11 Penn Plaza
New York, NY 10001
(212) 967-8800

The Ins and Outs of Medical Insurance Billing
by Eric Durak, MSC & Andrew Shapiro, MA
Medical Health and Fitness
P.O. Box 29
Santa Barbara, CA 93102

The Theory and Practice of Therapeutic Massage by Mark Beck
Milady Publishing Company
3839 White Plains Road
Bronx, NY 10467-5394

Trager Mentastics: Movement as a Way to Agelessness by Milton Trager, M.D. with Cathy
Guadagno, Ph.D.
Station Hill Press
Station Hill Road
Barrytown, NY 12507
(914) 758-5840

Understanding Medical Insurance by Jo Ann C. Rowell
Medical Economics Books
Five Paragon Drive
Montvale, NJ 07649
(201) 358-7500

Your Successful Massage/Bodywork Practice and the Massage Marketing Kit
by Jefferson Saunders, L.M.P. and Deborah Nucci, CHT.
Superior Publishing Company
1202 E. Pike Street, Suite 900
Seattle, WA 98122-3934
(206) 329-3566

IMPORTANT JOURNALS AND NEWSLETTERS

Alternative and Complementary Therapies Journal
Mary Ann Liebert, Inc. Publishers
2 Madison Avenue
Larchmont, NY 10538
1-800-M-LIEBERT

Alternative Medicine Digest
Future Medicine Publishing
21 1/2 Main Street
Tiburon, CA 94920
(415) 789-8700

Alternative Therapies in Health and Medicine
InnoVision Communications, Publisher
101 Columbia
Aliso Viejo, CA 92656
1-800-899-1712

Hospital Based Massage Network Newsletter
c/o Rocky Mountain Therapeutics
5 Old Town Square
Suite 205
Fort Collins, CO 80524
(970) 407-9232
FAX (970) 225-9217

Journal of Soft-Tissue Manipulation
Ontario Massage Therapy Association
324 Oakdale Ave.
Ottowa, Canada K1YOE4
(613) 722-8588
FAX (613) 722-5186

Massage and Bodywork Magazine
Associated Bodywork and Massage Professionals
28677 Buffalo Park Road
Evergreen, CO 80439-7347
(303) 674-8478
1-800-458-2267

Massage Magazine, Inc.
1315 Mallon
Spokane, WA 99201
(509) 324-8117 or 1-800-872-1282

Massage Therapy Journal
American Massage Therapy Association
820 Davis Street, Suite 100
Evanston, IL 60201-444
(847) 864-0123

Nurse's Touch
Newsletter of the National Association of Nurse Massage Therapists
167 Carl Street
Jupiter, FL 33477-5022

Somatics Magazine-Journal of the Bodily Arts and Sciences
1516 Grant Avenue, Suite 220
Novato, CA 94945

St. Anthony's Business Report on Alternative and Complimentary Medicine
St. Anthony Publishing, Inc.
11410 Isaac Newton Square
Reston, VA 20190
1-800-632-0123

Soft-Tissue Review (previously the *Body Mind Journal*)
7223 6th Ave. N.E.
Olympia, WA 98506
(360) 956-7238

St. John News
St. John Neuromuscular Pain Relief Institute
11211 Prosperity Farms Road, D-325
Palm Beach Gardens, FL 33410-3487
1-800-232-4668, Ext. 8907

The Bodywork Entrepreneur
584 Castro Street, Suite 373
San Francisco, CA 94114
(415) 861-4746

The Trager Journal, Volumes I and II
The Trager Institute
10 Old Mill Street
Mill Valley, CA 94941-1891

Touch Therapy Times
Jack Thomas
13407 Tower Road
Thurmont, MD 21788
(301) 271-4812

Update-A Publication of the Upledger Institute
The Upledger Institute, Inc.
11211 Prosperity Farms Road, D-325
Palm Beach Gardens, FL 33410-3487
1-800-233-5880, Ext. 8905

REFERENCE MATERIALS FOR INSURANCE BILLING

ICD-9-CM Diagnostic Code Book, Volumes 1 & 2
1997 5th edition
Order from
Saint Anthony's Publishing
11410 Issac Newton Square
Reston, VA 20190
1-800-632-0123

Physician's Current Procedural Terminology - CPT Coding Book 1998/1999
Available in doctors' offices, medical bookstores or from:
American Medical Association
Order Department:
515 North State Street
Chicago, IL 60610-9986

State of California, Worker's Compensation Handbook

Order from:
Department of Industrial Relations
Division of Worker's Compensation
455 Golden Gate Avenue, Room 5182
San Francisco, CA 94102

INSURANCE COMPANIES OFFERING COVERAGE FOR ADJUNCTIVE AND ALTERNATIVE SERVICES

The following list is for the practitioner and/or client interested in purchasing health insurance that recognizes and pays for alternative and adjunctive services such as acupuncture, neuromuscular re-education and chiropractic. Great variations exist among states and companies as to who pays and for what. Call the company you are interested in. As always in dealing with insurance companies, make sure you use terminology they understand; for example, neuromuscular re-education and soft-tissue mobilization instead of massage.

Alliance for Alternatives in Healthcare, Inc.
P.O. Box 6279
Thousand Oaks, CA 91359-6279
(805) 347-6003
FAX (805) 379-1580
1-800 966-8467

This company provides information and referral to a variety of health insurance plans that cover alternative and adjunctive services. As of 1998, the Alternative Health Insurance Group is establishing a nationwide network of alternative providers. Contact them to find out how you can join and become part of this exciting opportunity to work with many more clients interested in complementary health care services.

Oxford Health Plans

Contracts with massage therapists in the Northeastern States including New Jersey, New York and Connecticut

Write to:
Kerry MacKenzie
Oxford Health Plans, Inc.
800 Connecticut Avenue
Norwalk, CT 06854

HHC Health

2625 Alcatraz Avenue, Suite 303, Berkeley, California 94705
1-888-314-4632

As of 1998 contracting with California therapists and planning to contract nationwide in 1999.

Alternare of Washington
1-800-500-0997

Minnesota's Health Partners
1-800-883-2177

Axis Health Care
Portland, Oregon
(503)295-2983

Sloans Lake Managed Care
Denver, Colorado
(303) 691-2200

Harvard Pilgrim Health Care
Massachusetts
(800)742-8326

Consensus Health Corp
San Francisco, Calif.
(650)777-0334

AlternaNet, LLC
Santa Cruz, California
1-888-ALT-7576

PROFESSIONAL ORGANIZATIONS AND RESOURCES

American Holistic Health Association
Department C, P. O. Box 17400
Anaheim, CA 92817
(714) 779-6152

American Holistic Medical Association
4101 Lake Boon Trail, Suite 201
Raleigh, NC 27607
(919) 787-5181

American Massage Therapy Association
820 Davis St, Suite 100
Evanston, IL 60201-4444
(847) 864-0123

Associated Bodywork and Massage Professionals
28677 Buffalo Park Road
Evergreen, CO 80439-7347
(303) 674-8478

Association for Humanistic Psychology
Somatics and Wellness Community
P. O. Box 2123
San Anselmo, CA 94979-2123
(415) 346-7929

Bodywork Research Institute
Richard Van Why, Director
123 E. 8th Street, Suite 121
Frederick, MD 21701
(301) 698-0932

California Health Practitioners Association
P.O. Box 90875
San Diego, CA 92109

Health Insurance Association of America
1025 Connecticut Avenue., N.W.
Washington, D.C. 20036

Hospital Based Massage Network
c/o Rocky Mountain Therapeutics
5 Old Town Square, Suite 205
Ft. Collins, CO 80524
(970) 407-9232

International Massage Association
3000 Connecticut Avenue, N.W., Suite 308
Washington, D.C. 20008
(202) 387-6555
1-800-933-7113

International Myomassethics Federation, Inc.
15251 Purdy Street
Westminster, CA 92683
1-800-433-4463

National Association of Nurse Massage Therapists
167 Carl Street
Jupiter, FL 33477
(407) 746-8860

National Certification Board for Therapeutic Massage and Bodywork
1735 N. Lynn Street, Suite 950
Arlington, VA 22209
(800) 296-0664 or (703) 524-9563

Personal Fitness and Bodywork Professionals Association
121 W. 17th Street, Suite 8D
New York, NY 10011
(212) 620-4321

The California Coalition on Somatic Practices
P. O. Box 5611
San Mateo, CA 94402-0611
(415) 637-1233

COMPUTERIZED/ELECTRONIC BILLING PROGRAMS FOR THE BODYTHERAPY PROFESSIONAL

Easy Billing
Marla Productions
524 Don Gaspar
Santa Fe, NM 87501
1-800-618-6136

Medi-Soft
Phoenix Consultant
Authorized Dealers for Medi-Soft
P.O. Box 1016
Gainesville, GA 30503
1-800-679-7442

NEBS - The Small Business Resource
500 Main Street
Groton, MA 01471
1-800-225-6380

RESOURCE LIST OF BUSINESS/INSURANCE MATERIALS AND ELECTRONIC BILLING SERVICES

Bodyworker Business Forms
Carol Abernathy, LMT
P. O. Box 1016
Gainesville, Georgia 30503
1-800-295-7085

Comp. Med. Billing for Complimentary Medicine
16172 Parkside Drive
Suite 101
Parker, CO 80134
(303) 840-7500
FAX 303-840-7575

Electronic Billing Software: Who Is Out There Selling?
Zimmerman and Associates, Inc.
P. O. Box 407
Hales Corners, WI 53130

Healing Arts Forms, Inc.
7040 W. Palmetto Park Road
Suite 2103
Boca Raton, FL 33433
(561) 347-6430

PEACENERGY
P. O. Box 846
Edwards, CO 81632
970-926-2639
970-926-9090

LIABILITY INSURANCE ASSOCIATIONS
FOR BODYTHERAPY PRACTITIONERS

American Massage Therapy Association
820 Davis St, Suite 100
Evanston, IL 60201-4444
(847) 864-0123

Associated Bodywork and Massage Professionals
28677 Buffalo Park Road
Evergreen, CO 80439-7347
(303) 674-8478

International Massage Association
3000 Connecticut Avenue, N.W., Suite 308
Washington, D.C. 20008
(202) 387-6555
1-800-933-7113

Magginis and Associates
332 S. Midigan Avenue
Suite 1400
Chicago, IL 60604
1-800-621-3008

Massage Laws Nationwide & Resource List of State Boards/ Agencies

Massage Laws Nationwide & Resource List of State Boards/Agencies

As of Spring 1998, 22 states plus the District of Columbia offer some type of credential to practicing massage therapists—usually a license, certification or registration. Even if your state is listed here, contact your city or county officials about local requirements and ordinances. The Update Service (**1-800-888-1516**) through Bodytherapy Business Institute will update this information on a regular basis to reflect changes to the requirements and additions of states.

Call Bodytherapy Business Institute today to subscribe to the Update Service to keep you current.

Alabama

Alabama State Licensing Board for Massage Therapy
660 Adams Avenue
Suite 150
Montgomery, Alabama 36104
(334)269-9990

Arkansas

Arkansas State Board of Massage Therapy
P. O. Box 34163
Little Rock, Arkansas 72203
(501)623-0444

Connecticut

Department of Public Health
410 Capitol Avenue
P. O. Box 340308
Hartford, Connecticut 06134-0308
(860)509-7570

Delaware

Delaware Board of Massage and Bodywork
Cannon Building
Suite 203
861 Silver Lake Blvd.
Dover, Delaware 19904
(302)739-4522, ext. 205

Florida

Department of Professional Regulations
Board of Massage
Northwood Centre
1940 N. Monroe Street
Tallahassee, Florida 32399-0774
(850) 488-0595
(904) 488-6021

Hawaii

Department of Commerce and Consumer Affairs
Professional and Vocational Licensing Division
P. O. Box 3469
Honolulu, Hawaii 96801
(808) 586-3000

Iowa

Massage Therapy Board
c/o Department of Public Health
Lucas Building, 4th floor
312 E. 12th Street
Des Moines, Iowa 50319-0075
(515)281-6959

Louisiana

Louisiana State Board of Massage Therapy
P. O. Box 1279
Zachary, Louisiana 70791
(504) 658-8941

Maine

Department of Professional and Financial Regulations
35 State House Station
Augusta, Maine 07333
(207)624-8624

Nebraska

Nebraska Board of Massage Therapy
P. O. Box 94986
Lincoln, Nebraska 68509
(402) 471-2117

New Hampshire

Department of Public Health
Bureau of Health Facilities Administration
6 Hazen Drive
Concord, NH 03301
(603) 271-4594

New Mexico

Board of Massage Therapy
P. O. Box 25101
Santa Fe, NM 87504
(505)827-7013

New York

State Education Department
Division of Professional Licensing Services
Massage Unit, Room 3041
Cultural Education Center
Albany, NY 12230
(518) 473-1417

North Dakota

Massage Therapy Clinic
P. O. Box 701
Dickinson, North Dakota 58601
(701)225-3906

Ohio

Ohio State Medical Board
77 South High Street, 17th Floor
Columbus, OH 43266-0315
(614) 466-3934

Oregon

Oregon Board of Massage Technicians
800 N.E. Oregon Street, #21
Suite 407
Portland, OR 97232
(503) 731-4064

Rhode Island

Department of Health
Cannon Building
Three Capitol Hill
Providence, RI 02908
(401) 222-2827 X112

South Carolina

Board of Massage Therapy
P. O. Box 11329
Columbia, South Carolina 29210
(803) 896-4830

Tennesse

Board of Massage
1st floor
Cordell Hall Building
425 Fifth Avenue
North Nashville, Tennessee 37247-1010
(615) 532-5083

Texas

Texas Department of Health
Professional Licensing and Certification
Massage Therapy Registration Program
1100 W. 49th Street
Austin, TX 78756-3183
(512) 834-6616

Utah

Department of Business Regulation
Division of Occupational and Professional Licensing
Heber M. Wells Building
160 E. 300 South
Salt Lake City, UT 84114-6741
(801)530-6628

Virginia

Virginia Board of Nursing
Dept. of Health Professions
6606 West Broad Street
Richmond, Virginia 23230
(804)662-9909

Washington

Department of Licensing
Division of Professional Licensing
P. O. Box 47869
Olympia, WA 98504-7869
(206) 586-6351

Washington, D.C.

D.C. Board of Massage Therapy
Room 921
614 H. Street, N.W.
Washington, D.C. 20001
(202)727-7450

PROMOTIONAL MATERIALS FOR WORKING WITH A DOCTOR'S OFFICE

Promotional Materials for Working With a Doctor's Office

In order to establish yourself with a healthcare professional you have to clearly demonstrate the purpose of your work and how it can help his or her patients. You need to demonstrate a high level of skill and expertise in your chosen specialty. The following pages give you information you can use to best present the value of your work to a healthcare practice.

Read **The Bodywork Book**, **Discovering the Body's Wisdom** and **The Encyclopedia of Bodywork** for further information on how to define your specific type of bodywork. Also, *Massage Magazine* regularly features articles by experts on the various bodywork sub-specialities. High-quality photocopies of such supportive articles will add credibility to your overall presentation.

Besides presenting the benefits of your speciality, you also must keep yourself up-to-date on medical terminology and new developments both in your field and in healthcare in general. Attend continuing education seminars in a specialized area of clinical bodywork that you are interested in. For example, study neuromuscular therapy or trigger-point therapy which is a series of seminars on working with specific clinical problems. See Suggested Readings and Reference Materials after Chapter 17 for information on these and other helpful resources.

As part of your promotional effort, be prepared to show the doctor certificates of educational programs you have attended and letters of reference both from satisfied clients and healthcare professionals you have worked with. These letters should specifically state your qualifications, what you do, and how your sessions have benefitted clients. This appendix contains two sample letters from doctors and one from a client.

Finally, design an excellent brochure about your work and yourself which you can both send in advance and leave with the doctor after an interview.

The following example illustrates the benefits of two types of body therapy (massage and Trager®). Adapt this model as appropriate to your practice.

Benefits of Massage Therapy

Skeletal System

1. Maintains posture and body balance

2. Reduces muscular tension that may eventually cause structural problems

3. Increases the flow of nutrients to the bones

4. Promotes elimination of waste matter

Muscular System

1. Relieves muscle tension

2. Increases the supply of blood and nutrients to the muscles

3. Helps to eliminate waste matter from muscles (especially lactic acid)

4. Helps restore tone to flaccid muscles and partially compensates for lack of exercise and inactivity because of illness or injury

5. Eliminates or prevents muscle adhesions resulting from injury

6. Increases flexibility and strength of joints

Circulatory System

1. Improves blood circulation and relieves congestion

2. Increases supply of oxygen and nutrients to cells throughout the body

3. Eases the strain on the heart by helping to return blood to vital organs, especially in cases of forced inactivity due to illness or injury

4. Pushes the movement of lymph through the body, thereby strengthening the immune system and eliminating toxic wastes

Nervous System

1. Can either sedate or stimulate the nervous system, depending on the technique used

2. By balancing the nervous system, massage affects all systems of the body

Respiratory System

1. Improves breathing patterns

2. Aids in relief of many long-term respiratory difficulties such as asthma and bronchitis

Digestive System

1. Improves the function of the liver

2. Acts as a mechanical cleanser, pushing out waste products, particularly in those who suffer from constipation

3. Relieves spastic colon

Urinary Tract System

1. Massaging the kidneys can cleanse the blood and tone the entire system

2. Massage can affect the elimination of fluids in problems of swelling in the body

The American Massage Therapy Association presents the benefits of massage therapy as they affect physical, emotional and mental health.

PHYSICAL BENEFITS

Deep Relaxation & Stress Reduction

Relief of Muscle Tension & Stiffness

Reduced Muscle Spasms

Greater Joint Flexibility & Range of Motion

Increased Efficiency of Movement

Reduced Blood Pressure

Improved Posture

Strengthened Immune System

Disease Prevention

Health Maintenance

EMOTIONAL BENEFITS

Enhanced Self-Image

Reduced Levels of Anxiety

Increased Awareness of the Mind/Body Connection

Greater Ease of Emotional Expression

MENTAL BENEFITS

Relaxed State of Alertness

Reduced Mental Stress (A Calmer Mind)

Greater Ability to Monitor and Respond to Stress Signals

Increased Capacity for Clearer Thinking

THE TRAGER® APPROACH

- is the innovative learning approach to movement re-education developed over 60 years ago by Milton Trager, M.D.
- is designed to increase range of motion and flexibility.
- facilitates the client to access and incorporate a state of deep relaxation.
- releases stress and tension throughout the body.
- modifies old postural habits and gait patterns.
- is an important adjunct to chiropractic adjustments and total health care.

What Happens During a Trager® Session?

During a session of Trager® Psychophysical Integration the practitioner rhythmically and gently guides the client through a series of movements designed to increase range of motion and flexibility. The gentle, rhythmic movements allow the client to access and incorporate a state of deep relaxation. The sensations of movement become new habits of movement that can be recalled and, over time, automatically take precedence. Accumulated stress is released. The new patterns of movement are maintained by daily practice of Mentastics, a series of simple, effortless movements to enhance the client's sense of lightness, freedom and flexibility.

Trager® and Chiropractic*

- Trager relaxes and releases tension in your muscles to prepare you for your chiropractic adjustment.
- Trager enhances your response to chiropractic treatments.
- Old postural and gait habit patterns are replaced with normal motion and movement patterns.
- Tight and restricted areas of your body will be more accessible to chiropractic treatments.
- Trager assists you in maintaining your new postural movement patterns.
- Trager is available in this office as a 15-minute adjunct to your chiropractic adjustment and for 30-minute and 1-hour sessions.

*Adapted from *The Trager® Journal*, Volume I, Fall 1982.

Doctor's Letter Recommending Trager® Bodywork

(Dr.'s Letterhead)

Date:

To Whom It May Concern:

As a medical doctor specializing in preventive medicine and women's health care, I treat many patients with premenstrual syndrome, stress and eating disorders and a variety of complaints, including chronic pain, muscle spasms, limited range of motion and neuromuscular disorders.

I have found Trager® neuromuscular re-education to be an effective adjunct in my medical practice. After a series of 10 weekly Trager sessions, patients report excellent results, including increased flexibility and range of motion and freedom from pain and muscle spasms. Patients say they are able to maintain the relaxation and freedom of movement.

Trager psychophysical integration is an approach to movement re-education created and developed by Milton Trager, M.D., more than 60 years ago. Since his retirement in 1977 from medical practice, Dr. Trager has devoted his time to research, writing and training. Trager practitioners are trained and certified by Dr. Trager and the Trager Institute. Their certification is renewable annually through continuing education seminars.

During a Trager session, the practitioner rhythmically and gently guides the client through a series of movements designed to release deep-seated holding patterns and stress. The Trager movements help the client access and incorporate a deep state of relaxation. The sensations of movement become new movement habits which can be recalled at any time through a series of exercises taught at the end of each session.

I highly recommend this approach to medical doctors and healthcare professionals.

Sincerely,

Doctor's Letter Recommending Practitioner

(Dr.'s Letterhead)

Date:

To Whom It May Concern:

I have worked with (Practitioner's Name) since September, 1987, with a variety of patients. (Practitioner) is a certified practitioner of Hellerwork® and massage therapy. Her work has been an effective adjunct to my medical treatment program for patients with tension state, headaches, chronic neck and back pain as well as arthritis.

Patients report that as a result of (Practitioner)'s work they are able to release chronic neck, back and shoulder tension and muscle spasms. After several sessions with (Practitioner) they report having much less pain and discomfort. After a series of 10 sessions they are frequently pain-free, demonstrate increased flexibility and range of motion and are able to resume normal activities. Patients utilize daily exercises to maintain their progress.

Using neuromuscular re-education and massage as an adjunctive therapy in my medical practice has significantly improved patients' health and reduced excessive costs of repeat visits.

I highly recommend (Practitioner). Please contact me if I can be of further assistance.

Sincerely,

Client's Letter Recommending Practitioner

Date:

To Whom It May Concern:

When I first came to see (Practitioner), I had chronic headaches, insomnia and daily pain in my back and shoulders. My doctor suggested that I contact (practitioner) for sessions of massage therapy to release chronic shoulder and neck muscle spasms.

After several sessions, my pain decreased and I was able to sleep at night without medication for the first time in months. After two months of weekly sessions, my neck and shoulder discomfort had improved and I was able to resume my daily activities without pain. The massage therapy has also helped me recognize the sources of my stress and tension, and how to release stress before it becomes physical pain. I am able to recall how it feels to be relaxed quickly and easily.

I am continuing my improvements with monthly sessions and am maintaining the progress I have made.

Sincerely,

Client's Name
Address
City, State, Zip
Telephone number

Appendix C

Glossary of Insurance-Related Terms

Glossary of Insurance-Related Terms

ABMP - Associated Bodywork and Massage Professionals

A.M.A. - American Medical Association- national professional society of physicians

A.M.T.A. - American Massage Therapy Association

ASSIGNMENT OF BENEFITS - An authorization for an insurance company to pay a claim to someone other than the insured person, usually the doctor or the therapist treating the insured. To assign benefits to the doctor, the client signs the appropriate box on the insurance claim form or superbill. At the time of the visit, the client pays the co-payment amount, usually 20% of the bill, which is not paid by the insurance company.

BLUE CROSS - An independent, not-for-profit membership corporation providing protection against the costs of hospital care and, in some policies, protection against the costs of surgical and professional care.

BLUE SHIELD - An independent, not-for-profit membership association providing protection against the costs of surgery and other items of medical care.

BUSINESS LICENSE - Permission by your city to do business at your office. Must be renewed at specified intervals, depending on city ordinances and regulations.

C.A. - Certified Acupuncturist

CAPITATION - System of payment used by managed care plans in which physicians and licensed providers are paid a fixed, per capita amount for each patient enrolled over a stated period of time, regardless of the type and number of services provided.

CARRIER - An insurance company that underwrites policies that cover health care services.

CLEARINGHOUSE SYSTEM - Insurance claims transmitted to a clearinghouse, referred to as a third-party administrator, who redistributes the claims electronically to various insurance carriers.

CPT - Current Procedural Terminology. A Reference Procedural Code Book using a numerical system for procedures. Established by the American Medical Association primarily for insurance billing purposes.

D.C. - Doctor of Chiropractic

D.O. - Doctor of Osteopathic Medicine

DOWN CODING - Occurs when the coding system used on a claim form does not match that used by the insurance company receiving the claim.

ELECTRONIC CLAIM - Insurance claims submitted to the insurance carrier via a central processing unit (CPU), tape diskette, direct data entry, direct wire, dial-in telephone, digital fax, or personal computer download or upload.

ELECTRONIC CLAIMS SUBMISSION - Insurance claims prepared on a computer and submitted via modem (telephone lines) to the insurance carrier's computer system.

EXCLUSIVE PROVIDER ORGANIZATION - Type of managed health care plan in which subscriber members are eligible for benefits only when they use the services of a limited network of providers. EPO's are regulated under state health insurance laws.

EXPLANATION OF BENEFITS - An explanation of services periodically issued to recipients or providers on whose behalf claims have been paid. It shows the dates of service, allowable charge, amount billed, the amount paid, how much deductible has been paid and the patient's cost share.

FEDERAL TAX IDENTIFICATION NUMBER - A number is issued by the Internal Revenue Service to a medical group or solo practitioner physician and used for income tax purposes.

FEE FOR SERVICE - Method of payment in which the patient pays the physician or therapist for each professional service performed from an established schedule of fees.

FEE SCHEDULE - A listing of established allowances for medical services and procedures.

GATEKEEPER SYSTEM - System by which a primary care physician controls the amount of care a patient receives from an IPA (Independent Practice Association) plan. The physician receives a fixed monthly payment for each plan to cover his own and any specialist services.

HEALTH INSURANCE - A contract offering reimbursement for specified medical expenses in return for a fixed premium. Usually covers hospital and professional fees. Blue Cross/Blue Shield is the major U.S. non-profit private insurer.

HEALTH MAINTENANCE ORGANIZATION (HMO) - A type of health care program in which enrollees receive benefits when they obtain services that are provided or authorized by selected providers, usually with a primary care physician as the "gatekeeper." In general, enrollees do not receive coverage for the services of providers who are not in the HMO network, except for emergency service. An example is Kaiser Permanente in California.

ICD-9 - International Classification of Diseases is a numeric code system for diagnosis and procedures. Lists approximately 10,000 diagnoses and 5,000 procedure codes used by doctors and licensed healthcare providers.

INDEPENDENT PRACTICE ASSOCIATION - A type of HMO in which a program administrator contracts with a number of physicians who agree to provide treatment to subscribers in their own offices for a fixed capitation payment per month.

INSURANCE CLAIM FORM - A standard form provided by the insurance company to the client to be submitted when seeking reimbursement. The claim form is completed by the client and the doctor, and signed by the supervising healthcare provider.

INSURANCE DEDUCTIBLE - The amount of loss which the insured person must pay from his own funds before the insurance company will pay anything. A deductible is a type of cost sharing which lowers the amount insurance companies pay out in claims.

ITEMIZED BILL - A detailed list of all charges of services provided by a facility.

LICENSED HEALTHCARE PROVIDER - A person giving medical or health-related services who has passed the licensing exam required by a state board and completed other necessary degree/professional requirements.

LIEN - A legal agreement giving someone preference for payment before an owner has complete use of his property. In insurance reimbursement and personal injury disputes, a lien gives someone other than the insured first rights to money coming from a settlement or judgment. The lien document states who will be paid for which services related to a personal accident/injury case. It is an essential document, which must be kept on file in the client's chart and the attorney's office, because it protects your right to be paid for your services once the case is settled.

M.D. - Medical Doctor

MANAGED CARE - Arrangements made by payors to promote cost-effective health care through establishing selective relationships with health care provides, developing coordinated delivery systems, and conducting medical management activities.

MEDICAL CAPITATION PLAN - A program that provides a number of basic medical services at no charge, with additional charges on more costly procedures. Subscribers to these plans have limited or no choice of physicians. Treatment is delivered via a clinic or an independent practice association.

MEDICAL NECESSITY - Specific diagnostic or therapeutic requirements, for a specific service. Medical necessity MUST be established (via diagnostic or other information presented on the claim form) before the carrier can make payment.

MODIFIER - In CPT coding, a two-digit add on to a five digit number, representing the modifier, placed after the usual procedure code number.

NEUROMUSCULAR RE-EDUCATION - Movement of muscles and joints through range of motion exercises which re-educates the muscles/joints and the nervous system to function more effectively.

PARTIAL DISABILITY- When an illness or injury prevents an insured person from performing one or more of the functions of his or her regular job.

PENDING CLAIM - Insurance claims held in suspense due to review or other reasons. These claims may be cleared for payment or denied.

PPO - Preferred Provider Organization, such as Blue Shield Preferred. This type of insurance arrangement acts as a broker between the purchaser and the provider of care. Providers usually receive payment on a discounted fee-for-service basis. Enrollees are given incentives to use providers within the PPO, (for example, no co-payment) and they may receive covered services outside the PPO, but at lower rates of reimbursement.

PROCEDURE CODE - The code that describes each service the doctor or therapist renders to a patient.

SCOPE OF PRACTICE - Legal definition by state licensing and professional boards specifying what a healthcare practitioner is allowed to do.

SOAP - An abbreviation for Subjective complaints, Objective findings, Assessment of status, and diagnostic, or therapeutic Plan; a method of structuring progress notes.

STATE LICENSE - A license to practice a profession after completing degree and educational requirements and passing an examination given by the state regulating agency or professional board.

SUPERBILL - A form used by the doctor's office which contains all the necessary procedure coding, diagnostic coding and doctor's identification numbers, as well as signature blocks for billing the insurance company. Many offices that ask the patient to pay at the time of the visit give this form to the patient to submit to his/her insurance company.

SUPPLEMENTAL BENEFITS - Disability insurance provisions that allow benefits to the insured to increase the monthly indemnity or to receive a percentage of the policy premiums if an individual keeps a policy in force for 5 or 10 years or does not file any claims.

TEMPORARY DISABILITY - The recovery period following a work related injury during which the employee is unable to work and the condition has not stabilized; a schedule of benefits payable for the temporary disability.

THIRD-PARTY PAYMENT - Money for a service paid by someone other than the person receiving the service, that is, those who reimburse providers for healthcare services, as distinguished from the patient and the provider (the first two parties). In the U.S. the major third parties are the U.S. Government (which is responsible for Medicare and Medicaid), the non-profit Blue Cross/Blue Shield plans, and insurance companies.

TOTAL DISABILITY - A term that varies in meaning from one insurance policy to another. A liberal definition might read: "The insured must be unable to perform the major duties of his or her occupation."

SOFT-TISSUE MOBILIZATION - Movement (or mobilization) of the muscles and soft tissues.

UCR - Usual, Customary and Reasonable; A method used by insurance companies to establish their fee schedules. UCR uses the conversion factor method of establishing maximums.

UTILIZATION REVIEW - A process, based on established criteria, of reviewing and controlling the medical necessity for services and providers' use of medical care resources. Reviews are carried out by allied health personnel at predetermined times to determine medical necessity.

WAITING PERIOD - For disability insurance, the initial period of time when a disabled individual is not eligible to receive benefits even though unable to work.

WORKER'S COMPENSATION INSURANCE - A contract that insures a person against on-the job injury or illness. The employer pays the premium for his or her employees.

Appendix D

Sample Forms for Insurance Billing/Working in a Medical Office

Listing of Forms:

- Health Insurance Claim Form
- Phone Verification of Insurance Coverage
- Client Intake Form
- Client Personal Health Information
- Client Progress Notes with Body Diagram
- Low Back Pain Disability Questionnaire
- Neck Pain Disability Index
- Insurance Communication Log
- Request for Claim Review
- Insurance Complaint Form
- Comprehensive Client Intake Form for Worker's Compensation

APPROVED OMB-0938-0008

CARRIER

HEALTH INSURANCE CLAIM FORM

PICA | | | | | PICA | |

| PICA | | |

1. MEDICARE   MEDICAID   CHAMPUS   CHAMPVA   GROUP HEALTH PLAN (SSN or ID)   FECA BLK LUNG (SSN)   OTHER (ID)

(Medicare #)   (Medicaid #)   (Sponsor's SSN)   (VA File #)

1a. INSURED'S I.D. NUMBER   (FOR PROGRAM IN ITEM 1)

2. PATIENT'S NAME (Last Name, First Name, Middle Initial)

3. PATIENT'S BIRTH DATE   MM | DD | YY   SEX   M | F

4. INSURED'S NAME (Last Name, First Name, Middle Initial)

5. PATIENT'S ADDRESS (No., Street)

6. PATIENT RELATIONSHIP TO INSURED   Self | Spouse | Child | Other

7. INSURED'S ADDRESS (No., Street)

CITY   STATE

8. PATIENT STATUS   Single | Married | Other

CITY   STATE

ZIP CODE   TELEPHONE (Include Area Code) ( )

Employed | Full-Time Student | Part-Time Student

ZIP CODE   TELEPHONE (INCLUDE AREA CODE) ( )

9. OTHER INSURED'S NAME (Last Name, First Name, Middle Initial)

10. IS PATIENT'S CONDITION RELATED TO:

11. INSURED'S POLICY GROUP OR FECA NUMBER

a. OTHER INSURED'S POLICY OR GROUP NUMBER

a. EMPLOYMENT? (CURRENT OR PREVIOUS)   YES | NO

a. INSURED'S DATE OF BIRTH   MM | DD | YY   SEX   M | F

b. OTHER INSURED'S DATE OF BIRTH   MM | DD | YY   SEX   M | F

b. AUTO ACCIDENT?   PLACE (State)   YES | NO

b. EMPLOYER'S NAME OR SCHOOL NAME

c. EMPLOYER'S NAME OR SCHOOL NAME

c. OTHER ACCIDENT?   YES | NO

c. INSURANCE PLAN NAME OR PROGRAM NAME

d. INSURANCE PLAN NAME OR PROGRAM NAME

10d. RESERVED FOR LOCAL USE

d. IS THERE ANOTHER HEALTH BENEFIT PLAN?   YES | NO   If yes, return to and complete item 9 a-d.

READ BACK OF FORM BEFORE COMPLETING & SIGNING THIS FORM.

12. PATIENT'S OR AUTHORIZED PERSON'S SIGNATURE I authorize the release of any medical or other information necessary to process this claim. I also request payment of government benefits either to myself or to the party who accepts assignment below.

SIGNED _____ DATE _____

13. INSURED'S OR AUTHORIZED PERSON'S SIGNATURE I authorize payment of medical benefits to the undersigned physician or supplier for services described below.

SIGNED _____

PATIENT AND INSURED INFORMATION

14. DATE OF CURRENT: MM | DD | YY   ILLNESS (First symptom) OR INJURY (Accident) OR PREGNANCY(LMP)

15. IF PATIENT HAS HAD SAME OR SIMILAR ILLNESS. GIVE FIRST DATE   MM | DD | YY

16. DATES PATIENT UNABLE TO WORK IN CURRENT OCCUPATION   MM | DD | YY   FROM   TO   MM | DD | YY

17. NAME OF REFERRING PHYSICIAN OR OTHER SOURCE

17a. I.D. NUMBER OF REFERRING PHYSICIAN

18. HOSPITALIZATION DATES RELATED TO CURRENT SERVICES   MM | DD | YY   FROM   TO   MM | DD | YY

19. RESERVED FOR LOCAL USE

20. OUTSIDE LAB?   YES | NO $ CHARGES

21. DIAGNOSIS OR NATURE OF ILLNESS OR INJURY. (RELATE ITEMS 1,2,3 OR 4 TO ITEM 24E BY LINE)

1. |___.___|
2. |___.___|
3. |___.___|
4. |___.___|

22. MEDICAID RESUBMISSION CODE   ORIGINAL REF. NO.

23. PRIOR AUTHORIZATION NUMBER

24. A			B	C	D		E	F	G	H	I	J	K
DATE(S) OF SERVICE			Place of Service	Type of Service	PROCEDURES, SERVICES, OR SUPPLIES (Explain Unusual Circumstances)		DIAGNOSIS CODE	$ CHARGES	DAYS OR UNITS	EPSDT Family Plan	EMG	COB	RESERVED FOR LOCAL USE
From MM DD YY	To MM DD YY				CPT/HCPCS	MODIFIER							
1													
2													
3													
4													
5													
6													

25. FEDERAL TAX I.D. NUMBER   SSN | EIN

26. PATIENT'S ACCOUNT NO.

27. ACCEPT ASSIGNMENT? (For govt. claims, see back)   YES | NO

28. TOTAL CHARGE $

29. AMOUNT PAID $

30. BALANCE DUE $

31. SIGNATURE OF PHYSICIAN OR SUPPLIER INCLUDING DEGREES OR CREDENTIALS (I certify that the statements on the reverse apply to this bill and are made a part thereof.)

SIGNED _____ DATE _____

32. NAME AND ADDRESS OF FACILITY WHERE SERVICES WERE RENDERED (If other than home or office)

33. PHYSICIAN'S, SUPPLIER'S BILLING NAME, ADDRESS, ZIP CODE & PHONE #

PIN#   GRP#

PHYSICIAN OR SUPPLIER INFORMATION

(APPROVED BY AMA COUNCIL ON MEDICAL SERVICE 8/88)   **PLEASE PRINT OR TYPE**

FORM HCFA-1500 (12-90)
FORM OWCP-1500   FORM RRB-1500
x29426
Use with Envelope #14145 (gummed) or #14146 (self-seal)

PHONE VERIFICATION OF INSURANCE COVERAGE

CALL INSURANCE COMPANY and say that you want to verify the coverage of a client for their doctor.

Date of call _____ Time of call _____ Person making this call _____

Client's name _____ Insured's name _____

Client's Insurance Co. _____ Policy # _____ Group # _____

Insurance Co. address _____ Phone # _____

QUESTIONS TO ASK:

1. Is there a deductible? ☐ Yes ☐ No How much is it? _____

2. Has it been met? ☐ Yes ☐ No When is another deductible due? _____

3. Does the policy cover soft-tissue therapy or neuromuscular re-education? ☐ Yes ☐ No

4. Is there a maximum number of visits per year? ☐ Yes ☐ No

5. What percentage does this policy pay per session? _____

6. Is there a lifetime maximum on soft-tissue therapy? ☐ Yes ☐ No

7. If so, has any been used? ☐ Yes ☐ No

8. Are there any limitations, clauses or riders on this policy? ☐ Yes ☐ No

9. If so, what? _____

10. Do you honor Assignment of Payments? ☐ Yes ☐ No

11. Address where claim should be mailed to: _____

12. To attention of: (Name of person) _____ Dept. _____

13. Name of person you spoke with: _____ Title _____

NOTES:

CLIENT INTAKE FORM

WELCOME TO THE OFFICE OF _____

Client Information
(please print)

Name : _____   Sex: M __ F __

Address:_____

City:_____   State _____ Zip_____

Telephone Number: (____)_____

Soc. Sec. No. _____   Driver's Lic. No. _____

Age: ____ Date of Birth:_____ Number of Children:____

Marital Status: Single ( )   Married ( )   Widow(er) ( )   Divorced ( )   Separated ( )

Occupation _____   Employer _____

Address:_____

City:_____   State_____ Zip_____

Telephone Number: (___)_____

Spouse's Name: _____

Occupation _____

Employer _____   Address: _____

City:_____   State _____ Zip_____

Telephone Number: (___)_____

Family Physician _____

Address:_____

City:_____   State _____ Zip _____

Telephone Number: (___)_____

CLIENT INTAKE FORM (Continued)

Insurance Information:

*Primary Carrier*_____

Address:_____

City:_____ State _____ Zip_____

Telephone Number: (___)_____

Subscriber's Name_____ ID# _____ Policy# _____

*Secondary Carrier*_____

Address:_____

City:_____ State_____ Zip_____

Telephone Number: (___)_____

Subscriber's Name_____ ID#_____ Policy#_____

Who referred you to this office? _____

Have you ever been treated by a counselor? No ( ) Yes ( ) Last Visit_____

In case of emergency, please notify:_____

Telephone Number: (___)_____

Financial Policy: We ask our clients to pay at the end of each visit, unless other specific arrangements are made.

Cancellation Policy: The time of your appointment is reserved for you.
Please give us 24 hours notice if you are unable to keep your appointment. Appointments cancelled less than 24 hours beforehand will be charged for payment in full.

Signature:_____ Date_____

Witness:_____ Relationship (if minor client) _____

CLIENT PERSONAL HEALTH INFORMATION

Date _____

Name _____

How did you hear of my services? _____

Describe reason for this visit: _____

Date of last medical examination:_____

Are you currently under a doctor's care?_____ If yes, give name of physician and reason for consulting

him/her: _____

Are you presently taking any medications?_____

If yes, please describe: _____

Are you now or have you ever been under the care of a psychotherapist? _____ If yes, give name and

reason for care: _____

Have you ever received bodytherapy? ____ If yes, please describe _____

_____

List any other therapies you are receiving _____

_____

Have you ever had any type of accident?_____

If yes, please describe _____

_____

_____

Do you have trouble with varicose veins or blood clots?_____

Have you had any type of surgery?_____

Do you have any limitations of mobility?_____

_____

CLIENT PERSONAL HEALTH INFORMATION (continued)

Are you on an exercise program?_____

Describe type of excercise & frequency: _____

_____

_____

Describe methods you use to manage your stress: _____

_____

_____

Any additional comments regarding your health:_____

_____

_____

CLIENT PROGRESS NOTES

Client's NAME

DATE			TIME	SESSIONS AND REMARKS	
MO.	DAY	YEAR			

BODY DIAGRAM

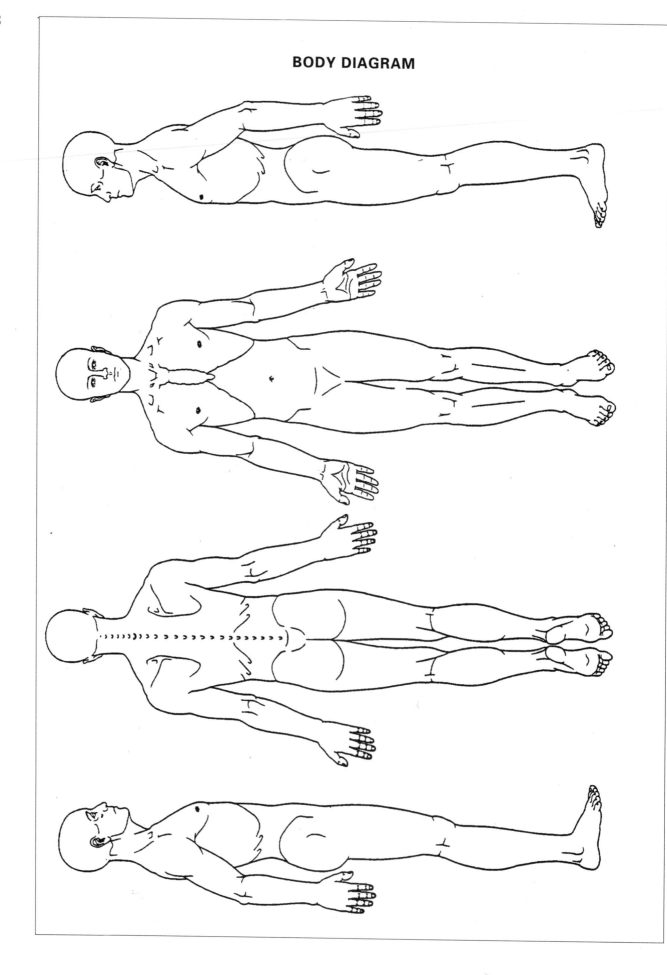

LOW BACK PAIN AND DISABILITY QUESTIONNAIRE (revised Oswestry)

Name: _____   Date: _____

This questionnaire has been designed to give the health care provider information as to how your back pain has affected your ability to manage everyday life. Please answer every section and mark in each section only the **ONE** box which applies to you. We realize you may consider that two of the statements in any one section relate to you, but please just mark the box which most closely describes your problem today.

SECTION 1- PAIN INTENSITY
- ☐ The pain comes and goes and is very mild.
- ☐ The pain is mild and does not vary much.
- ☐ The pain comes and goes and is moderate.
- ☐ The pain is moderate and does not vary much.
- ☐ The pain comes and goes and is very severe.
- ☐ The pain is severe and does not vary much.

SECTION 2- PERSONAL CARE
- ☐ I would not have to change my way of washing or dressing in order to avoid pain.
- ☐ I do not normally change my way of washing and dressing even though it causes some pain.
- ☐ Washing and dressing increase the pain but I manage not to change my way of doing it.
- ☐ Washing and dressing increase the pain and I find it necessary to change my way of doing it.
- ☐ Because of the pain I am unable to do some washing and dressing.
- ☐ Because of the pain I am unable to do any washing and dressing without help.

SECTION 3- LIFTING
- ☐ I can lift heavy weights without extra pain.
- ☐ I can lift heavy weights but it causes extra pain.
- ☐ Pain prevents me from lifting heavy weights off the floor.
- ☐ Pain prevents me from lifting heavy weights off the floor, but I manage if they are conveniently positioned (e.g. on a table).
- ☐ Pain prevents me from lifting heavy weights but I can manage light to medium weights if they are conveniently positioned.
- ☐ I can only lift very light weights at the most.

SECTION 4- WALKING
- ☐ I have no pain on walking.
- ☐ I have some pain on walking but it does not increase with distance.
- ☐ I cannot walk more than one mile without increasing pain.
- ☐ I cannot walk more than 1/2 mile without increasing pain.
- ☐ I cannot walk more than 1/4 mile without increasing pain.
- ☐ I cannot walk at all without increasing pain.

SECTION 5- SITTING
- ☐ I can sit in any chair as long as I like.
- ☐ I can only sit in my favorite chair as long as I like.
- ☐ Pain prevents me from sitting more than one hour.
- ☐ Pain prevents me from sitting more than 1/2 hour.
- ☐ Pain prevents me from sitting more than 10 minutes.
- ☐ I avoid sitting because it increases my pain straight away.

SECTION 6- STANDING
- ☐ I can stand as long as I want without pain.
- ☐ I have some pain on standing but it does not increase with time.
- ☐ I cannot stand for longer than one hour without increasing pain.
- ☐ I cannot stand for longer than 1/2 hour without increasing pain.
- ☐ I cannot stand for longer than 10 minutes without increasing pain.
- ☐ I avoid standing because it increases the pain straight away.

SECTION 7- SLEEPING
- ☐ I get no pain in bed.
- ☐ I get pain in bed but it does not prevent me from sleeping well.
- ☐ Because of pain my normal night's sleep is reduced by less than 1/4.
- ☐ because of pain my normal night's sleep is reduced by less than 1/2.
- ☐ Because of pain my normal night's sleep is reduced by less than 3/4.
- ☐ Pain prevents me from sleeping at all.

SECTION 8- SOCIAL LIFE
- ☐ My social life is normal and gives me no pain.
- ☐ My social life is normal but increases the degree of pain.
- ☐ Pain has no significant effect on my social life apart from limiting my more energetic interests, e.g. dancing, etc.
- ☐ Pain has restricted my social life and I do not go out very often.
- ☐ Pain has restricted my social life to my home.
- ☐ I have hardly any social life because of the pain.

SECTION 9- TRAVELLING
- ☐ I get no pain while traveling.
- ☐ I get some pain while travelling but none of my usual forms of travel make it any worse.
- ☐ I get extra pain while travelling but it does not compel me to seek alternate forms of travel.
- ☐ I get extra pain while travelling which compels me to seek alternative forms of travel.
- ☐ Pain restricts all forms of travel.
- ☐ Pain prevents all forms of travel except that done lying down.

SECTION 10- CHANGING DEGREE OF PAIN
- ☐ My pain is rapidly getting better.
- ☐ My pain fluctuates but overall is definitely getting better.
- ☐ My pain seems to be getting better but improvement is slow at present.
- ☐ My pain is neither getting better or worse.
- ☐ My pain is gradually worsening.
- ☐ My pain is rapidly worsening.

NECK PAIN AND DISABILITY INDEX (Vernon-Mior)

Name: _____   Date: _____

This questionnaire has been designed to give the health care provider information as to how your neck pain has affected your ability to manage everyday life. Please answer every section and mark in each section only the **ONE** box which applies to you. We realize you may consider that two of the statements in any one section relate to you, but please just mark the box which most closely describes your problem today.

SECTION 1- PAIN INTENSITY
- ☐ I have no pain at the moment.
- ☐ The pain is very mild at the moment.
- ☐ The pain is moderate at the moment.
- ☐ The pain is fairly severe at the moment.
- ☐ The pain is very severe at the moment.
- ☐ The pain is the worst imaginable at the moment.

SECTION 2- PERSONAL CARE (washing, dressing etc.)
- ☐ I can look after myself normally without causing pain.
- ☐ I can look after myself normally but it causes extra pain.
- ☐ It is painful to look after myself and I am slow and careful.
- ☐ I need some help but manage most of my personal care.
- ☐ I need help every day in most aspects of self care.
- ☐ I do not get dressed, I wash with difficulty and I stay in bed.

SECTION 3- LIFTING
- ☐ I can lift heavy weights without extra pain.
- ☐ I can lift heavy weights but it gives extra pain.
- ☐ Pain prevents me from lifting heavy weights off the floor, but I can manage if they are conveniently positioned, for example on a table.
- ☐ Pain prevents me from lifting heavy weights, but I can manage light to medium weights if they are conveniently positioned.
- ☐ I can lift very light weights.
- ☐ I cannot lift or carry anything at all.

SECTION 4- READING
- ☐ I can read as much as I want to with no pain in my neck.
- ☐ I can read as much as I want to with slight pain in my neck.
- ☐ I can read as much as I want to with moderate pain in my neck.
- ☐ I can't read as much as I want because of moderate pain in my neck.
- ☐ I can hardly read at all because of severe pain in my neck.
- ☐ I cannot read at all.

SECTION 5- HEADACHES
- ☐ I have no headaches at all.
- ☐ I have slight headaches which come infrequently.
- ☐ I have moderate headaches which come infrequently.
- ☐ I have moderate headaches which come frequently.
- ☐ I have severe headaches which come frequently.
- ☐ I have headaches almost all of the time.

SECTION 6- CONCENTRATION
- ☐ I can concentrate fully when I want to with no difficulty.
- ☐ I can concentrate fully when I want to with slight difficulty.
- ☐ I have a fair degree of difficulty in concentrating when I want to.
- ☐ I have a great deal of difficulty in concentrating when I want to.
- ☐ I cannot concentrate at all.

SECTION 7- WORK
- ☐ I can do as much work as I want to.
- ☐ I can do my usual work but no more.
- ☐ I can do most of my usual work but no more.
- ☐ I cannot do my usual work.
- ☐ I can hardly do any work at all.
- ☐ I can't do any work at all.

SECTION 8- DRIVING
- ☐ I can drive my car without any neck pain.
- ☐ I can drive my car as long as I want with slight pain in my neck.
- ☐ I can drive my car as long as I want with moderate pain in my neck.
- ☐ I can't drive my car as long as I want because of moderate pain in my neck.
- ☐ I can hardly drive at all because of severe pain in my neck.
- ☐ I can't drive my car at all.

SECTION 9- SLEEPING
- ☐ I have no trouble sleeping.
- ☐ My sleep is slightly disturbed (less than one hour sleepless).
- ☐ My sleep is mildly disturbed (1-2 hrs. sleepless).
- ☐ My sleep is moderately disturbed (2-3 hrs. sleepless).
- ☐ My sleep is greatly disturbed (3-5 hrs. sleepless).
- ☐ My sleep is completely disturbed (5-7 hrs. sleepless).

SECTION 10- RECREATION.
- ☐ I am able to engage in all my recreation activities with no neck pain at all.
- ☐ I am able to engage in all my recreation activities, with some pain in my neck.
- ☐ I am able to engage in most, but not all of my usual recreation activities because of pain in my neck.
- ☐ I am able to engage in a few of my usual recreation activities because of pain in my neck.
- ☐ I hardly do any recreation activities because of pain in my neck.
- ☐ I can't do recreation activities at all.

INSURANCE COMMUNICATION LOG

Patient _____ File No. _____

1. Employer _____
   Address _____
   Phone No. _____ Length of Employment _____

2. Insurance Carrier _____
   Address _____
   Phone No. _____ Adjuster _____
   Subscriber _____
   Certificate No. _____ Group No. _____
   Claim No. _____ % Paid by Insurance _____
   Deductible _____ Amount of Deductible Met _____
   Is Deductible Per Year ☐ Yes   ☐ No   Per Illness ☐ Yes   ☐ No

3. Attorney _____ Case No. _____
   Address _____
   Phone No. _____ Secretary _____

COMMUNICATION LOG

Date	Time	In/Out	1/2/3	Person Spoken to	Conversation

#1070

REQUEST FOR CLAIM REVIEW

☐ Worker's Comp   ☐ Private Pay   ☐ Group Ins.   ☐ Other_____

Date _____

TO: Claims Department of _____ Insurance Company.

Address _____

Client's Name _____   Insured's Name _____

Policy No. _____   Date(s) of Service _____

Date of Original Claim _____   Claim No. _____

On behalf of your contract-holder (insured) _____ We REQUEST a review **on the above claim handled by your office. We have enclosed a signed Authorization from the client for you to release information directly to our office.**

Our client is not satisfied with the payment of $_____ you sent him/her. We do not understand how you arrived at this figure.

Our client's sessions were longer than usual due to the following circumstances

_____

The enclosed photocopies of his/her records support that claim. We believe this information should have your special attention in reviewing this claim.

Would you please tell us whether or not there should be a correction in your original benefits payment. If not, could you please respond with an explanation of how your payment of $_____ was decided upon.

Sincerely,

Name _____

Address _____   Phone _____

CLIENT'S AUTHORIZATION TO RELEASE INFORMATION

I request your Claims Department to release information on the above claim directly to the above named practitioner.

Client's Signature _____   Date _____

INSURANCE COMPLAINT FORM

TO: Department of Insurance   Date: _____

Address _____
               STREET   CITY   STATE   ZIP

FROM: _____   Phone _____
               HEALTH CARE PROVIDERS NAME

Address _____
               STREET   CITY   STATE   ZIP

We have filed a claim (copy attached) with the _____ insurance company
                                           NAME OF CARRIER

on _____ . It has not been paid or denied.
       DATE

Please accept this letter as a formal written complaint against the below named insurance company.

COMPLAINT AGAINST: _____
                             NAME OF CARRIER

Address: _____   Phone _____
           STREET   CITY   STATE   ZIP

Policy Number _____   Claim/File Number _____

The following is a brief statement of what the above insurance has done or failed to do: (Use reverse side if more space is needed.)

_____

_____

_____

_____

_____

_____

_____

_____

_____

_____

_____

_____

_____

Authorized signature _____

COMPREHENSIVE CLIENT INTAKE FORM
FOR WORKER'S COMPENSATION

Name : _____   Claim Number _____

Address:_____   Social Security Number_____

City:_____   Referring Doctor:_____

Zip Code: _____   Insurance Co. Name: _____

Telephone Number: (____)_____

Date of Injury: _____   Legal Case: _____

Describe Injury:_____

_____

Physical Activities at Work: Indicate Percentage (%) of time spent at each of the following activities:

_____ Sitting	_____ Lifting	_____ Typing
_____ Standing	_____ 10-Key	_____ Mousing
_____ Twisting	_____ Writing	_____ Drawing
_____ Reaching	_____ Carrying	_____ Talking

Indicate the percentage of time spent on the telephone per day:

Please circle one:	Headset	Yes	No
	Do you use it	Yes	No
	Touch Typist	Yes	No
	Trackball	Yes	No
	Mouse on left	Yes	No

HIERARCHY OF SYMPTOMS: (Please list symptoms from most severe to least severe, describing the specific body area involved and the percentage (%) of time symptoms are present).

LOCATION OF SYMPTOMS:	(% of time present)	Flares with Task
_____	_____	_____
_____	_____	_____
_____	_____	_____

COMPREHENSIVE CLIENT INTAKE FORM
FOR WORKER'S COMPENSATION (continued)

Do tasks make the symptoms worse?   Yes   No

What other therapies have you tried? _____ -

_____

_____

Describe your regular sleep patterns: _____

How do you feel when you wake up in the morning? Do the symptoms wake you up at times?

_____

_____

_____

Fatigue Level (1-10 where 10 is the most fatigued)

Fatigue level at the beginning of the day: ____

Fatigue level at the end of the day: ____

Stress Level (1-10 where 10 is the highest level of stress)

Indicate stress level at the beginning of the day: ____

Indicate stress level at the end of the day: ____

Do you drink caffeinated beverages? ____ If yes, how often and how many:

_____

_____

Do you exercise? ____   What type and how often? _____

What do you do regularly to relax? _____

Book Evaluation Form

BOOK NAME:
The Insurance Reimbursement Manual

Please complete **BOTH SIDES** of this form (check boxes on this side... written comments on other side); Please mail completed form to address below.

PLEASE RATE:	Excellent	Very Good	Good	Fair	Poor	Remarks
1. Usefulness of material learned	☐	☐	☐	☐	☐	_____
2. Author's knowledge of subject	☐	☐	☐	☐	☐	_____
3. Organization and ease-of-use	☐	☐	☐	☐	☐	_____
4. Clear and understandable writing	☐	☐	☐	☐	☐	_____
5. Value of insurance industry background	☐	☐	☐	☐	☐	_____
6. Value of insurance claims information	☐	☐	☐	☐	☐	_____
7. Value of insurance procedure codes	☐	☐	☐	☐	☐	_____
8. Value of legal / licensing information	☐	☐	☐	☐	☐	_____
9. Value of tax information	☐	☐	☐	☐	☐	_____
10. Value of marketing information	☐	☐	☐	☐	☐	_____
11. Value of chart/recordkeeping information	☐	☐	☐	☐	☐	_____
12. Value of sample forms	☐	☐	☐	☐	☐	_____
13. Value of sample letters	☐	☐	☐	☐	☐	_____
14. Value of examples and illustrations	☐	☐	☐	☐	☐	_____
15. Value of lists and directories	☐	☐	☐	☐	☐	_____
16. Value of glossaries	☐	☐	☐	☐	☐	_____
17. Value of suggested reference materials	☐	☐	☐	☐	☐	_____
18. Value of state law summaries	☐	☐	☐	☐	☐	_____
19. Usefulness as a future reference manual	☐	☐	☐	☐	☐	_____
20. Value received for price paid	☐	☐	☐	☐	☐	_____
21. _____	☐	☐	☐	☐	☐	_____
22. _____	☐	☐	☐	☐	☐	_____
YOUR OVERALL EVALUATION	☐	☐	☐	☐	☐	_____

PLEASE TURN OVER →

Christine Rosche, Director • Bodytherapy Business Institute • 4157 El Camino Way, Suite C • Palo Alto, California 94306 • (415) 856-3151

PLEASE SHARE YOUR COMMENTS ABOUT THIS BOOK

■ What 3 things about this book did you **LIKE MOST**?

1. _____

2. _____

3. _____

■ What 3 things about this book did you **LIKE LEAST**?

1. _____

2. _____

3. _____

■ What specific things would you **ADD TO** this book to improve it?

_____

_____

_____

■ What specific things would you **REMOVE FROM** this book to improve it?

_____

_____

_____

_____

■ **WHAT ELSE** do you think could improve this book? _____

_____

_____

_____

■ **COMMENTS** — Please share your comments / suggestions / critiques / compliments about this book _____

_____

_____

_____

■ **FOLLOW-UP QUESTIONS** — We may want contact you about your responses to these questions. Thank you.

Name _____   Occupation_____

Address _____   Telephone (_____)_____

City _____   State _____ Zip_____

READER'S FEEDBACK FORM

Please help make this book even more useful.
Use this form to send us your freedback, updates and improvements so we can make this publication even better.

Send to:

■ Bodytherapy Business Institute
4157 El Camino Way, Suite C
Palo Alto, CA 94306
Telephone: (415) 856-3151

Purpose:

❑ Add — New material to be included
❑ Delete — Materials to be removed
❑ Change — Revisions / Updates / Errors
❑ Suggestions / Ideas / Brainstorms
❑ Comments / Concerns / Critiques
❑ Other: _____

From:

Name _____

Title _____

Company _____

Type of Business _____

Address _____

City / State / Zip _____

Phone _____ FAX _____

Date _____ Reply Requested? ❑ Yes ❑ No